WORLD AIR POWER

JOURNAL

Aerospace Publishing Ltd

Airtime Publishing Inc.

Published quarterly by
Aerospace Publishing Ltd
179 Dalling Road
London W6 0ES
UK

Copyright © 1992 Aerospace
Publishing Ltd

Cutaway drawings
copyright © 1992 Greenborough
Associates Ltd

ISSN 0959-7050

Aerospace ISBN 1 874023 17 4
            (softback)
            1 874023 18 2
            (hardback)
Airtime ISBN 1-880588-07-2
            (hardback)

Published under licence in USA and
Canada by Airtime Publishing Inc.,
10 Bay Street, Westport,
CT 06880, USA

Editorial Offices:
WORLD AIR POWER JOURNAL
Aerospace Publishing Ltd
179 Dalling Road
London W6 0ES
UK

Publisher: Stan Morse
Editors: David Donald
        Jon Lake
Production Editors:
    Trisha Palmer
    Karen Leverington
Design: Barry Savage
        Robert Hewson
Typesetting: SX Composing Ltd
Origination and printing by
Imago Publishing Ltd
Printed in Italy

Europe Correspondent:
    Paul Jackson
Washington Correspondent:
    Robert F. Dorr
USA West Coast Correspondent:
    René J. Francillon
Asia Correspondent:
    Pushpindar Singh

The editors of WORLD AIR
POWER JOURNAL welcome
photographs for possible
publication, but cannot accept any
responsibility for loss or damage to
unsolicited material.

World Air Power Journal is a
registered trademark in the
United States of America of
Airtime Publishing Inc.

World Air Power Journal
is published quarterly
and is available by
subscription

SUBSCRIPTION AND BACK
NUMBERS:

UK and World (except USA and
Canada) write to:
Aerospace Publishing Ltd
FREEPOST
MARLBOROUGH
Wilts SN8 2BR
UK

(No stamp required if posted
within the UK)

USA and Canada, write to:
Airtime Publishing Inc.
Subscription Dept
10 Bay Street
Westport, CT 06880
USA

Prevailing subscription rates are
available on request.
For single and back issues of the
soft-cover edition (subject to
availability):
$17.95 each for delivery within
mainland USA, Alaska and
Hawaii. $21 (Can) each for
delivery to Canada. $21 (US)
each for delivery overseas.
Please enclose payment with
your order. Visa and MasterCard
accepted. Include your card
number, expiration date and
signature.
Hard-cover subscription rates
available on request.

Publisher, North America:
    Melvyn Williams
Subscription Director:
    Linda DeAngelis
Charter Member Services Managers:
    Jill Brooks
    Janie Klanit

The publishers gratefully
acknowledge the assistance given by
the following people:
Lon O. Nordeen and Tom Downey
of McDonnell Douglas for their help
with the F-15 feature.
Lt Cdr Rick Burgess, USN, Lt Fred
Henney, USN, Mr Norman
Polmar, Major Rick DeChaineau,
USMC, and Master Sergeant Paul
Earle, USMC, for their help with
the Air Power Analysis feature.

WORLD AIR POWER®
JOURNAL

CONTENTS

Military Aviation Review

International

NATO Sentries redouble watch

Following modernisation at Boeing Field, Seattle, NATO E-3A LX-N90442 returned to Geilenkirchen in October fitted with AN/AYR-1 ESM equipment. Unlike RAF Sentries with their Loral 1017 'Yellow Gate' wingtip pods, the NATO aircraft will have a canoe-shaped bulge on each side of the forward fuselage for collecting and analysing electronic signals transmitted by other aircraft. The USAF's temporary testbed JE-3C (31674) has also flown to Geilenkirchen for trials of the same equipment. Closure of the Boeing 707 line has forced Boeing to consider an alternative platform for countries (such as Japan) still seeking a large AEW aircraft. Installation of the E-3's Westinghouse AN/APY-2 early warning avionics is currently being considered in a Boeing 767 airliner.

Sidewinder-armed Mirage 5BAs of No. 8 Squadron are seen in Turkey during Operation Desert Shield, the closest these ageing fighters ever came to action.

Western Europe

BELGIUM:

8 Squadron disbands

Once comprising four squadrons, the FAeB/BLU Dassault Mirage 5 force was reduced to one when 8 Squadron disbanded at Bierset on 13 September. The unit's 12 Mirage 5BAs and five 5BD trainers have been placed in storage or passed to co-located No. 42 Squadron, which will operate up to 20 Mirages due to undergo modernisation, if funding can be found. No. 42 is now the sole component of 3 Wing, but will be transferred to Florennes and be controlled by 2 Wing.

FINLAND:

Fighter evaluations

The Ilmavoimat completed a 16-sortie evaluation of the McDonnell Douglas F/A-18C Hornet at MCAS El Toro on 23 October prior to beginning detailed assessments of competitors for its 67-aircraft requirement. Others under consideration are the SIG Gripen and General Dynamics F-16 Fighting Falcon.

FRANCE:

Air force reorganised

Changes in the higher command of the Armée de l'Air were implemented on 1 September, affecting both the Air Regions and the nuclear and air defence units. The former four numbered Regions Aériennes were reduced to three to conform with the army's administrative areas and now comprise RA Nord-Est with HQ at Villacoublay and 19 air bases, approximating to the old 1 RA; RA Atlantique, HQ Bordeaux, and 17 bases, combining almost all the previous 2 and 3 RAs; and RA Mediterranée at Aix-en-Provence, having 12 bases of the former 4 RA.

In a re-alignment of nuclear forces, Commandement des Forces Aériennes Stratégiques (CoFAS) has augmented its Mirage IVPs (ASMP nuclear missiles), S-2 silo-launched IRBMs and C-135FR tankers with two squadrons of ASMP-armed Mirage 2000Ns of 4ième Escadre de Chasse. These have come from the Tactical Force

(FATac – Force Aérienne Tactique) which became non-nuclear on 1 September when the AN52 free-fall nuclear bombs of the Jaguar force were withdrawn. FATac has been more than compensated by its absorption of the entire manned fighter component of the air defence organisation, Commandement 'Air' des Forces de Defense Aérienne (CAFDA). Four wings of Mirage F1s and Mirage 2000Cs were involved in the transfer, leaving CAFDA to fly only four Boeing E-3F Sentry AWACS, although it retains its SAMs and ground radar sites. Transport and training commands are unchanged, except that the former is administratively transferred to the Atlantic Air Region.

Rafale re-think

Uncertainty was rife over the optimum configuration for the Dassault Rafale during the closing months of 1991 as lessons of the Gulf War were studied. The original requirement for 225 single-seat Rafale Cs and 25 dual-control trainer Rafale Bs became increasingly unlikely to be fulfilled as the merits of carrying a weapon systems officer (WSO) became apparent. Contracts are expected to be amended accordingly, but the navy remains set on the single-seat Rafale M. Deliveries of the latter, formerly scheduled to begin on 1 July 1996, will be put back by two years, as will the air force variant, from 1998 to 2000.

Budget cuts and increases

The Armée de l'Air was seen to have received mixed news in the defence appropriations placed before Parliament on 13 November, most seriously involving an unexpectedly early end to Mirage 2000C interceptor procurement. No more of the variant will be ordered, thereby limiting orders to 146, instead of 169. The 23 Mirage 2000B trainers are not affected, nor are – at least for the moment – 75 2000Ns and 105 2000Ds. There will also be a stretch-out in Mirage 2000 deliveries. By contrast, the final 14 conversions of Mirage F1C to ground-attack F1CT standard have been reinstated as a result of Gulf War ex-

perience, restoring the programme to 55. The 1992 budget contains funds for 20 EMBRAER Tucanos from 50 required as Fouga Magister replacements, following the initial order for two in the 1991 budget. It seemed unlikely, however, that the Tucano order would be extended to the originally-planned 80 in order to provide 30 aircraft for use as continuation trainers and liaison aircraft at fighter bases.

The army learned in October that it would receive the simplified Horizon version of the Orchidée helicopter-borne battlefield radar surveillance system. Orchidée was originally cancelled on 1 August 1990 – the day before Iraq invaded Kuwait – but the prototype's performance in the Gulf War prompted a re-evaluation. Horizon will be 30 per cent cheaper than the planned system because of economies such as deletion of a data-link. The system used in Saudi Arabia and Kuwait was mounted in an Aérospatiale Puma, but the Cougar (Super Puma) will carry the definitive version.

GERMANY:

Eurofighter cuts threatened

In common with Italy and Spain, Germany was revising downwards its commitment to the Eurofighter EFA as the year drew to a close, leaving only the UK officially still intending to take up its full allocation of 250. Having begun by announcing a need for 250 aircraft, Germany reduced this to 200 and in latest statements was speaking of 150 as the maximum affordable within the Luftwaffe's budget unless costs are reduced. Germany is waiting until 1993, when a firm price can be quoted, before committing itself to buying EFAs, the implication being that it will look elsewhere if costs are too high. Present estimates are DM98.98 million ($57 million) per aircraft, which Germany says is unacceptably high. As a means of limiting the price, proposals were being made for the planned four assembly lines to be reduced to one or two. The four-nation commitment to EFA was originally 765 aircraft, but this appears to have dropped to about 510.

AMRAAM trials begin

Firing trials began in the USA during October of the Hughes AIM-120 Advanced Medium-Range AAM (AMRAAM) launched from a German

F-4E-ICE Phantom. ICE (Improved Combat Efficiency) F-4Es are due to enter service in April, fitted with a Hughes AN/APG-65 pulse-Doppler radar in place of the Westinghouse AN/APQ-120 with which they were delivered in the mid-1970s. Previously able to launch only the short-range, heat-seeking AIM-9 Sidewinder AAM, Luftwaffe Phantoms will now gain BVR (beyond visual range) capability.

GREECE:

US arms offered

Having just received the first of an additional 28 McDonnell Douglas F-4E Phantoms to be delivered before the end of 1991, Greece revealed in October that the US was to supply it with 26 surplus LTV A-7 Corsair attack aircraft to augment 36 promised by the same source a few months before and to reinforce the survivors of 60 A-7Hs originally supplied. The US announced in September that the batch of 36 A-7/TA-7 Corsairs would be reworked at NAS Jacksonville, Florida, before delivery.

Army aviation will receive a considerable boost in effectiveness – notably in its night capabilities – following an offer by the US to supply 20 McDonnell Douglas AH-64 Apache attack helicopters equipped with 446 Rockwell AGM-114 Hellfire anti-tank missiles and the TADS/PNVS infra-red system for night-flying and target-finding. Other Apache export orders comprise 18 for Israel, 12 (plus 36 options) for Saudi Arabia and 24 for Egypt. The Apache offer followed almost immediately on a US decision to deliver 15 Bell AH-1 Cobras to the Greek army.

ITALY:

Defence cuts threatened

A programme of planned economies presented to Parliament for approval nominates five squadrons and four air bases of the Aeronautica Militare Italiana for dissolution. The AMI will be reduced from 76,460 to 63,100 personnel and slim down to six F-104S-ASA Starfighter squadrons (including one mostly equipped with TF-104Gs); three interdictor squadrons, all with Tornados; five attack/reconnaissance squadrons (eventually all equipped with AMX); and one maritime patrol squadron combining the 16 Atlantics formerly operated by two. Partly redressing the balance,

Above: The F-4F ICE testbed serves with **ETD61** at Manching, and has recently begun **AMRAAM** firing trials.

Below: Latest Italian Tornado unit is 155° Gruppo of 50° Stormo, which now wears a 50° Stormo badge on the tailfins of its Tornados.

Left above: A Greek air force PZL Dromader. One of these aircraft was lost during late 1991.

a new squadron will be formed with two AEW aircraft of a type yet to be decided.

Confirming what had been suspected earlier, the plan reduces single-seat AMX procurement from 187 to 135 and limits the Eurofighter EFA programme to 130 aircraft instead of 165 – the latter as Starfighter replacements. On the positive side, the army is to get 30 more scout-configured Agusta A 129 Mangustas to augment 60 in anti-tank roles, whilst the navy is to receive a second V/STOL carrier and 10 more AV-8B+ Harriers to add to a dozen on order. Bases nominated for closure are Grazzanise (home of 10 Squadron and its F-104S-ASAs); Treviso/San Angelo (14 Squadron, G91R); Brindisi (13 Squadron, G91Y); and Cagliari/Elmas (86 Squadron, Atlantic).

New army aircraft

Army Light Aviation (ALE – Aviazione Leggera dell'Esercito) took delivery in November of the first four Agusta-Bell 412SP helicopters from a follow-on batch of six – plus six Meridionali-Boeing CH-47C Chinooks also on order – which it will operate for the National Civil Protection Agency (SNPC – Servizio Nazionale Protezione Civile). On completion of deliveries, SNPC will have five (civil-registered) Canadair CL-215s, one Lockheed C-130H Hercules, three Alenia G222s, nine CH-47s, six AB 412s and two AB 212s. With the exception of the CL-215s, aircraft are normally operated by the Italian armed forces and made available (with crews) to the SNPC when required. Also supplied – making its public debut on 5 October – was the first of eight Dornier 228-212 light twin transports (including two with survey equipment for the Istituto Geografico).

The three major helicopter wings of the Italian army were re-titled on 5 October from Raggruppamenti to Regimenti and are now 1° Regimento 'Antares' at Viterbo; 4° Regimento 'Altair' at Bolzano; and 5° Regimento 'Rigel' at Casarsa. Each regiment contains between eight and 12 flights, typically of six helicopters each.

NETHERLANDS:
Last F-16 squadron forms

No. 316 Squadron, the last Netherlands unit to convert to General Dynamics F-16s, re-formed at Eindhoven on 1 October. Officially stood-down as an NF-5 unit on 1 May 1991, No. 316 underwent conversion training at Gilze-Rijen with No. 314 Squadron. On 26 September, F-16A J-136 was delivered to Eindhoven and the squadron began flying on 30 September with eight aircraft. Now with the planned strength of four F-16As and eight F-16B trainers, No. 316 (which has the badge of a hawk descending on its prey) is responsible for Theatre Operational Conversion of pilots.

SAR requirement

Three new rescue helicopters – Aérospatiale Dauphins, Agusta AB 412s or MBB/Kawasaki BK-117s – are to be bought by the Royal Netherlands Air Force to replace four Alouette IIIs of the SAR Vlucht at Leeuwarden. Other military Alouettes are due to be supplanted by a combat helicopter, which will not be suitable for rescue duties.

PORTUGAL:
T-Birds' farewell

Portugal retired its last six Lockheed T-33As on 14 October, the type having served with 103 Esquadra at Beja. The PAF received 35 T-Birds from 1953 onwards, including two RT-33As and five Canadian

Left: An Agusta-Sikorsky HH-3F Pelican of 15° Stormo at Agusta's Vergiate facility, seen with new camouflage scheme, RWRs and chaff/flare dispensers.

CT-133s. Greece and Turkey have the only European air forces still flying T-33s but a few are based with the Canadian contingent at Söllingen.

SPAIN:
Defence cuts revealed

Economies being imposed on the EdA were revealed as likely to reduce its commitment to the Eurofighter EFA from the previously announced 108 to 72. A further casualty is likely to be the planned avionics upgrade for the Mirage IIIEE fleet.

SWEDEN:
Fifth Gripen airborne

SIG Gripen 39-5, the fifth prototype, was first flown at Linköping on 23 October by Weikko Sunell, bringing the total of Gripen test missions to 216. Because of the early loss of 39-1, first production aircraft 39101 will also be assigned to trials. The air force has also learned that Parliament will allow development of the two-seat version of SIG Gripen (JAS 39B).

Elint upgrade planned

A further manifestation of stronger defence policies is the announcement of plans to replace the two veteran Tp 85 Caravelles operated by F 13M at Malmslätt on electronic intelligence (Elint)-gathering missions. The choice of a successor will be announced before next July from a shortlist including McDonnell Douglas MD-87, Gulfstream IV, Fokker 100 and Canadair Challenger.

SWITZERLAND:
Last Hawk delivered

Deliveries of 20 BAe Hawk Mk 66s were completed in November when the last (U-1270) was handed over to General Werner Jung, the aviation commander. First aircraft, U-1251, was built by BAe at Dunsfold and delivered to Switzerland on 8 November 1989. Remaining Hawks have been assembled locally by F+W from BAe kits, their RR/Turboméca Adour 861A engines provided by Schulzer Bros under a similar assembly agreement.

Fighters train in UK

BAe's privately-operated instrumented air combat range above the North Sea was used by the Swiss for the first time for a three-week deployment beginning on 4 October. Eight Northrop F-5s and five Mirage IIISs used RAF Waddington as a base for dissimilar adversary training of Militia (reservist) pilots who spent one week in the UK before being replaced by others from their units. Switzerland has previously exercised from Solenzara (Corsica) under the codename of Exercise SAKA, but is believed to have found its visit to Waddington (Exercise NORKA) more profitable and is likely to make regular annual visits.

TURKEY:
Anti-guerrilla attacks

Despite being host to allied air forces dissuading Saddam Hussein from attacking the Kurdish people in Iraq's northern territory, Turkey twice during October sent its own aircraft to attack targets in the area in retaliation for raids on its territory by Kurdish separatists. In the first air strike on 11 October, eight aircraft attacked targets about four miles from the Turkish border. On 25 October, in the third assault since early August, aircraft from Diyarbakir made a post-dawn raid lasting 20 minutes on a guerrilla base. This was followed by a one-hour helicopter attack, while further jet sorties were mounted later in the day.

Military Aviation Review

UNITED KINGDOM:
EH.101 confirmed for RN

Long anticipated, formal announcement of a Royal Navy order for 44 EHI EH.101 Merlin helicopters worth £1,500 million was made by the government on 2 September when Westland (half the EHI partnership, with Agusta of Italy) and IBM of the USA 'were chosen as joint prime contractors. Westland/IBM was selected in competition with a rival bid by BAe/GEC, which would have relegated EHI to the status of a sub-contractor providing airframes. By insisting that an avionics firm should be an integral part of the programme management, the MoD was stressing the importance of the helicopter's anti-submarine equipment and hoping to prevent a recurrence of the Nimrod AEW.Mk 3 fiasco, in which airframe and avionics were in separate worlds.

Destined to replace the Westland-built Sea King, Merlin will have a new dipping sonar to be developed by Ferranti-Thomson and an ESM suite from Racal, code-named Orange Reaper. Although IBM is a US firm, the winning consortium has declared that 100 per cent of the Merlin's hardware will originate in Europe and 98 per cent of the programme sub-contracts will be assigned in the UK or Italy. Deliveries will begin in 1995 – five years later than planned.

ASTOR returns to square one

After several years of assessing the relative merits of battlefield surveillance radars in Canberra and Defender (Islander) testbeds, the UK MoD was reported during October to be looking at the Gulfstream SRA-4 – which has a side-looking airborne radar – to satisfy its ASTOR (Airborne STand-Off Radar) requirement. Meanwhile, the bulbous-nosed ASTOR demonstrator Defender, fitted with a development of the Thorn-EMI Searchwater radar and now known as MASTOR, is being offered to Middle Eastern countries.

German QRA ends

RAF Germany made its final Quick Reaction Alert 'scramble' at Wildenrath on 2 October when two blue-painted Phantom FGR.Mk 2s of No. 19 Squadron (XT899 'B', plus XV408 'Z' which was still wearing the insignia of recently disbanded No. 92) were launched for a pre-planned mission. The sortie ended 45 years of such flights to police the Air Defence Identification Zone along what was previously the border between East and West Germany.

Base changes planned

Unconfirmed reports of possible base changes were circulating during October, including transfer of Wittering's Harriers (No. 1 Squadron and No. 233 OCU/No. 20 [Reserve] Squadron) to Bentwaters and movement of the Coltishall Jaguar force (Nos 6, 41 and 54 Squadrons) to nearby Woodbridge. The twin bases of Bent-

waters and Woodbridge are due to be vacated by the USAF before late 1993 and would provide hardened aircraft shelters not available at Coltishall and Wittering. RAF Wattisham is to close as an RAF base after the last Phantoms are withdrawn in March 1993. Resident No. 56 Squadron is due to be down-declared from NATO on 1 July 1992, followed by No. 74 in January 1993.

RAF Germany Tornado cuts

The RAF disbanded a Tornado GR.Mk 1 unit for the first time on 11 September when No. 16 Squadron at Laarbruch held its final parade. The traditions of the squadron will be maintained by allocating its 'number plate' to No. 226 OCU, the Jaguar training unit at Lossiemouth. Continuing the halving of RAF Germany, No. 2 Squadron transferred from Laarbruch to Marham on 3 December with its Tornado GR.Mk 1A tactical reconnaissance aircraft. Similarly-tasked No. 13 Squadron at Honington will move to Marham in 1992.

Lynx AH.Mk 9 in service

No. 673 Squadron, Army Air Corps, received its first two Westland Lynx AH.Mk 9s at Dishforth on 30 November although two (ZG886 and 887) had already flown in the September Exercise Certain Shield in Germany. Fitted with a wheel undercarriage and new-technology rotor blades which increase their cruising speed by 20 kt, the 16 new AH.Mk 9s on order are being delivered at the rate of two per month, alongside eight more converted from AH.Mk 1s. Dishforth re-opened as an army base on 21 February 1991 and is the home of 9 Regiment, AAC. Also due to re-equip with the uprated Lynx, No. 672 Squadron has been operating from the same base with Lynx AH.Mk 7s as an interim measure.

Fast ladies

Armed Forces Minister Archie Hamilton announced on 2 December that women will be trained to fly RAF combat aircraft. Those currently under instruction are limited to second-line duties, but the restriction has been dropped by the RAF after the Royal Navy recently allowed women to train for Sea King and Lynx helicopter flying, in which role they could come under enemy fire. The first woman to gain her wings after joining the RAF specifically for aircrew duties (as distinct from being transferred to flying from another branch) was Pilot Officer Jane Crowther, who qualified at No. 3 FTS, Cranwell, on 11 October and is to receive multi-engined training in 1992.

First ladies

Cadet Pilot Kate Sanders of Cambridge University Air Squadron reluctantly made RAF history on 24 September when she ejected from the rear seat of a No. 233 OCU Harrier T.Mk 4A (XZ147) which crashed during a low-level flight over

Below: A Norwegian air force DHC-6 Twin Otter of No. 719 Skvadron, based at Bodø, in a new two-tone colour scheme with toned-down national markings. This was a rare visitor to Britain.

Above: Various Dutch fighter squadrons have celebrated important anniversaries by painting up their F-16s. Above is 312's 40th anniversary aircraft, while above right is 311's.

Humberside. Sanders was only the second woman known to have used an ejection seat and was only narrowly beaten by Lieutenant Linda Heid, USN, who vacated a Grumman A-6E in February 1991.

25-year jamming session

While other squadrons have been celebrating 75 years since their formation, Wyton-based No. 360 marked its 25th anniversary

over the weekend of 9/10 November – rather belatedly, as the unit was actually formed on 1 April 1966. Equipped with BAC Canberra T.Mk 17/17As, No. 360 is 25 per cent manned by the Royal Navy for its role of giving air defence radar operators on land, sea and in the air experience of working in an offensive jamming environment. The squadron will disband in 1993 or 1994 and has already withdrawn the first of its dozen aircraft.

Eastern Europe

COMMONWEALTH OF INDEPENDENT STATES (FORMER SOVIET UNION):
Separate armed forces

Accelerating breakdown of the former USSR, the Ukraine declared formation late in October of its own armed forces and decreed itself independent on 2 December following a referendum. Some anxiety was caused in the West by the prospect of several breakaway republics gaining control of the nuclear missiles on their territory, but less importance was attached to the air forces which have been called into being by the declarations of independence. Russia, the dominant republic, houses most of the strategic bomber force and the majority of nuclear missiles, comprising 331 SS-11s, 40 SS-13s, 47 SS-17s, 204 SS-18s, 170 SS-19s, 43 SS-24s (10 in silos; 33 on rail-cars) and 207 SS-25s. Ukraine (130 SS-19s and 46 silo-based SS-24s) and Belorussia (54 SS-25s) agreed to pool their weapons with Russia, each republic having

power of veto on their use. Kazakhstan (104 SS-18s) was expected to join the agreement, although there was uncertainty as to which individual would be supreme commander, as Mr Gorbachev was by then in the unenviable position of president of an empire which had ceased to exist.

Military reductions confirmed

US intelligence estimates, released in September, of military aviation in the former USSR, indicate that aircraft production in almost every category has decreased 25 per cent since 1988, one important exception being bomber manufacture, which shows a smaller dip. Conversely, helicopter building is down by 40 per cent.

The potential size of the combat element in any autonomous air force which might be established by the republics is suggested by a breakdown of aircraft distribution released by the US. Dispositions of interceptor and tactical attack aircraft (excluding reserves and those in storage) are

Above right, right and below right: Portugal has now retired the last of its T-33s. One aircraft carried the legend '38 years' on one side and '65,000 hours' on the other. Standard training aircraft wore light grey and Dayglo colours. The T-33 remains in use with fellow NATO member Greece.

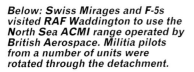

Below: Swiss Mirages and F-5s visited RAF Waddington to use the North Sea ACMI range operated by British Aerospace. Militia pilots from a number of units were rotated through the detachment.

estimated to be: Armenia nil and nil; Azerbaijan 30/100; Belorussia 110/360; Georgia 50/190; Kazakhstan 100/240; Kirgizia and Moldavia, no aircraft; Russia 1,400/980, plus the majority of strategic bombers; Tajikistan nil and nil; Turkmenistan 70/90; Ukraine 230/620; and Uzbekistan 20/260. In addition, the Baltic states claiming independence from Moscow may have to return military equipment on their territory as a condition.

Tupolev troubles

In an unprecedented interview, air force Commander in Chief Colonel General Piotr Dienekin revealed that design shortcomings in the Tupolev Tu-160 'Blackjack' were having a serious effect on the aircraft's ability to perform its bombing mission. Two years ago, Dienekin unsuccessfully attempted to have the Tupolev bureau prosecuted over alleged deficiencies in both the Tu-160 and earlier Tu-22M 'Backfire'.

'Russian Knights' make Western debut

On 18 September – exactly four weeks to the day after the coup attempt against President Gorbachev failed – a new chapter in aviation history was opened at RAF Scampton as six Sukhoi Su-27 'Flanker' long-range interceptors of the Russkiye Veetyaze ('Russian Knights') aerobatic team arrived for a goodwill visit to the United Kingdom. Scampton is the home of the Hawk-equipped 'Red Arrows' aerobatic team, whose 1990 tour of the USSR inspired the Soviet Air Force (Voyenno-Vozdushnyye Sily) to form its own equivalent. Fittingly, the team's first visit abroad was to the 'Red Arrows'.

Led by Lieutenant General Nikolai Timofeyevich Antoshkin, who is also Commander of the Air Force of the Moscow Military District, the 'Russian Knights' are drawn from the No. 1 Squadron of the Proskurovskii Guards Regiment at Kubinka Air Base, near Moscow.

The team line-up of a precision, close-formation four-ship plus a single aerobatic aircraft was demonstrated at two Battle of Britain displays (Leuchars and Finningley).

Yak-141 disaster

Hopes of continuing with development of the Yakovlev Yak-141 supersonic V/STOL fighter for export (following its cancellation in September by the navy) appear to have been eliminated in November when one of the two prototypes was destroyed in a crash. While landing aboard the carrier *Admiral Gorshkov* in Severomorsk harbour in November, the aircraft struck the deck heavily and was destroyed by fire, although the pilot ejected safely.

Naval 'Flanker' trials

Happier naval landings were enjoyed on 26 September when the Sukhoi Su-27K 'Flanker-D' made its first arrested landings aboard the *Admiral Kuznetsov* (formerly *Tbilisi*), cruising in the Black Sea. Over a two-day period, Lieutenant Colonel Apakidze, Colonel Artemyev, Colonel Yakovlev and Colonel Yedush all flew from the vessel.

YUGOSLAVIA:

Air actions continue

Aerial attacks by the Serbian-dominated national armed forces progressively diminished during the autumn as areas of Croatia were occupied – allegedly for incorporation in a 'greater Serbia'. Zagreb, Karlovak, Vukovar and Osijek were among towns and cities bombed – principally by MiG-21s, Super Galebs and Jastrebs, although a MiG-29 was reportedly

shot down near Osijek on 17 October. Several civilian airfields were attacked during September, including Osijek, Varazdin, Hvar and Senj, as well as the airport at Zagreb, and some light aircraft were destroyed. A Galeb crashed off Mlat on 5 September, killing the pilot.

A major land assault in mid-September was supported by air strikes. On 16 September, four MiG-21s violated Hungarian airspace and five jet aircraft were claimed shot down by Croat militia near Petrinja and Sisak – of which two MiG-21s and a Jastreb (near Donji Miholjac) were independently confirmed. An SA-7 missile destroyed a Galeb near Varazdin on 17 September and two further MiG-21s were lost on 18 September (near Ogulin and Petrinja). Two Oraos fell on 19 September, near Jakovo and Novska, followed by a Jastreb lost to an SA-7 near Sibenik on the next day. (A helicopter was claimed destroyed at the same location and date.) Early in October, two more MiG-21s fell to ground fire whilst attacking Dubrovnik, bringing claimed shoot-downs by the forces of Croatia to 41 – a figure some observers suggest should be reduced by at least two-thirds. A MiG-21 pilot flew his aircraft to Klagenfurt in Austria on 25 October and claimed political asylum. Croatia and Slovenia ratified their earlier declarations of independence from Yugoslavia on 8 October, Macedonia having become the third republic to secede, on 8 September.

The federal air force has transferred aircraft from bases in Croatia, some moving to reserve airfields at Bajna Baäta, Glamou, Udbina and Zalueane. The latter took J-22 and reconnaissance IJ-22 Oraos from Cerklje, while IJ-1 recce Jastrebs from the latter moved to Tuzla. Jastrebs and G2-A Galebs from the training school at Zemunik were installed at Ubidna. MiG-21s and G4 Super Galebs are believed to have left Pula.

Middle East

EGYPT:

Third-batch F-16s arrive

The EAF took first delivery on 24 October of its third GD Fighting Falcon batch (Peace Vector III), which will comprise 40 F-16Cs and seven F-16Ds to equip two squadrons and make good attrition. All are to block 40 standard and fitted with General Electric F110 engines. In two previous orders, the EAF received 34 F-16As, seven F-16Bs, 36 F-16Cs and four F-16Ds from 1982 onwards, these having Pratt & Whitney F100s. A fourth batch of 46 block 50 aircraft is in prospect for 1994.

ISRAEL:

Surprise deliveries

Deliveries of two unannounced aircraft orders to the IDF/AF caused surprise in military circles, the most notable being of second-hand McDonnell Douglas F-15As. Apparently to redress the 1990 emergency supply of F-15Cs to Saudi Arabia, F-15As

formerly with the 122nd TFS, Louisiana ANG, began passing through Bitburg, Germany, bound for Israel, where the first four were received on 23 October. By the following month, eight had been supplied from up to 25 expected.

KUWAIT:

First Hornet

Ordered prior to the Iraqi invasion of August 1990, the first of 40 McDonnell Douglas Hornets on order was handed over at St Louis on 8 October. The aircraft was one of eight F/A-18D two-seat trainers which will later be joined by 32 F/A-18Cs. The Kuwaiti batch is also of significance in being the first to be powered by the –402 version of the General Electric F400 reheated turbofan. Delivery schedules called for the first F-18s to be flown to Kuwait in January 1992, but because of extensive damage at Ahmed al Jaber AB, the aircraft will initially operate from Ali al Salem. An assessment of occupation and war damage suggests that Kuwait's military facilities suffered 83-85 per cent destruction.

Military Aviation Review

SAUDI ARABIA:
UK arms contracts

Deliveries began in the autumn of six reconnaissance-configured Panavia Tornados (similar to the RAF's GR.Mk 1A) as part of the batch of 48 IDS variants included in the 1985 Al Yamamah I defence contract with the UK government. Operating unit is No. 66 Squadron, following complete equipment of No. 7 Squadron at Dhahran with 24 aircraft between 1986 and 1989. At the same time, the Saudi Ambassador to the USA stated the long-postponed Al Yamamah II will be implemented shortly. Compared with original proposals for 36 Panavia Tornado ADV interceptors, 12 Tornado IDSs, 60 BAe Hawk 200s and 88 Westland-Sikorsky Black Hawks, 'AY II' is now understood to involve 48 IDSs, 60 Hawks and only 40 Black Hawks. The RSAF is said to have abandoned its requirement for ADVs because of the aircraft's alleged poor performance in the Gulf War. Instead, Saudi Arabia let it be known that it would ask the US for 72 McDonnell Douglas F-15Fs and two-seat F-15Gs, these being projected air-superiority developments of the multi-role F-15E Strike Eagle. After objections by the pro-Israeli lobby in Washington, Saudi Arabia backpedalled the proposals.

Right: A Sukhoi Su-27 'Flanker-B' of the 'Russian Knights' aerobatic team, part of the Kubinka-based Proskurovskii Guards Regiment. This specialised demonstration unit also includes the MiG-29-equipped 'Swifts' aerobatic team. The 'Russian Knights' visited the RAF's 'Red Arrows' at RAF Scampton in September.

Above: No. 360 Squadron, the RAF's youngest, celebrated 25 years' existence, all on the Canberra T.Mk 17. One aircraft received a red tailfin in celebration. Replacement by cheaper-to-run biz jets is around the corner.

Right: One of the Royal Navy's 'Sharks' display team Gazelles prepares to take off under a very threatening sky at Redhill's prestigious Helitech exhibition.

Southern Asia

AFGHANISTAN:
'Fencers' boost AAF

Reports from Kabul indicated that the former USSR was continuing to support the government against rebel forces, despite having withdrawn its own combat units, in the form of 15 recently-delivered Sukhoi Su-24MK 'Fencer-Ds'. Optimised for all-weather interdiction, the sophisticated Su-24 would appear to be over-complicated for the roles of close air support and COIN which are the main tasks of the AAF.

Far East

CHINA:
J-9's maiden flight

In a rare contemporary announcement of a significant military aviation event, China revealed that the prototype of a new combat aircraft, designated J-9, had flown for the first time at Sichuan on 5 September. Commentators linked the aircraft to the 'completely new' single-seat fighter which was believed to be under development in the late 1980s, drawing on Israeli data from the cancelled Lavi programme. Features are said to include canards, composite construction and fly-by-wire controls.

JAPAN:
Local Seahawks delivered

Production deliveries were begun in the autumn to the Maritime Self Defence Force of the first Mitsubishi-built Sikorsky SH-60J Seahawks, launching the process of replacing 167 SH-3 Sea Kings built by the same firm. The helicopter, initial examples of which are to be operated by the trials unit, No. 51 Squadron at Atsugi, features a high proportion of local avionics, including the submarine detection equipment. General Electric T700 turboshaft engines – two of which power each SH-60 – are built under licence by Ishikawajima-Harima.

TAIWAN:
Turbo Trackers accepted

Re-delivery was achieved of two RoCAF Grumman Trackers modified by the manufacturer in the US to S-2T standard with a pair of Garrett TPE331-15AW turboprop engines, Litton AN/APS-504(V)-5 radar, FLIR and other improved avionics. Also covered by the 1986 contract is local conversion by AIDC at Taichung of a further 30 aircraft.

THAILAND:
Aircraft commitments

Commitments were made to two combat aircraft orders in September, the first involving a US offer of 14 General Dynamics F-16As and four F-16Bs powered by Pratt & Whitney F100 engines and accompanied by six sets of Martin LANTIRN night-navigation and -targetting pods. The RTAF also announced that its attack aircraft requirement was to be fulfilled by the Italo-Brazilian AMX, 38 of which are needed, including 12 two-seat trainers. It was also revealed that six Pacific Aerospace Corporation CT-4 Airtrainers were on order for the RTAF, for 1992 delivery.

Above: This blue-painted Phantom FGR.Mk 2 (wearing the colours of No. 92 Squadron) was one of a pair which flew the last RAF Germany QRA (better known as 'Battle Flight') scramble on 2 October 1991. Nos 19 and 92 Squadrons then disbanded.

Australasia

AUSTRALIA:
Tanker crashes

Delivery during October of the third of four planned tanker conversions of its Boeing 707 fleet was marred by the loss of one aircraft which dived into the sea near East Sale on 29 October, killing all six aboard. Remaining 707s were temporarily grounded.

Seahawk line completed

Following the army's receipt of its 39th and last Sikorsky S-70A-9 Black Hawk in February, the Royal Australian Navy achieved full strength of 16 S-70B-2 Seahawks on 11 September when the last was delivered from ASTA at Avalon. The initial eight aircraft had been produced by Sikorsky and delivered from October 1989 after Hawker-de Havilland, the intended local assembly contractor, withdrew from the agreement. ASTA (Aerospace Technologies of Australia) was then engaged to complete the final eight. Operated by HS-816 at Nowra, NSW, the Seahawks participated in the naval embargo of Iraq before and during the Gulf War.

BRUNEI:
Aircraft sales firmed up

Brunei's small air arm re-confirmed during September that it planned to proceed with purchases of BAe Hawks and four maritime patrol/transport aircraft. The long-standing Hawk requirement is now stated to be for 16 two-seat Srs 100 air-

Above: This Yugoslavian air force Mikoyan-Gurevich MiG-21 defected to Klagenfurt in Austria on 25 October 1991, its pilot claiming political asylum. The aircraft is to remain in Austria until hostilities cease. Interestingly, the three-digit nose code has been painted out, but the aircraft serial number remains on the tailfin. MiG-21s have played a part in operations against Croatian positions.

craft instead of a mixture of these and single-place Srs 200s. Airtech CN.235s, built in Indonesia by IPTN, are understood to have been chosen for the second requirement and will comprise one transport and three CN.235MPAs delivered in 1994 with Litton AN/APS-504(V)-5 search radar, GEC TICM II forward-looking infra-red and Marconi Sky Guardian Srs 300 ESM. In recognition of its expansion plans, the Air Wing was re-named in October as the Royal Brunei Air Force.

Africa

SOUTH AFRICA:
Turbo-Dakota revealed

Foreshadowed by earlier statements affirming that the SAAF would shortly have no piston-engined aircraft, the first turbo-conversion of the military Douglas DC-3/C-47 fleet was unveiled in September. With Pratt & Whitney Canada PT6A turboprops, Hartzell five-bladed propellers and a fuselage 'stretch', the aircraft emerging from production lines at two SAAF bases are similar to the Basler conversions produced at Oshkosh. When the programme is completed in 1994, the SAAF will have given each of its 40 Dakotas a 1-tonne increase in payload, 80 km/h (50 mph) additional cruising speed and 402 km (250 miles) in extra range. Following retirement of its Piaggio P.166S maritime patrollers, the SAAF is planning to develop a special Turbo-Dakota in the same role with radar and additional tankage to extend endurance to 12-14 hours.

ZAÏRE:
Europeans evacuated

French paratroopers were flown to Zaïre on 24 September to seize the airport at Kinshasa as an airhead for the evacuation of some 4,000 Europeans. Belgian troops and aircraft also joined in a two-month airlift, which was prompted by a mutiny by the Zaïre army and the collapse of public order.

South America

BOLIVIA:
Turbo DC-3s

Following the lead set by El Salvador, Bolivia became the second Latin-American nation to adopt turboprop conversion as a means of keeping its venerable Douglas DC-3s and C-47s operational. One Basler Turbo-67 conversion was delivered to the FAB in September, the aircraft having Pratt & Whitney Canada PT6A-67 turboprops and a 1-m (3-ft 4-in) fuselage 'stretch' to maintain its centre of gravity. Basler, which has its production line at Oshkosh, has a further order from the Colombian air force. Replacement of P & W Twin Wasp radial piston engines by turbines extends the availability of the DC-3/C-47 in most of the Third World, where aviation gasoline is scarce.

North America

CANADA:
European withdrawal timetable

HQ Canadian Forces announced that Baden-Söllingen will close in 1994 when Nos 421 and 439 Squadrons return with their 32 CF-18s and 1,400 personnel to Canada. Nearby Lahr – the European airhead and home of No. 444 Squadron's CH-136 Kiowas – will cease operations in 1995. A third Hornet unit, No. 409, disbanded in 1991, donating some of its aircraft to Nos 421 and 439.

Once Europe-based aircraft have returned home, the CF-18 force will be reduced from seven to four squadrons, two of which will be on notice for return to Europe in an emergency and two assigned to support of maritime operations. Prime role, however, will be air defence of Canada.

Maritime air expansion

Modernisation of Canada's maritime air units was announced in the form of an expansion of utility squadrons VU-32 at Shearwater (Atlantic) and VU-33 at Comox (Pacific). Each currently has six Canadair/Lockheed CT-133s and two Bell

BRAZIL:
Tucano-H first flight

EMBRAER attempts to give a new lease of life to the Tucano production line in its home country resulted in the first flight on 9 September of the EMB-312H version (PT-ZTW). Characterised externally by a 1.4-m (4-ft 7¾-in) fuselage extension, the new Tucano has a 1,508-eshp Pratt & Whitney Canada PT6A-67 turboprop engine which doubles its installed power, compared with the original EMB-312. To this extent, the EMB-312 re-invents the Shorts Tucano used by the Royal Air Force to train students on an aircraft with jet-like performance, the prize sought for the EMB-312H being the USAF's JPATS requirement. For this, EMBRAER is planning a 'glass cockpit' and even more power (1,600 eshp from a PT6A-68), but it has yet to secure the most important aspect: a US partner firm.

AMX passes 1,000 hours

Two years after the first locally-built EMBRAER A-1 AMX was delivered to 1°/16° GAv (1 Squadron/16 Wing) of the FAB on 17 October 1989, the type achieved its 1,000th hour of service flying. 16° GAv had received 11 aircraft by October 1991 and was expecting delivery of the first two-seat AMX-T from 14 included in the initial 79 aircraft to be ordered.

(Model 212) CH-135s, but will replace its veteran T-33s through purchase of 11 new combat support aircraft of unspecified type. Additionally, up to nine inshore patrol aircraft will belatedly replace the withdrawn DHC/Grumman Trackers and reduce pressure on the CP-140 Aurora force. SAR units are expected to share some 15 EHI EH.101 helicopters from Anglo-Italian production, while a further 35 of the type, fitted with more-advanced avionics, will replace Sikorsky CH-124 Sea Kings in the anti-submarine role.

Training privatised

Award of contracts for the privatised training of CF aircrew was announced in October to Canadair for a five-year period beginning July 1992. Leading a consortium of nine other firms, Canadair will be responsible for fixed-wing primary, multi-engined and continuation training, plus basic helicopter instruction and provision of related ground-support services. New equipment to be obtained comprises 12 Slingsby T.67C Firefly primary trainers from the UK and 12 Beech 90A King Airs for the multi-engined component. Two King Airs have also been leased for the CF's Central Flying School at Winnipeg

and designated CT-145. Helicopter instruction will be on 14 military Bell CH-139 JetRanger IIIs which Canadair is leasing back from the CF. The training package is to operate from Portage la Prairie, where Fireflies will provide 27 hours of screening to 50 students per year before they progress to Canadair CT-114 Tutors at No. 2 FTS, Moose Jaw. Helicopter trainees – again 50 per year – are to have 90 hours of training on CH-139s, while a similar number will receive the King Air course.

UNITED STATES:
British army helicopter tested in US

The British army's Westland Lynx AH.Mk 9 LBH (Light Battlefield Helicopter) underwent high-altitude and hot-weather tests in the western United States in the summer of 1991. The helicopter (XZ170) was evaluated for high-altitude performance during the summer at Leadville, Colorado, and Alamosa, Colorado, at elevations from 7,000 to 10,000 ft (2167 to 3096 m). Thereafter, the same airframe conducted extreme high-temperature testing at Yuma, Arizona, where summer temperatures routinely exceed 38°C (100°F). XZ170 was equipped with the pneumatic undercarriage, powerplant modifications, and infra-red fixtures intended for British Army use.

A-10 'Warthog' scores top honours at Gunsmoke 91

The Fairchild A-10 'Warthog' attack aircraft took top honours in the individual and team categories at the US Air Force's Gunsmoke 1991 bombing and strafing competition at Nellis AFB, Nevada, in October 1991. In team standings, the 175th Tactical Fighter Group, Maryland Air National Guard, stationed at Baltimore, finished first. A-10 pilots from two units also finished first and second in the individual 'Top Gun' category, an F-16 pilot third. The Gunsmoke competition is held every two years.

The Fairchild A-10 'Warthog' attack aircraft's success is largely credited to the LASTE (Low-Altitude Safety Targeting Enhancement) modification developed and kit-built by General Electric and installed at the Sacramento (California) Air Logistics Center.

The USAF has postponed plans to retire the A-10 and plans to keep two wings of the aircraft for the attack role and two more of OA-10A FAC (forward air control) aircraft. The LASTE package gives the A-10 an autopilot feature it previously lacked, tied into the targetting computer to provide a CCIP (continuously-computed impact point) pipper on the pilot's HUD (head-up display) for both bomb release and cannon fire. The CCIP compensates for wind, dive angle, speed and bomb characteristics. While fighter-bombers at Gunsmoke 89 managed a CEA (circular error average) of around 3.5 m (11 ft 6 in) overall, the A-10s in 1991 scored a 2.25-m (7-ft 4-in) CEA.

In late 1991, 153 A-10s had been equipped with LASTE.

Military Aviation Review

F-117 upgrades

The US Air Force is improving the Lockheed F-117's sensor system. The F-117's FLIR (forward-looking infra-red), only recently revealed to have been built by Texas Instruments, is being improved to generate 'photographic quality' images on cockpit cathode ray terminals and liquid-crystal displays. The modification will "ease pilot workload in identifying and designating targets," says Lockheed's Paul Martin. At the same time, the USAF appears to have abandoned its hopes to re-engine the F-117. The aircraft uses the General Electric F404 but is unlikely to get the newer F414, which delivers 37 per cent more thrust.

Lockheed has also disclosed that 48 of the 56 F-117s have been retrofitted with a new thermoplastic fin set. The fin was redesigned after an older version came off an F-117 in flight, without mishap.

The manufacturers and the USAF are also looking at installing the ATARS reconnaissance system in the F-117. Rather than be loaded as a pod in the weapons bay, ATARS could be installed in existing space, according to Lockheed: new apertures in the weapons bay would be needed but ordnance load would be unchanged.

Recently declassified testimony by US Air Force officers describes technical problems in the F-117 programme that drove costs up and delayed the programme by nearly two years. Problems have been acknowledged in correlating the upper and lower FLIR (forward-looking infra-red) systems on the F-117, as well as its increased tail size. Pentagon officials also acknowledged that in its eagerness to sell stealth technology, the USAF 'distorted' the amount of assistance from conventional aircraft that the F-117 received during the Gulf War.

Instead of acknowledging that the F-117 benefited from the support of Air Force and Navy electronic warfare aircraft and missiles designed to blind Iraq's air defence network, the USAF claimed repeatedly that the F-117 "did all their bombing themselves."

Saudi purchase of more F-15s 'premature'

McDonnell Douglas has retracted a 5 November 1991 announcement that Saudi Arabia "intends to purchase" 72 new F-15 Eagle fighters, reportedly a mix of F-15Cs and F-15Fs, in addition to its current 98-plane F-15 force. The announcement, made at the Dubai 91 Air Show, is being called premature and provoked strong opposition from some members of the US Congress. The manufacturer also said that the United Arab Emirates have asked for 'pricing' of 26 F-15s, which it says is "one step away from announcing [an] intent to purchase."

In 1990, President Bush waived a congressional cap of 60 on the number of F-15s the Saudis can buy, but the Pentagon's position is that the current force is sufficient.

New Apaches for US Army, foreign buyers

US Army plans for upgrade of its AH-64 Apache fleet call for conversion of 254 AH-64A Apaches to AH-64B standard with near-term improvements based on Operation Desert Storm experience, and 535 to the AH-64C/D Longbow Apache configuration. McDonnell Douglas is converting four AH-64 Apache helicopters with Longbow Fire Control Radar and Hellfire Longbow missile seekers to act as proof-of-concept aircraft for the modernised AH-64C/D. Following completion of the Army's Longbow Apache Critical Design Review (CDR) in November 1991, first flight of the first converted Apache is scheduled for the second quarter of 1992.

McDonnell Douglas Helicopter has received limited funding to accelerate development of the AH-64C Apache to enable production deliveries to begin in mid-1995, a year ahead of the AH-64D. The AH-64C and AH-64D are identical except for radar and engine. The AH-64D

Above: A new nose radome, engine filters and Super Puma-style ventral fin identify this aircraft as an Oryx, a South African upgrade.

Below: Nigeria operates the Aermacchi M.B.339 in the advanced training and light strike roles.

has Longbow Fire Control Radar and General Electric T700-GE-701C engines in place of the -701 now used.

Foreign sales of the AH-64A Apache include 24 to Egypt, 20 to Greece, 18 to Israel, and an initial 12 for Saudi Arabia. Other countries interested in acquiring the Apache include the United Arab Emirates (20), South Korea (37), and Kuwait (32). The UAE was in the process of finalising a purchase in December 1991 and was expected to take delivery of six Apaches in 1993, 14 the following year.

First F-16C block 50 accepted by USAF

In November 1991, the US Air Force accepted the first F-16C block 50 Fighting Falcon, which is capable of employing the AGM-88B HARM (high-speed anti-radiation missile) and the new AGM-137 TSSAM (tri-service stand-off attack missile). F-16C block 50 aircraft have the General Electric F110-GE-129 IPE (improved performance engine), Hughes AN/APG-68(V5) radar with advanced signal processing capabilities, AN/ALR-56M radar warning receiver, and AN/ALE-47 chaff/flare dispenser system.

The F-16 was at the centre of a contentious budget battle between the two houses of the US Congress in late 1991. The two sides debated whether to fund 72 F-16C block 50s or new production of 24 Lockheed F-117 'Stealth Fighters'. The eventual compromise funded 48 F-16s and 12 F-117s in fiscal year 1992 (though start-up of the latter aircraft was later 'zero'-funded) and advance procurement for 24 additional F-16s in FY 1993.

Strategic Air Command chain of command reorganised

Strategic Air Command (SAC) implemented a major reorganisation on 1 September when it activated two additional

numbered Air Forces to streamline its chain of command, with each responsible for a particular activity. Prior to restructuring, the 8th Air Force at Barksdale AFB, Louisiana, and the 15th Air Force at March AFB, California, were responsible for virtually all SAC assets roughly on a geographical basis, with the former administering operations within the eastern half of the United States and Europe while the latter Air Force controlled those of the western USA and the Pacific region. Subordinate to the 8th Air Force were three air divisions, which in turn were responsible for 15 operational wings in addition to the Strategic Warfare Center at Ellsworth AFB, South Dakota. The 15th Air Force had 14 operational wings organised into four air divisions. Of the seven air divisions, five were eliminated, consisting of 14th AD at Beale AFB, California, 40th AD at Malmstrom AFB, Montana, 42nd AD at Grand Forks AFB, North Dakota, 57th AD at Minot AFB, North Dakota, and 100th AD at Whiteman AFB, Missouri, leaving just the 3rd AD at Hickam AFB, Hawaii, and 7th AD at Ramstein AB, Germany, to administer overseas activities.

The two new units are the 2nd Air Force at Beale AFB, California, which has been created to control all SAC reconnaissance assets such as the RC-135, U-2R and TR-1 aircraft, and the 20th Air Force at Vandenberg AFB, California, with responsibility for the Intercontinental Ballistic Missile (ICBM) fleet. The two existing AFs had their responsibilities realigned, with the 8th Air Force now assigned all of the manned bombers (B-1B and B-52G/H) while the 15th Air Force has assumed all front-line tankers (KC-10A and KC-135, plus EC-135s other than those at Offutt AFB).

Of the 29 operational wings, 15 are equipped with more than one specific type, such as the KC-135R and B-52H, and now report to more than one numbered Air Force. However, this should not present too many problems, as the AF's function is to exercise administrative control rather than to define policy.

Above: The first of Kuwait's F/A-18 Hornets have now been handed over, but remained in the USA for training until they were delivered.

Below: After a long grounding, Ghana's Short Skyvans were extensively refurbished by Airwork, and fitted with new avionics and radar.

SAC Unit Review

2nd Air Force (Beale AFB, CA)

6th Wing	24th SRS	Eielson AFB, AK	RC-135S/X, TC-135S
9th Wing	5th SRTS	Beale AFB, CA	T-38A, TR-1A/B, U-2R(T)
	5th SRS	RAF Akrotiri, Cyprus	U-2R
	6th SRS	Osan AB, RoK	U-2R
	95th SRS	RAF Alconbury, UK	TR-1A
	99th SRS	Beale AFB, CA	TR-1A, U-2R
	349th ARefS	Beale AFB, CA	KC-135Q
	350th ARefS	Beale AFB, CA	KC-135Q
55th Wing	1st ACCS	Offutt AFB, NE	E-4B
	2nd ACCS	Offutt AFB, NE	EC-135C
	38th SRS	Offutt AFB, NE	C-135A, NKC-135A
	343rd SRS	Offutt AFB, NE	KC-135E, RC-135U/V/W, TC-135W

8th Air Force (Barksdale AFB, LA (bombers)) & **15th Air Force** (March AFB, CA (tankers))

2nd Wing	62nd BS	Barksdale AFB, LA	B-52G
	596th BS	Barksdale AFB, LA	B-52G
	32nd ARefS	Barksdale AFB, LA	KC-10A
	71st ARefS	Barksdale AFB, LA	KC-135A/Q
5th Wing	23rd BS	Minot AFB, ND	B-52H
	906th ARefS	Minot AFB, ND	KC-135A
7th Wing	9th BS	Carswell AFB, TX	B-52H
	20th BS	Carswell AFB, TX	B-52H
	7th ARefS	Carswell AFB, TX	KC-135A
28th Wing	37th BS	Ellsworth AFB, SD	B-1B
	77th BS	Ellsworth AFB, SD	B-1B
	4th ACCS	Ellsworth AFB, SD	EC-135A/C/G/L
	28th ARefS	Ellsworth AFB, SD	KC-135R
42nd Wing	69th BS	Loring AFB, ME	B-52G
	42nd ARefS	Loring AFB, ME	KC-135R
	407th ARefS	Loring AFB, ME	KC-135R
92nd Wing	325th BS	Fairchild AFB, WA	B-52H
	43rd ARefS	Fairchild AFB, WA	KC-135R
	92nd ARefS	Fairchild AFB, WA	KC-135R
93rd Wing	328th BS	Castle AFB, CA	B-52G
	329th CCTS	Castle AFB, CA	B-52G
	93rd ARefS	Castle AFB, CA	KC-135A/R
	924th ARefS	Castle AFB, CA	KC-135A/R
96th Wing	337th BS	Dyess AFB, TX	B-1B
	338th BS	Dyess AFB, TX	B-1B
	917th ARefS	Dyess AFB, TX	KC-135A
319th Wing	46th BS	Grand Forks AFB, ND	B-1B
	905th ARefS	Grand Forks AFB, ND	KC-135R

379th Wing	524th BS	Wurtsmith AFB, MI	B-52G
	920th ARefS	Wurtsmith AFB, MI	KC-135A
384th Wing	28th BS	McConnell AFB, KS	B-1B
	384th ARefS	McConnell AFB, KS	KC-135R
410th Wing	644th BS	K. I. Sawyer AFB, MI	B-52H
	46th ARefS	K. I. Sawyer AFB, MI	KC-135A
	307th ARefS	K. I. Sawyer AFB, MI	KC-135A
416th Wing	668th BS	Griffiss AFB, NY	B-52G
	41st ARefS	Griffiss AFB, NY	KC-135R

15th Air Force (March AFB, CA)

19th Wing	99th ARefS	Robins AFB, GA	KC-135R
	912th ARefS	Robins AFB, GA	KC-135R
22nd Wing	6th ARefS	March AFB, CA	KC-10A
	9th ARefS	March AFB, CA	KC-10A
301st Wing	91st ARefS	Malmstrom AFB, MT	KC-135R
305th Wing	70th ARefS	Grissom AFB, IN	KC-135R, EC-135G/L
	305th ARefS	Grissom AFB, IN	KC-135R
340th Wing	11th ARefS	Altus AFB, OK	KC-135R
	306th ARefS	Altus AFB, OK	KC-135R
376th Wing	909th ARefS	Kadena AB, Okinawa	KC-135A
380th Wing	310th ARefS	Plattsburgh AFB, NY	KC-135A/Q
	380th ARefS	Plattsburgh AFB, NY	KC-135A/Q

20th Air Force (Vandenberg AFB, CA)

44th SMW	66th SMS	Ellsworth AFB, SD	LGM-30F
	67th SMS	Ellsworth AFB, SD	LGM-30F
	68th SMS	Ellsworth AFB, SD	LGM-30F
90th SMW	319th SMS	FE Warren AFB, WY	LGM-30G
	320th SMS	FE Warren AFB, WY	LGM-30G
	321st SMS	FE Warren AFB, WY	LGM-30G
	400th SMS	FE Warren AFB, WY	LGM-118A
91st SMW	740th SMS	Minot AFB, ND	LGM-30G
	741st SMS	Minot AFB, ND	LGM-30G
	742nd SMS	Minot AFB, ND	LGM-30G
321st SMW	446th SMS	Grand Forks AFB, ND	LGM-30G
	447th SMS	Grand Forks AFB, ND	LGM-30G
	448th SMS	Grand Forks AFB, ND	LGM-30G
341st SMW	10th SMS	Malmstrom AFB, MT	LGM-30F to G
	12th SMS	Malmstrom AFB, MT	LGM-30F to G
	490th SMS	Malmstrom AFB, MT	LGM-30F to G
	564th SMS	Malmstrom AFB, MT	LGM-30G
351st SMW	508th SMS	Whiteman AFB, MO	LGM-30F
	509th SMS	Whiteman AFB, MO	LGM-30F
	510th SMS	Whiteman AFB, MO	LGM-30F

SAC alert discontinued

President Bush announced on 17 September that all B-1B and B-52 manned bombers held on alert at their home bases, numbering approximately 40 aircraft, together with their KC-135s and tankers on alert at other SAC bases, would be stood down with immediate effect. SAC bombers and tankers have maintained a full-time alert for almost four decades with aircraft and aircrew on standby to be airborne within minutes of the alarm sounding. However, the missile force of LGM-118A Peacekeepers and LGM-30G Minuteman IIIs is not affected by the decision and will continue to be on 24-hour alert. The President also stated that the withdrawal of LGM-30F Minuteman IIs would be speeded up and all AGM-86B and AGM-129A air-launched cruise missiles would be removed from SAC aircraft and placed in storage. The LGM-30F was assigned to the 44th SMW at Ellsworth AFB, South Dakota, and 351st SMW at Whiteman AFB, MO, which are in the process of inactivating, while the 341st SMW will complete conversion to the LGM-30G from one of the remaining three wings, which will inactivate once transfer is complete.

Ongoing US operations in Middle East

The successful outcome of the Gulf War and the subsequent return home of the majority of US combat units permitted the spotlight to be shifted from Saudi Arabia and the Persian Gulf region to the resupply of the Kurdish refugees in the north of Iraq. However, as the exodus of US forces gathered pace, others arrived to act as a buffer against Saddam Hussein regaining ideas of expanding into neighbouring territory.

SAC reconnaissance aircraft have continued to operate daily sorties to monitor the situation inside Iraq, with TR-1A/U-2Rs detaching to Taif in south-west Saudi Arabia, while RC-135s have rotated to Riyadh Military City Airport. The 1704th Reconnaissance Squadron (Provisional) was established at Taif to co-ordinate operations of aircraft drawn from the 9th SRW at Beale AFB, California, and the 17th RW at RAF Alconbury, UK, although the provisional unit is believed to have been deactivated with the 9th SRW (now 9th Wing) being responsible for ongoing activities. The 55th SRW (now 55th Wing) has also continued to provide a presence in Saudi Arabia with RC-135V and W models rotating on a monthly basis to Riyadh while others have operated from the wing's detachment at Soudha Bay, Crete. This latter detachment was established to replace the one at Hellenikon Airport, Athens, and has been active monitoring events in the north of Iraq, while Riyadh-based aircraft monitor southern Iraq. Ongoing surveillance flights have continued primarily to ensure Saddam Hussein complies with United Nations orders to dismantle ballistic missile, nuclear, biological and chemical warfare production facilities and storage areas. The Stateside-based reconnaissance aircraft have transitted UK bases with the TR-1A/U-2Rs passing through Alconbury, while the RC-135s have staged via Mildenhall.

SAC has also retained tanker facilities at Riyadh, with some 15 KC-135Rs rotated regularly between the Saudi base and their Stateside homes with a stop-over at Mildenhall. The primary duty of these tankers is to provide air refuelling for US fighter aircraft remaining in the region.

However, the largest US presence in Saudi Arabia since the end of Desert Storm has been concentrated at Dhahran. The 4404th Composite Wing was established to co-ordinate the mixture of types drawn from SAC, TAC and USAFE. Amongst the types located at Dhahran during recent

Left: The prototype Tucano-H, an up-engined, stretched fuselage derivative of the basic EMB-312, made its maiden flight on 9 September 1991.

months have been the F-117A from 37th TFW (now 37th FW), with eight aircraft present (although this number was believed to have been increased during mid-September when President George Bush announced he was becoming increasingly frustrated by Iraqi intransigence). The 4th Wing from Seymour Johnson AFB, North Carolina, and the 347th TFW from Moody AFB, Georgia, have both maintained approximately a dozen aircraft in the region, with these two units operating at Dhahran by May. Air defence missions have been conducted by F-15As of the 49th TFW (now 49th FW) from Holloman AFB, New Mexico, while the 35th TFW from George AFB, California, has sent F-4Gs to the 4404th CW.

USAFE units assigned to the composite wing have included the 81st TFW from Bentwaters and Woodbridge (which has rotated A-10A squadrons with approximately a dozen aircraft at a time to Dhahran, in addition to supporting Operation Provide Comfort at Incirlik AB, Turkey), and the 42nd ECS from Upper Heyford with four EF-111As. The 52nd TFW from Spangdahlem AB, Germany, has bolstered the F-4G presence with four aircraft.

The 552nd AW&CW from Tinker AFB, Oklahoma, has maintained a detachment of three E-3B/C Sentries at Riyadh Military City Airport with a regular swopover taking place on a monthly basis. Additional E-3s have been rotated to Incirlik, enabling a complete overview of Iraq while orbiting from the safety of Turkish and Saudi Arabian airspace.

MAC has provided a number of Hercules squadrons to the Middle East with nine 463rd TAW C-130Hs assigned to Dhahran in late June/early July, which were replaced by nine 317th TAW C-130Es at the end of August. Air Force Special Operations Command has also had an ongoing presence with 1st SOW MH-53Js being located in Saudi Arabia during the summer, while a pair of 7th SOS MC-130Es from Rhein Main AB, Germany, were stationed at Dhahran between June and August. The 9th SOS at Eglin AFB, Florida, stationed a pair of HC-130Ns in the region during August.

The relief of the Kurdish refugees along the Turkish/Iraqi border under Operation Provide Comfort has continued unabated since April, with several USAF squadrons detaching to Incirlik. As mentioned earlier, the 81st TFW sent a dozen A-10As to provide close air support (CAS) to the MAC C-130s flying low-level resupply sorties over the mountainous region. Added to these were the 86th FW from Ramstein AB, Germany, which sent a small detachment of F-16Cs also to conduct CAS missions. A dozen F-111Fs from 494th TFS (now 494th FS) from Lakenheath and four 42nd ECS EF-111As were flown to Incirlik in late September as part of the overall increase in forces.

During October the US reached agreement with the Bahraini and Kuwaiti governments over future access to facilities, joint exercises and the storage of equipment. Similar talks were being conducted with the United Arab Emirates and Oman as the Saudis were concerned about the continued US presence on their soil, and it is likely that all remaining forces will relocate to these countries bordering the Persian Gulf.

Right: This Westland Lynx AH.Mk 9 underwent high altitude and high temperature trials in Colorado during the summer of 1991. The type entered service in November with No. 673 Squadron, part of 9 Regiment AAC, at Dishforth.

Above: No. 419 Squadron, Canadian Forces, has painted one of its CF-5A Freedom Fighters in this attractive colour scheme, complete with the unit's charging moose insignia on the tailfin.

Above: An anonymous-looking HH-3, serial number overpainted. This was one of the least well-known USAF participants in Operation Desert Storm.

Below: With the impending Canadian withdrawal from Europe, the Canadair CL-66 Cosmopolitan (known as the CC-109 in CF service) will become an increasingly rare sight. Canada will lose three of its seven Hornet units when the two Baden-based squadrons move home.

Major commands to be axed

Air Force Secretary Donald Rice announced on 17 September that the USAF is to undergo the largest reorganisation in its history. Under the plan the three major commands of Military Airlift Command (MAC), Strategic Air Command (SAC) and Tactical Air Command (TAC) will all disappear during mid-1992 and be replaced by two organisations tentatively identified as Air Combat Command (ACC) and Air Mobility Command (AMC). The former will be responsible for deterrence and air campaign operations and will include fighters and command, control and communications types from TAC, bombers, reconnaissance types and Intercontinental Ballistic Missiles (ICBMs) from SAC, as well as former SAC tankers and some tactical airlifters of the composite wings. AMC will be assigned the missions of intercontinental and theatre airlift, and air refuelling employing the majority of transport and the remaining tanker aircraft, plus all front-line rescue and aeromedical evacuation assets. ACC will have its headquarters at Langley AFB, Virginia, occupying the complex currently housing HQ TAC, while AMC will have its HQ at Scott AFB, Illinois, which is currently home to HQ MAC. AMC will establish a central tanker and airlift control centre to maximise assets and mission requirements, enabling the best use of limited resources.

The giant underground headquarters of SAC at Offutt AFB, Nebraska, will be the site of Strategic Command, which is the new joint service command due to be formed on 1 June 1992 with operational control of all USAF and US Navy nuclear weapons. General Lee Butler, who is currently CinC SAC, is expected to head the new command, although the position will alternate between the Air Force and Navy.

The reorganisation has been made possible due to the concept evaluated on a small scale at Incirlik AB, Turkey, during Desert Storm, when different types were successfully operated under a single manager as a composite wing. This led not only to the establishment of additional composite wings but also to the amalgamation of assets from different commands. The primary advantage is seen as a way of increasing flexibility and reducing the reaction time to deploy overseas with a simplified chain of command. Once established, these composite wings will gear their training towards rapid movement as an integrated package.

The two new Commands will be responsible for units based in the continental United States, although their area of operations will continue to be worldwide. However, those MAC and SAC units which are currently stationed overseas in Europe and the Pacific, together with those whose complement is made up of rotational aircraft on a regular basis from the USA, will be transferred to either USAFE or PACAF. This will include KC-135 tankers, C-130 theatre airlifters, and VIP types including the C-12F, C-20A, C-21A and UH-1N.

Unit designation changes

The Air Force recently adopted a change in designation system with the elimination of the prefix identities 'Military', 'Strategic' and 'Tactical' to most MAC, SAC, TAC, PACAF and USAFE units. One of the first to adopt the new system was MAC, whose commander, General H. T. Johnson, authorised the amalgamation of the 89th MAW (with a variety of VIP types) and the 1776th ABW (a non-flying administrative unit) both at Andrews AFB, Maryland, as the 89th Airlift Wing (89th AW) on 12 July. Subsequently, the 60th, 62nd, 63rd, 436th, 437th, 438th and 443rd MAWs, together with the 375th AAW, have all had their prefix designations removed and are now simply airlift wings. As yet, the four tactical airlift wings and the variety of military airlift groups have not changed, although they are due to be redesignated shortly. The individual flying squadrons will also change designation in due course.

Above: With tailcodes removed, but retaining USAF serial and star and bar, this former 163rd TFS F-4E was pictured at NAS Willow Grove on delivery to the Greek air force. A small Hellenic flag is just visible on the intake. Only a handful of recce and 'Wild Weasel' Phantoms remain in USAF, AFRes and ANG service.

Right: The proposed new F/A-18F features a stretched fuselage, enlarged wing, extra hardpoints, non-afterburning engines and square-section air intakes. Intended as a carrierborne light/medium strike aircraft for the US Navy, many believe that the new type would also be an excellent F-16 replacement for the USAF.

On 1 October 1991 all SAC flying wings changed designation with the deletion of the prefix titles 'Bombardment', 'Air Refueling' and 'Strategic Reconniassance'. The 23 major flying units are now simply identified as wing, which is abbreviated to Wg. For example, the 2nd Bombardment Wing is now 2nd Wing, while the 55th Strategic Reconnaissance Wing is now 55th Wing. The squadrons have not changed their designations as there are several whose numerical identity would clash in abbreviated format but for the allocation of role, i.e. 9th Bombardment Squadron at Carswell AFB, TX, and 9th Air Refueling Squadron at March AFB, CA.

The tactical fighter community in the Pacific and Europe, as well as the USA, has commenced changes to their designation system with the F-16C/D-equipped 432nd TFW at Misawa AB, Japan, being one of the first units to remove the prefix 'tactical' and become the 432nd Fighter Wing, while the 13th and 14th TFSs have changed to Fighter Squadrons.

However, the majority of other units which are known to have changed appear to have implemented the new designation on 1 October. In Europe, the 20th FW at Upper Heyford, 48th FW at Lakenheath and 36th FW at Bitburg have all been confirmed, and it is probable the 52nd TFW at Spangdahlem AB, Germany, and the 32nd

TFG at Soesterberg AB, the Netherlands, have also altered their designations. The squadrons assigned to the 20th, 36th and 48th FWs have also removed the 'tactical' prefix to their designations. The 10th and 81st TFWs remain unchanged, as apart from primarily being tactical units operating the A-10A, both are scheduled to cease operations during 1992/1993. The 86th FW at Ramstein AB, Germany, adopted its revised title during the spring of 1991 as one of the spearhead units.

Many TAC units have removed the word 'tactical', while some training units have changed designation altogether, which in two instances has involved the amalgamation of two wings into one. Those Tactical Fighter Wings which are confirmed as having changed designation are the 1st, 27th, 37th, 49th, 363rd and 388th, while the 31st, 33rd, 56th, 67th (TRW), 347th, 366th have probably adopted the new unit title also. At Davis-Monthan AFB, Arizona, the 355th TTW has become a Fighter Wing, as the unit is likely to retain the A-10A within the new Air Combat Command. However, the 23rd and 354th TFWs are scheduled to deactivate once their A-10As have retired, and therefore will not alter their designations.

At Luke AFB, Arizona, the 405th TTW was assigned three squadrons of F-15s, while the 58th TTW had three F-16C/D

squadrons. However, the F-15A/Bs of 555th TFTS are in the process of transferring to 325th TTW to consolidate Eagle training at Tyndall AFB, Florida, with the exception of the F-15E which will continue at Luke AFB. The two F-15E squadrons at Luke AFB – 461st and 550th TFTSs – are being reassigned from the 405th TTW to the 58th FW joining the 310th, 311th and 314th FSs. The 49th FW at Holloman AFB, New Mexico, has added the AT-38Bs of the former 479th TTW to its complement. The latter unit had four squadrons of Talons assigned, although the majority have been retired or transferred elsewhere as the lead-in fighter training role has diminished, with just the 433rd TFTS remaining. The 479th was downgraded to tactical training group status in March 1991, and has probably become simply a training group with responsibility for liaison between its single squadron and the parent wing. The 49th FW is to transition to the F-117A beginning in January 1992.

Skywarrior withdrawn from operational service

VQ-2 at NAS Rota, Spain, staged their 'Warrior Retirement' ceremony on 20/21 September to commemorate the withdrawal of the EA-3B from the squadron. The last five aircraft were ferried back to the USA during October for storage with AM&RC at Davis-Monthan AFB, Arizona. Among these final examples of the Skywarrior in Europe was TA-3B 144865/JQ-011, which was employed in the communications and training roles, sparing valuable flying hours of the EA-3Bs for operational duties.

One week later VAQ-33 at NAS Key West, Florida, held a retirement banquet on 27 September for the 'Whale', to officially mark the withdrawal of the type from operational service. During the same week the Naval Weapons Center at NAS China Lake, California, prepared their sole NA-3B for retirement. However, 14 aircraft remain in service with defence contractors, or as a source of spares, to conduct a variety of test roles.

Installation closure timetable

The President confirmed the timetable for the closure of the military installations announced earlier in 1991. A dozen USAF bases are to close within the next four years, with their assigned units being disbanded some months prior. Bases which will close in September 1993 are Bergstrom AFB, Texas, Carswell AFB, Texas, Eaker AFB, Arkansas, Myrtle Beach AFB, South Carolina, Williams AFB, Arizona, and Wurtsmith AFB, Michigan. Twelve months later Grissom AFB, Indiana, Loring AFB, Maine, Lowry AFB, Colorado, Richards Gebaur AFB, Missouri, and Rickenbacker ANGB, Ohio, will shut, while Castle AFB, California will close in September 1995. Of these, Carswell and Grissom will remain open as Reservist facilities.

At Eaker AFB the 97th Wing will inactivate at the end of 1991, while the 23rd TFW

at England AFB, 354th TFW at Myrtle Beach AFB and 82nd FTW at Williams AFB will inactivate by September 1992. The 379th Wing at Wurtsmith AFB will retire its B-52Gs by December 1992 and their KC-135As by March 1993, with the 7th Wing at Barksdale AFB following a similar timescale, although their B-52Hs are to be transferred to Barksdale AFB for reassignment to the 2nd Wing. The 67th TRW at Bergstrom AFB will inactivate by September 1992 with the retirement of the last front-line RF-4C Phantoms, followed six months later by the transfer of HQ 12th Air Force to Davis-Monthan AFB, Arizona.

Three bases are to be re-aligned, including Mountain Home AFB, Idaho, which will lose the EF/F-111As of the 366th TFW (to be 366th FW) prior to the formation of the first fully-integrated composite wing. Re-alignment is due to take place by September 1992 and will be followed one year later by Goodfellow AFB, Texas, and six months later by MacDill AFB, Florida. Goodfellow AFB conducts various non-aviation technical training courses and would appear not to have any aircraft units assigned in the future. MacDill AFB is home to the 56th TFW (to be 56th FW) with four squadrons of F-16C/Ds performing tactical fighter training, although the commitment is to transfer to Luke AFB in 1994.

With the Navy, NAS Chase Field, Texas, is to transfer its three squadrons – VT-24, VT-25 and VT-26 – to NAS Kingsville, Texas, and NAS Meridian, Mississippi, before the end of 1992, permitting the station to close the following year. NAS Moffett Field, California, was due to close within a similar timeframe, although the transfer of the P-3 Orion squadrons to NAS Barbers Point, Hawaii, NAS Brunswick, Maine, and NAS Jacksonville, Florida, will not be completed until 1996. In California the Pacific Missile Test Center (PMTC) at NAS Point Mugu and the Naval Weapons Center (NWC) at NAS China Lake will consolidate their activities in 1992, with both changing name to Naval Air Warfare Center (Weapons). The only Marine Corps facility affected by the closure plan is MCAS Tustin, California, whose helicopters will be redistributed between MCAS Camp Pendleton and a new facility being constructed at Twenty Nine Palms, both in California.

The Army occupies a large number of facilities and quite naturally several locations are earmarked for changes. Fort Devens, Massachusetts, is to become a training ground for Reservists following the transfer in 1992 of the 10th Special Forces Group to Fort Carson, Colorado, and the Intelligence School to Fort Huachuca, Arizona, by October 1995. The 7th Infantry Division will move to Fort Lewis, Washington, from Fort Ord, California, during 1993, while across San Francisco Bay Hamilton AAF will transfer the 6th Army Aviation Detachment to Fort Carson by September 1995, along with the HQ 6th US Army from Presidio to San Francisco. Despite not being affected by the closures, Fort Polk, Louisiana, will lose the 5th Infantry Division to Fort Hood, Texas, by September 1993. These changes will not involve any large-scale movement of aviation assets, although there will be some transfer of helicopter units.

BRIEFING

Above: An A-50 in flight, streaming powerful wingtip vortices. The tail turret is replaced by dielectric fairings serving the ESM system.

Below: The A-50 carries its rotodome above the rear fuselage, roughly level with the trailing edge of the wing. Clearly visible here is the dorsal 'canoe' in front of the wing.

Ilyushin A-50 'Mainstay'

Red Star AWACS

The first Soviet AWACS platform, the Tupolev Tu-126, code-named 'Moss' by NATO's Air Standards Co-ordinating Committee, emerged in the mid-1960s. Converted from Tu-114 airliner airframes, these aircraft combined long endurance with excellent crew accommodation, making them extremely popular. The Tu-126's replacement was based upon the airframe of the Il-76 heavylift transport (known as 'Candid' to NATO), and entered service in 1984.

By comparison with the basic Il-76, 'Mainstay' mounts a large rotodome above the rear fuselage, but also differs in less obvious ways. The tail gun turret is absent, replaced by various antennas, and the navigator's nose glazing is replaced by non-transparent fairings. A large dorsal antenna fairing projects forward from the leading edge above the fuselage, and a huge cooling air intake is located at the base of the tailfin.

Recently, details have begun to emerge about the development and deployment of the new aircraft, through *Krasnaya Zvesda* (the Soviet military newspaper) reports of military exercises in which 'Mainstay' has been involved, and through interviews with senior project engineers. Despite the fact that the A-50 represents a considerable advance over the old Tu-126, and despite its success in exercises, some criticism has arisen.

Vladimir Ivanov of the Vega NPO (Scientific Industrial Enterprise), the company responsible for systems design and integration, was the chief designer of the A-50's radar systems. He has compared the Soviet aircraft to the US E-3 Sentry. Like the Sentry, the A-50 carries a rotodome (rotating radome) some 9 m (30 ft) in diameter on twin, aerodynamically-faired struts above the rear fuselage, and according to Ivanov carries out the same basic missions with the same sized crew.

Ivanov does not pretend that the A-50 is as capable as the Sentry, and acknowledges some weaknesses. Because the Soviet electronics industry lags behind Western companies, many computers and display systems had to be developed from scratch specifically for the A-50, while the E-3 was able to use much existing equipment. This has often meant that Soviet equipment has been bulkier and heavier than its Western equiva-

Below: The port undercarrriage fairing incorporates an aerofoil-type winglet.

lents. Achieving the same performance has been an amazing leap, sometimes at the expense of lightness and simplicity. Hybrid silicon chips have had to be used instead of monolithic ones.

Weight growth has also been caused by the dissociation of the separate branches of the Soviet Armed Forces, which has necessitated the installation of duplicate systems to cope with different navy and air force command systems, data exchange formats and IFF interrogators. All decoding and interfacing are done on board, whereas much of the latter is undertaken on the ground for the E-3 Sentry.

Ivanov has estimated that the Soviet electronics equipment is some 50 per cent heavier than that fitted to the Sentry, and this is enough for landing gear weight limitations to prevent the A-50 from taking off with full fuel, reducing maximum endurance by about half an hour. This is not in itself especially significant, but the endurance problem is aggravated by the A-50's extremely poor air-to-air refuelling characteristics. Disturbed airflow from the rotodome reportedly makes it practically impossible to use the nose-mounted inflight-refuelling probe.

The designers of the A-50 have admitted that it is inferior to the E-3 in terms of absolute detection range and in terms of the number of interceptors which the aircraft can control. Above all, crew conditions are markedly inferior. This is a particular bugbear for A-50 crews, many of whom were used to the luxury of the Tu-126. Incredibly, for an aircraft with a crew of 15 and designed for missions of many hours' duration, the A-50 has neither crew rest bunks nor even a properly equipped toilet. Noise levels in the cabin are extremely high.

An A-50 'Mainstay' on the ground at its Pechora base. The 'Mainstays' were moved here from the Baltic region some two years ago.

Another A-50 weakness is reliability. The disintegration of the Soviet Union, and its economy, has led to severe disruption to the supply of spares, and the training of ground-crew has also suffered. It is routine for the flight engineer to remove and change electronic black boxes in flight. All of the shortcomings that have emerged are being rectified in a new modification and modernisation programme, although this is being threatened by budget cuts. Air defence commanders are reportedly supporting the programme very strongly, however.

The 'Mainstay' does, according to Soviet sources, enjoy some advantages over the E-3 Sentry. They claim better performance against ground clutter and claim an ability to gather and re-transmit (to aircraft and ground stations) data from satellites.

The main A-50 operating base is now at Pechora, in the Polar region, the move from the Baltic having been made some two years ago. It was necessary in order to station the aircraft at what Lieutenant General Timokhin, first deputy chief of the Main Air Defence Staff, described as the 'most dangerous direction'. Poor accommodation and social facilities at the new base have led to some morale problems.

The A-50 played a major part in re-

cent large-scale exercises in the Soviet Far East involving ships, submarines and aircraft from the IA-PVO, Long Range Aviation, Frontal Aviation and naval units. Operating from FOBs in the Far East, the A-50s guided MiG-31 interceptors to intercept naval cruise missiles flying at heights of between 36 and 61 m (120 and 200 ft), while supplying submarines with tactical information and simultaneously controlling engagements between interceptors and Naval Aviation Tu-26s and their escorts. The A-50s typically fly a figure-eight racetrack pattern at

about 10058 m (33,000 ft), with the distance between the two 'circles' of the pattern being about 100 km (62 miles).

Two of the A-50s operated from a base in the Black Sea area during Operation Desert Storm. Captained by Majors Alexei Serebrov and Vasilii Kubasov, the aircraft were on duty constantly, monitoring the US aircraft and even cruise missiles taking off or being launched from bases in Turkey. The A-50s acted as the main Soviet advanced listening and intelligence post.

Sikorsky SH-60F Ocean Hawk

The Navy's next-generation inner zone ASW platform

Having begun development in 1985, the Sikorsky SH-60F anti-submarine helicopter is now beginning to replace the SH-3H Sea King in US Navy service. Its initial fleet deployment was made with HS-2, part of Air Wing Seven, aboard the USS *Nimitz* (CVN-68). The squadron began transitioning to its new aircraft in October 1989, and initial service deliveries began in March 1990. During the *Nimitz*'s refresher training period, five of the squadron's new Ocean

Hawks flew 434 hours from the carrier. In their first six months of operation HS-2 achieved a total of 2,000 hours day and night, qualifying all aircrew in deck landings from both aircraft-carrier and destroyer decks. A detachment to NAS Fallon achieved the necessary strike rescue qualifications. Such rapid progress with a brand-new aircraft type spoke volumes for the SH-60F, and the professionalism of HS-2.

The first Atlantic Fleet squadron to

receive SH-60Fs, HS-3 'The Tridents' (CVW-7/NG) have greeted it with enthusiasm. Currently there are five on strength, undergoing integration into the squadron. A cousin of the SH-60B Seahawk, the new SH-60F has a much cleaner appearance, with the exterior AN/ALQ-142 ESM equipment, AN/ARQ-44 data-link antenna and AN/ASQ-81 MAD bird all absent. Neither has it the anti-ship capability, cargo hook or RAST (Recovery Assist Secure and Traverse)

deck landing equipment of the LAMPS III. While aircraft are flying from the parent carrier, the SH-60F can serve as a plane guard, equipped with a winch, but its primary function as a 'CV-helo' remains inner zone protection of the carrier battle group against submarine threats.

Looking inside the rear section of the cabin, most of the space is taken up by the Allied Signal (Bendix Oceanics) AN/AQS-13F Dunking Sonar and its associated reel mechanism. Directly in front of it sits the sensor operator. The great advantage of the new system, explained to *World Air Power Journal* by Sensor Operator AW-2 Roger Anderson, is that the sonar transducer itself contains the computer required to process the vast amount of signals it receives. Finished data is now transmitted via the thin connecting cable directly to the computer displays inside the cabin. The SH-3 has to carry its processing computer inside the cabin, which is an indication of how far micro-technology has progressed in the intervening years. Also, because there is consequently more room for the winch and the cable used is thinner, the SH-60F can carry a significantly longer amount of dunking line.

The Ocean Hawk can lower its sonar to a depth of 4576 m (1,500 ft (as opposed to 137 m/450 ft with the Sea King). This makes it much more capable of penetrating the various temperature layers in the ocean which submarines use to mask their presence. The reel assembly can propel the transducer through the water at a rate of 17 ft per second (FPS) when

Above: A Sikorsky SH-60F of HS-3 'Tridents' taxis past the tower at 'Navy Jax'. This aircraft carries the 'AJ' tailcodes of CVW-8, but the titles of CVW-17 on USS Saratoga, the squadron's usual ship, whose aircraft usually carry an 'AA' tailcode!

Below: Pictured at Patuxent River, this anonymous-looking test SH-60F shows the clean lines of its belly, with the large dipping sonar housing amidships.

being lowered, and at 22 FPS when being recovered. Normally the SH-60F would hover at 60 ft, using its Doppler auto-hover avionics, while in a dunking operation, with each dip lasting between three and five minutes. The AN/AQS-13F sonar, coupled to its MIL-STD 1553B data-bus, is the helicopter's primary means of underwater detection.

To augment the primarily active sonar the SH-60F, like the SH-60B, carries a small complement of sono-buoys. The 'Foxtrot' carries eight, as opposed to the 'Bravo's' 25. Located in a carousel behind the pilot's seat,

the sonobuoys have to be manually unloaded by the operator and placed in the tube from which they are dropped, not ejected. Normal prac-tice would be to deploy one or two as an exploratory measure; however, as the helicopter operates close to the battle group, inside a radius of 50 miles, the noise from the carrier can severely degrade the sonobuoy's effectiveness. The SH-60F does not use sonobuoys as its primary ASW device, and sonobuoy information processing capability is limited, but it can relay received data to other heli-copters in the ASW screen.

Above: This aircraft, possibly the SH-60F prototype, retains the undernose data-link and ESM, various radomes and antennas and the towed MAD pylon of the SH-60B.

Below: HS-2 made the SH-60F's first carrier deployment with CVW-9 aboard the USS Nimitz. Here the aircraft is seen in typical operational pose, about to 'dunk' its sonar.

Dominating the instrument panel in the cockpit is a large screen called the Multi-Function Display (MFD). There is an obvious absence of analogue instruments up front, with the glass cockpit concept much in evidence. Driven by dual Teledyne Systems AN/ASN-150 tactical navigation computers, the MFD presents the crew with all the operational information they need. There are two screens, the second at the Sensor Operators station, and four Central Display Units (CDUs). Accessible to all crew members, radio and navigation selections are done through the CDUs. This reduces the workload on the pilot, leaving him free to concentrate on flying. Another significant instrument is the Display Control Panel, or DCP, again located both in the cockpit and the cabin, which displays the TACAN navigation symbology and any alerts or warnings that warrant the crew's attention. Navigation equipment fitted includes TACAN and Doppler TacNav with provision for GPS. Communications are handled through a pair of ARC-182 V/UHF radios with secure voice capability.

On a typical mission, the crew numbers four: the pilot, co-pilot, air tactical officer and sensor operator. On a rescue or plane guard fight a rescueman in an immersion suit would also be carried. This still leaves two 'spare' seats in the cabin.

The simplification of the flight instrumentation represents a leap forward from the SH-3. Flight crew are no longer confronted with a battery of gauges, each of which had to be in-

Above: HS-2's SH-60Fs carried the 'NG' tailcode of the Nimitz, and a large 'toned-down' US flag on the rear fuselage. Carriage of a single long-range tank on the port pylon is typical.

Left: VX-1 conducted operational evaluations of the new aircraft. One of their SH-60Fs is pictured here during a stopover at Patrick AFB.

An SH-60F leads a pair of the SH-3Hs it is designed to replace on the flight deck of the Nimitz. The A-7 Corsairs in the background are now but a memory.

Sikorsky SH-60F Ocean Hawk

This SH-60F wears the markings of HS-3 'Tridents', shore-based at NAS Jacksonville, Florida, as part of Helicopter Anti-Submarine Warfare Wing One. The 'Tridents' are the first operator of the SH-60F in the Atlantic Fleet. The squadron formally accepted its first aircraft on 27 August 1991, and later transferred from CVW-17 (USS *Saratoga*) to CVW-8 (USS *Theodore Roosevelt*). Its first cruise will be aboard the *Roosevelt*.

Pylon
The port stores pylon can accommodate a 454-litre (120-US gal) fuel tank, and a Mk 50 torpedo, with another weapon on the starboard pylon.

Deployment
The SH-60F is replacing the ageing SH-3H Sea King in carrierborne ASW squadrons. They will be responsible for conducting the 'inner zone' ASW battle around a carrier. The SH-60F does have a SAR/Plane Guard capability, but these tasks will be handled by a pair of dedicated HH-60H 'Rescue Hawks' deployed with each fleet SH-60F unit.

Underfuselage contours
The SH-60F lacks the characteristic 'chin' radome and prominent ESM boxes of the SH-60B, giving the nose a much cleaner profile. The underfuselage RAST probe (used for securing the aircraft during landing on the pitching and rolling decks of small ships) is also deleted, replaced by the dipping sonar.

Folding tail
The tailwheel is moved forward on all naval H-60 variants, allowing the rear part of the tailboom, including the tail rotor pylon, to be folded forward. This allows the aircraft to use standard carrier lifts and eases storage problems.

Main rotor
The main rotor incorporates a powered folding system. The blades are rotated to an index position, then folded automatically to lie along the rear fuselage. The rotor blades have swept tips to improve performance and reduce noise.

Rescue hoist
A powerful winch is installed above the cabin door.

Tail rotor
As with all production members of the H-60/S.70 family, the SH-60F has a tail rotor that is canted to port, providing lift as well as an anti-torque force.

Powerplant
The SH-60F is powered by the same twin 1,900-shp General Electric T700-GE-401C turboshafts as late production SH-60B Sea Hawks. For the SH-60F, with its heavy load of sensors and weapons, the Rolls-Royce/Turboméca RTM322 would have provided useful extra power.

Sikorsky SH-60F

dividually checked to make sure no needles were in the red. Instead the pilot now needs only to look once around his office to ensure that all his displays are showing green and he knows he's good to go. This means that his attention can be focused outside the cockpit for longer and if a warning indicator does begin to flash, it will be far more obvious than before.

With folding rotor-blades, tailplane and tailboom the SH-60F takes up little room on the carrier flight deck or in the hangar below. The folding system is motor driven and controlled from the cockpit. Slowly rotated to an 'index' point, the blades are then folded back over the rear fuselge, the whole process taking about a minute. The swept tips, called 'tip caps', improve speed and also reduce noise.

The two new-technology, navalised General Electric T700-GE-401C engines have also proved themselves operationally, with hovering on a single engine now being carried out as a matter of course. This tremendous power allows the SH-60F to hover out of ground effect, at a maximum gross weight of 9927 kg (21,884 lb) even on a 35°C (95°F) day. During one endurance test, the helicopter was flown for 35 hours without shutting down. The SH-60F has two hydraulic systems and an additional backup. The flight controls are designed to absorb a 7.62-mm round hit anywhere in the circuit and remain oper-

The cramped cabin of an SH-60F, with the sonar winch and sensor operator's station. The SH-60F normally carries a crew of four, with two pilots and an air tactical officer in addition to the sensor operator.

ational. Maximum take-off weight has been increased to 10660 kg (23,500 lb), significantly more than that of the SH-60B. Up to 2132 kg (4,700 lb) of fuel can be carried, plus 363 kg (800 lb) in each of two external tanks. This gives an endurance of be-

tween 4½ and 6 hours with reserves.

Once a submarine has been hunted down the SH-60F moves in for the kill. Two types of current US Navy torpedoes can be carried, and the extra weapons pylon on the port side allows the carriage of up to three at once. The

Honeywell-built Mk 46 torpedo, which entered service in 1965, is a deep-diving high-speed weapon which enters a helical search pattern on hitting the water. It has a maximum range of 11000 m (36,090 ft) and a 44-kg (97-lb) warhead, but improvements in submarine technology mean it is beginning to show its age. Its replacement, now entering service, is the Mk 50, built by the same company. Of similar dimensions to the Mk 46, the new torpedo can catch faster submarines at greater depths and its revolutionary warhead can defeat even the most modern double-hulled submarines.

At present, the SH-60F has no self-defence capability; however, it has been designed to accommodate both passive ECM equipment and chaff/flare dispensers, which are likely to be retrofitted.

It is the Automatic Flight Control System which makes the SH-60F a uniquely effective sub-hunting platform. The AFCS combines several different sources of flight information and computes the best way to manoeuvre the aircraft. It moves the control stick and control surfaces, maintaining airspeed, attitude and altitude hold with reference to its AN/

Below: An HS-3 Ocean Hawk unfolds its main rotor blades before starting up. HS-3 is the first East Coast SH-60F unit. Some of the squadron's aircraft wear the title of CVW-8 from the USS Roosevelt.

Left and far left: Lieutenants Jeff Bartkoski and Dave Nelson hosted World Air Power Journal, and conveyed their great enthusiasm for the new aircraft – an impressive testament.

Right: The absence of an undernose radome and ESM and data-link fairings gives the SH-60F a distinctive appearance from head on. Here Lieutenants Bartkoski and Nelson prepare for a sortie.

APN-194V radar altimeter. It will also handle turn co-ordination, maintain a steady hover over one spot, automatically approach a hover and leave it again, as requested by the pilot. In effect, it keeps the aircraft in balanced flight no matter what the weather or operational conditions, which is vital for optimum sonar performance.

While it does not share the boat-shaped watertight hull of its predecessor the Sea King, the Ocean Hawk does carry flotation bags for use in the event of an unscheduled landing at sea. The housings for these are located near the nose, beside the cockpit steps at the pivot point for the main landing gear. However, once inflated, they obstruct the cabin enough to make escape from a flooding helicopter impossible. To get around this slight inconvenience, a 'towel rail' bar has been installed parallel to the cockpit doors. This provides the flight crew with enough room to open a door or

Right: An HS-3 SH-60F undergoing maintenance, showing its complex folding rotor hub to advantage. The SH-60F represents a major advance over the older SH-3 Sea King previously used in the Inner Zone ASW mission.

Below: The squadron's Trident is carried behind the Modex.

window, puncture the flotation bags with a survival knife and escape.

Operational plans call for six SH-60Fs to be deployed alongside a further two HH-60Hs. Despite, or rather because of, the Ocean Hawk's limited rescue capability, the latter type fulfils the role of dedicated combat SAR/special operations helicopters. This is more than evident from the equipment they carry, the HH-60H being armed with M60 machine-guns mounted in both the port cabin window and starboard cargo door. Designed to operate deep in hostile territory, they are also well protected, fitted with an AN/APR-39 radar warning receiver and the more exotic AN/AVR-2 laser warning re-

ceiver. They are unique among naval helicopters in carrying the AN/AAR-47 missile plume detector. On each side of the tail boom are AN/ALE-39 chaff and flare dispensers, and further anti-missile defence is provided by the AN/ALQ-144 'hot brick' infra-red jammer mounted above the engine exhausts, beside the rotor mast. Some aircraft do bow to their 'humble' SH-60B origins by retaining a cargo hook and RAST probe. Despite having an internal fuel capacity of only 1814 kg (4,000 lb) (plus the usual pair of 363-kg/800-lb external tanks) the HH-60H can accommodate up to 10 soldiers inside, the passengers usually being Navy SEAL teams. It is up to the potent Ocean Hawks, how-

ever, to protect the ships that provide a home from which the HH-60Hs can function.

The SH-60F has been designed for a specific task, which it carries out in an impressive fashion. It does not need to operate independently from the tiny deck of a lone frigate, but instead can call on all the resources of a full carrier battle group. In return for this help, it can quickly and effectively sanitise the surrounding ocean, leaving the capital ships free to concentrate on their primary mission. The equipment now employed and planned for the future ensures that Sikorsky's Ocean Hawk will remain at the forefront of anti-submarine warfare developments for some time to come.

BRIEFING

Armed Forces of Malta
Malta's Helicopter Flight

Adding to and amending the *Air Power Analysis* feature on Malta in *World Air Power Journal*, Volume 5, the following is a history of the Maltese helicopter force, together with the involvement of Libya and Italy.

The Malta Land Force received their first aircraft in May 1972, when four Bell 47G-2s were delivered from West Germany. The Germans also provided technical assistance and training during the establishment of Malta's Helicopter Flight. The four aircraft comprised three Agusta-built machines (9H-AAE/ex-74+02/c/n 225, 9H-AAF/ex-74+18/c/n 260 and 9H-AAG/ex-74+20/c/n 262) and one built by Bell (9H-AAH/ex-74+35/c/n 1991).

On 19 April 1973 the military became the Armed Forces of Malta, shortly before Agusta-Bell AB 206A JetRanger 9H-AAJ/c/n 8185 arrived with the Helicopter Flight on 4 June. All five aircraft are still in service, performing utility transport, medical evacuation and rescue duties.

Prior to 31 March 1979, Malta was used as a base by British forces, the main airfield at Luqa being in British hands. The Maltese helicopters flew from a hangar complex at St Patricks, but as this had no refuelling facilities, all five had to land at Luqa for refuelling. For about two years, starting from September 1978, the Helicopter Flight set up a base at HalFar, but contrary to many reports no military air-

craft have been used there, the Maltese government developing an industrial site on the field. With the departure of UK forces, the Helicopter Flight moved into Luqa, occupying Park No. 7, former home of No. 13 Sqn's Canberra PR.Mk 7s.

On 1 April 1980, all units of the 1st Regiment of the Armed Forces, in-

Right: The sole Maltese Agusta-Bell AB 206A JetRanger is seen in its original colour scheme.

Below: The same aircraft as it is today, re-painted and with the new '1' roundel, signifying the Helicopter Flight's parent organisation, the 1st Regiment.

cluding the Flight, became known as the Task Force, which had a separate commander from the Armed Forces, answering directly to the Prime Minister. The markings were also changed to a black 'TF' superimposed on a red and white circle. These were carried until 11 May 1988, when an amalgamation saw the units of the Task Force

Above: One of Malta's Agusta-Bell 47G-2s wearing the current markings, consisting of a white '1' superimposed on a red and blue disc.

Left: Two of the four Agusta-Bells at Luqa. They wear the original red and white 'TF' roundel used during the existence of the 'Task Force'.

once again brought under 1st Regiment control. Markings changed to a white '1' on a red and blue circle. The Labour government of the 1970s developed stronger ties with nearby Libya, which detached an Aérospatiale Super Frelon to the island on 30 January 1975. The single aircraft was rotated every three weeks, and was based at St Patricks, with regular refuelling stops at Luqa. In the autumn of 1978 three Aérospatiale Alouette IIIs were despatched from Libya in two Hercules transports. When Libyan forces were expelled in August 1980, the Alouettes were left behind, and put on the civil register for the Helicopter Flight. The three are 9H-AAV/ex-LC2288/c/n 2288, 9H-AAW/ex-LC2295/c/n 2295 and 9H-AAX/ex-LC2315/c/n 2315.

Since the Libyan departure, the Alouettes have remained in storage, one reason for this being that the Libyans took away the log books. However, on 11 June 1991, Staff Colonel El Rifi Ali El Sharif of the Libyan Defence Ministry formally returned the books to Brigadier John Spiteri, then Commander of the Armed Forces of Malta. There is no doubt that the Alouettes would greatly enhance the Helicopter Flight's capabilities, especially for rescue coverage, but extensive overhauls are required before they can fly again.

Italian assistance to the Helicopter Flight followed an aid agreement signed in April 1975, under which a Bell 47 and the JetRanger were flown by AMI Hercules to Bergamo for overhaul, followed in time by the other three Bell 47s. Italy was later to guarantee Maltese neutrality following the departure of the Libyans in 1980. Two years later, Italian air force AB 204Bs were detached to Malta as part of the Italian military mission stationed on the island. Contrary to

many reports, these flew from the Helicopter Flight area at Luqa, and not Hal Far. In October 1987 AB 212s replaced the AB 204Bs.

In the mid-1980s, the Armed Forces of Malta conducted a series of evaluations of fixed-wing types to extend the SAR and patrol cover. Aircraft demonstrated to the AFM were Pilatus Britten-Norman Turbine Islanders G-OPBN and G-DEMO in April 1985, Partenavia P.68 Observer I-OBSV in July, Lake Seawolf N1402J in October and Dornier Do 228 D-CBOL in July 1986.

However, in late 1991 the Armed Forces of Malta were finally awaiting their first fixed-wing equipment in the form of five Cessna Model 172s to be purchased in the United States. While nowhere near as capable as the aircraft types evaluated in the 1980s, the Cessnas will provide a useful and cheap coastal patrol asset, with training and liaison functions.

Left: Italian air force Agusta-Bell AB 212s have provided SAR cover since 1987, supporting an Italian military mission which guarantees Maltese neutrality.

Above: Before the AB 212s arrived, the Italian contingent used AB 204s, like the aircraft seen here. These operated from Luqa.

Schweizer RG-8A

Hunting for drugs

Three Schweizer RG-8A Condors were originally built for the US Army, the first making its maiden flight in 1986. The second aircraft was written off in an accident, and the remaining two were transferred to the US Coast Guard. Derived from the Schweizer SGM 2-37, a motor glider optimised for law enforcement and surveillance duties, the RG-8A was actually developed from the TG-7A, a two-seat motor glider built for the USAF academy at Colorado Springs. The RG-8A has a much more powerful 235-hp Textron Lycoming 10-54W3A5D engine driving a three-bladed 'quiet' propeller, and exhaust-silencing 'mufflers' on each side of the engine cowling. The aircraft maintains height using only 52 hp, giving a very low acoustic signature.

Fuel capacity is considerably increased by comparison with the original motor glider, giving a reported endurance in excess of eight hours. A new bulged cockpit canopy covers the two pilots, who sit side-by-side in a cockpit that is compatible with the use of night-vision goggles, and can be fitted with armour protection.

Behind the cockpit is a 65-cu ft payload bay which can accept a variety of pallet-mounted sensors, including low-light TV, optical cameras, imaging infra-red or radar. The Coast Guard are understandably tight-lipped about the sensor fits usually employed.

The Coast Guard's two Schweizer RG-8As are seldom seen together, and usually operate at fairly high altitude.

Right: The RG-8A has a high-technology 'quiet' propeller. Noise-reducing mufflers are mounted on the exhaust. The aircraft can maintain altitude using only a fraction of its installed engine power, allowing very low throttle to be used.

Right: The Coast Guard RG-8As wear toned-down insignia over an overall gunship grey colour scheme. Their operations are shrouded in secrecy.

Lockheed AC-130U and MC-130H

USAF Special Operations Hercules developments

Above: The AC-130U prototype on the ramp at Edwards in company with the first three MC-130H 'Combat Talon IIs'. The MC-130H has now entered USAF service, and AC-130 trials are progressing well. The distinctive nose radome shape of the MC-130H is immediately apparent. These two types will dramatically improve the capability of Special Forces transport and gunship forces.

Left and below: An overview of the AC-130U prototype. This aircraft wears traditional 'Spectre' artwork on its nose, consisting of a Minigun-toting skeleton using a crescent moon as cover. The European One camouflage scheme is less traditional for AC-130Us, which have previously been matt grey or even matt black.

The newest USAF Hercules variant (described briefly in *World Air Power Journal*, Volume 8) is now undergoing flight tests from Edwards AFB with the Special Operations Force Combined Test Group. One of our correspondents was given an unparalleled close-up look at this still 'top secret' aircraft.

Already being tentatively dubbed the 'U-Boat' by crews, the AC-130U takes into the 21st century the gunship concept explored and worked out in Vietnam. "You feel like Buck Rogers with real guns," joked one pilot. Fully all-weather capable, and able to simultaneously engage two targets, the AC-130U is fitted with an advanced Hughes APG-80 fire control radar, derived from the APG-70 carried by the F-15E. Other sensors include a Texas Instruments AN/

AAQ-117 FLIR, and a Ball Aerospace All Active Low Light Level TV with laser target designator and rangefinder. The four IBM IP-102 mission computers are linked by a 1553B databus. Navigation has never been easier in a Hercules gunship, with combined INS and GPS/Navstar. This effectively allows the twin INS to be updated by GPS satellites.

Carrying traditional 'Spectre' nose art, the first FSD AC-130U was the first of 12 aircraft to be converted by Rockwell from brand-new, standard C-130H airframes. Wearing European One camouflage rather than the gunship grey normally associated with the AC-130s, the first aircraft looks unlike its predecessors, with a different antenna and sensor configuration, and with only three guns. Ironically, ordinary Hercules transports (along with the C-141s and C-5s) are reportedly being painted in an overall matt grey colour scheme, so it will be interesting to see what scheme is adopted for the remaining AC-130Us.

Flight trials have reportedly gone well, drawing some unfavourable comparisons with the problems being experienced by Special Operations Command's other new C-130 variant, the MC-130H Combat Talon II. Four and a half years behind schedule, with costs having doubled to $1.9 billion, the first four MC-130Hs were formally accepted at Hurlburt Field in October, but problems are reportedly still being encountered with the ESCO APQ-170 radar. Supposedly able to 'look into the turn', the radar

---

has reportedly been seeing 'false terrain' and generating unnecessary 'pull-up' commands.

The surviving 14 MC-130E 'Combat Talon I' aircraft are being upgraded to virtual 'Combat Talon II' configuration (known as MOD 90 standard) under a programme costing $18 million per aircraft. This will not include the MC-130H's fully integrated FLIR, or the 'look into the turn' radar capability. The electronic warfare officer will continue to occupy a pallet-mounted station in the cargo compartment, whereas on 'Talon II' he sits in splendour on the flight deck. The system whereby all flight deck crew see the same display that the pilots see on their MFDs is being incorporated, minimising the need for intercom chatter. The MC-130E 'Combat Talon Is' will also gain a proper lavatory instead of what one pilot described as 'a bucket hanging on the wall', an important consideration on long-range insertion/recovery missions.

Above and above left: *The AC-130U's armament is reduced to only three guns. The 7.62-mm Minigun has disappeared completely, leaving a new 25-mm cannon forward of the Ball Aerospace ALLTV on the port landing gear sponson (above) with a 40-mm Bofors and a 105-mm Howitzer aft. These are not separated by a beacon tracking radome as they are on the AC-130H. These three guns nevertheless pack a powerful punch, and the AC-130U's advanced avionics allow them to engage two targets simultaneously. Flexible covers seal the fuselage.*

Left: *The AC-130U tailcone incorporates an ITT AN/ALQ-172 jammer and various RWRs.*

Below: *The AC-130U prototype in flight. Service entry will allow the AC-130Hs to be passed to the AFRes, and the ageing AC-130As to be retired or sold.*

A Texas Instruments AN/AAQ-117 FLIR is mounted in a gimballed turret on the port forward fuselage.

Joint STARS: The Eyes of the Storm

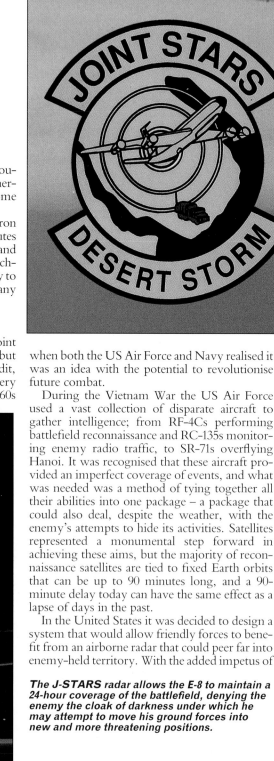

AWACS platforms such as the E-2 Hawkeye and E-3 Sentry have revolutionised the air battle, being able to provide a complete picture of the unfolding events and orchestrating the efforts of a multitude of friendly aircraft, whether their business be attack or defence. The US Army/US Air Force Joint STARS programme breaks new ground by attempting to do the same for the land battle. While still very much in the evaluation stage, the system was called on to go to war, where it proved to be a great success.

History has seen the rise of many solutions to the eternal question of the generals: what is the enemy doing, now? First balloons, next aircraft, then satellites; all of these have tried to provide their commanders with the answers they need, often at great risk to men and equipment. But always the problem was the same: how to get vital information into the hands of those who needed it before opportunities had been lost and the situation changed. Hard information that was often obtained at great cost became useless through confusion and delay. It was always apparent that faster ways of transmitting and disseminating intelligence must be developed. Beginning with the throwing of exposed canisters of film over the side of aircraft in 1917, to the introduction of geostationary reconnaissance satellites able to transmit real-time data to relay stations thousands of miles below, the delay between gathering and exploiting intelligence has become shorter and shorter.

However, for the infantry captain or squadron leader at the sharp end, even a delay of minutes can mean the difference between success and failure. What was needed was a means of watching the enemy from many miles and the ability to then share this vital information with as many friendly forces as possible.

Slow evolution

Enter the product of centuries of desire – Joint STARS. This system, still in development but now with combat experience to its credit, evolved slowly and faced cancellation at every point in its history. It was conceived in the 1960s when both the US Air Force and Navy realised it was an idea with the potential to revolutionise future combat.

During the Vietnam War the US Air Force used a vast collection of disparate aircraft to gather intelligence; from RF-4Cs performing battlefield reconnaissance and RC-135s monitoring enemy radio traffic, to SR-71s overflying Hanoi. It was recognised that these aircraft provided an imperfect coverage of events, and what was needed was a method of tying together all their abilities into one package – a package that could also deal, despite the weather, with the enemy's attempts to hide its activities. Satellites represented a monumental step forward in achieving these aims, but the majority of reconnaissance satellites are tied to fixed Earth orbits that can be up to 90 minutes long, and a 90-minute delay today can have the same effect as a lapse of days in the past.

In the United States it was decided to design a system that would allow friendly forces to benefit from an airborne radar that could peer far into enemy-held territory. With the added impetus of

***The J-STARS** radar allows the E-8 to maintain a 24-hour coverage of the battlefield, denying the enemy the cloak of darkness under which he may attempt to move his ground forces into new and more threatening positions.*

the Arab-Israeli wars, the 1970s saw the development of a radar system named 'Pave Mover', a project led by the USAF and the Defense Advanced Research Projects Agency (DARPA). Also on the drawing board at that time was an Army initiative dubbed Stand-Off Target Acquisition System (SOTAS). Mounted in the proposed EH-60B helicopter flying close to the Forward Line Of Troops (FLOT), SOTAS would have relayed data from the radar to ground stations. Alarming costs saw the cancellation of this programme in the early 1980s. Soon afterwards, in 1985, the Army and the Air Force merged their requirements and launched the project we now know as the Joint Surveillance and Target Acquisition Radar System (J-STARS).

Round-the-clock surveillance

Joint STARS detects, locates, identifies, classifies, tracks and targets hostile ground movements in any condition. It operates around the clock, always in touch with its Air Force command posts and Army mobile ground stations through secure data links. They, in turn, use this precise information to call on aircraft, missiles or artillery for fire support.

In 1985, after a full-scale competition, Grumman's Melbourne Systems Division was

awarded the contract to adapt the airborne equipment which would be carried by a pair of Boeing 707s, to be compatible with the Army's Ground Station Modules (GSMs) developed by Motorola. The aircraft were designated E-8A. The closure of the 707 production line has ensured that the projected new-build E-8B, powered by CFM International F108 (CFM56) turbofans, will not now come about. In a move to save money the definitive production version will be the E-8C, based on existing 707 airframes, although the option of re-engining these aircraft still exists. The two E-8As now being used both have a long history of airline service behind them, having

Above: A rare photograph catches both E-8As in the air together, illustrating the subtle differences in camouflage scheme between the two. Grumman's Melbourne Systems Division moved rapidly when it got the call to deploy the pair to Saudi Arabia, taking less than a month between initial notification of the impending operations and flying the first intelligence-producing mission.

Below: Being prepared for flight on Grumman's ramp at Melbourne, Florida, are both E-8A airframes. The darker grey aircraft on the right is the first conversion, registered USAF 86-0416/ N770JS, while the lighter grey machine on the left is USAF 86-0417/N8411. Both are ex-airline 707-320Cs.

Inside the E-8A

As with the E-3 AWACS, the USAF looked no further than the tried and trusted Boeing 707 airframe for the J-STARS platform. Gutted of airline paraphernalia, the cabin provides a perfectly-sized vehicle for the operator consoles, communications suite and associated equipment, while leaving sufficient space for rest areas and other crew facilities.

Right: Located on the starboard side of the cabin, facing aft, these are a pair of the large screen graphic displays where the radar data is presented. The left-hand screen below the main display is for menu options on a touch-sensitive surface. That on the right monitors the health of the system and the environmental control system. The panel at right is the communications interface, the keyboard working in conjunction with the ball to input data into the system, the ball directing a cursor on the main screen.

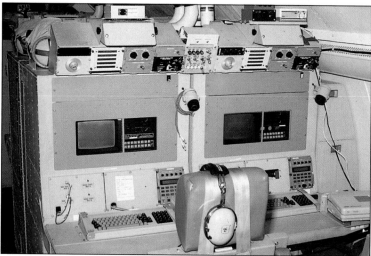
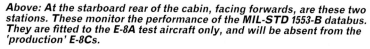

Above: At the starboard rear of the cabin, facing forwards, are these two stations. These monitor the performance of the MIL-STD 1553-B databus. They are fitted to the E-8A test aircraft only, and will be absent from the 'production' E-8Cs.

Above: Along the starboard side of the forward fuselage are these six bunks for crew rest, vital for the long missions envisaged for J-STARS (up to 20 hours with only one refuelling). On the left side are seats for take-off/landing positions.

Left: Opposite the main displays in the aft cabin is this high-speed printer, which can make hard copies of any screen display. On top is an RF amplifier.

Right: Another piece of equipment unique to the E-8A test aircraft is the CIRIS (Completely Integrated Range Instrumentation System). This has the task of verifying the accuracy of the on-board navigation suite, which needs precise positioning for radar plots. This is located at mid-cabin on the starboard side.

Ground Station Module

Above: This is one of a pair of operator consoles within the Ground Station Module, closely resembling those within the E-8 itself. The operator can call up any J-STARS mode without the E-8 crew having to make any input.

One of the Motorola TSQ-132S-280 Ground Station Modules, seen after its return to the US after Desert Storm but still wearing a sand camouflage. Alongside is the generator which provides power. Note the jacks for stability, and the large telescopic antenna, which is not fully extended.

flown for Qantas and Korean Airlines.

The contract for the third pre-production aircraft (the first E-8C) was placed in November 1990, and the full production award for (initially) five aircraft is anticipated at the time of writing in January 1992. The first of these aircraft should fly in 1995, with initial operating capability attained with five machines in 1997.

Radar system

The most obvious feature that sets the J-STARS aircraft apart from their civilian counterparts is the 7.3-m (24-ft) ventral canoe fairing underneath the fuselage, which houses the Norden-built phased-array multi-mode radar. It is this system which is the key to J-STARS' success. The antenna can be manoeuvred to look on each side of the aircraft, and it scans to determine the location and heading of moving targets. Azimuth scanning is achieved electronically, while elevation scan is mechanical.

A second, smaller, ventral fairing houses the FTDL, the high-gain directional Flight Test Data Link, known as the 'Fiddle'. This is to be fitted only for the duration of the development programme and will be absent on the definitive E-8. Just behind this is a small, black, stub antenna. This is the 'Skittle', the Surveillance and Control Data Link (SCDL). All data collected during the mission is transmitted through this to the waiting Ground Station Modules, although in the Gulf War the 'Fiddle' was used for data relay.

Inside, the aircraft has a standard 707/E-3A-type cockpit devoid of any modern innovations such as CRTs or EFIS, and no such modifications are planned. There are seats for electronics operators to occupy during take-off, and six bunks for a relief flight crew. The cabin houses large-screen graphics consoles, which can display both computer-processed imagery and pictures custom-generated by the operators for a specific task. Production aircraft will house up to 17 of

these systems, plus one for self-defence systems (which as envisaged will be purely warning in nature), but it is believed that the pair which went to war in Operation Desert Storm were only fitted with 10. The computing power behind the consoles is provided by four high-speed data processors each capable of completing 600 million operations per second.

Mission and capability

On a typical mission, the E-8 flies an elongated racetrack pattern, so that the aircraft is side-on to the area of interest for as long as possible. Some radar picture is lost during the turn away from, or towards, the area of interest. Each individual mission will have its profile tailored to meet the requirements, and to match geographic and political considerations. The standard surveillance

altitude is between 10670 m and 12800 m (35,000 ft and 42,000 ft).

A standard mission crew amounts to 21, in addition to the flight crew, with each electronics operator dealing with the individual needs of his 'customer'. Some may be interested in surveying the entire area visible to the system, while others may need to concentrate on a small, specific spot. For long-endurance patrols an augmented crew of 34 is envisaged. To achieve its unprecedented range of abilities, the J-STARS has the following radar modes available:

Wide-Area Surveillance/Moving Target

The second E-8A taxis for a test mission from Melbourne. Despite the considerable success of the system in Desert Storm, J-STARS has had to resume its time-consuming test programme, working towards IOC in 1997.

Indicator (WAS/MTI): This is the basic operating mode, which provides location and identification of slow-moving targets throughout a 512-km^2 (200-sq mile) search area. The area under surveillance can be radar- or ground-referenced, the former moving the surveillance area as the aircraft moves, and the area remaining constant in the latter mode. The system also includes the ability to differentiate between tracked and wheeled vehicles, achieving this by detecting the stationary lower portion of the track as it lays on the ground and the fast-moving upper portion as it travels across the rollers. Of great use is the velocity threshold function, which can discount fast-moving returns caused by cars to avoid a saturation of the screen information. In addition to this, J-STARS demonstrated the ability to track helicopters during Desert Storm, and also boasts a maritime capability, which has applications to drug-busting operations. The WAS/MTI mode is of particular use to force commanders, who want the 'big picture' across the battle zone.

Sector Search Mode (SSM): This mode employs a similar method to WAS/MTI, but allows the operator to concentrate on a much smaller area, typically 20 km^2 (7.7 sq miles). At this large scale, convoys of vehicles can be broken down to individual vehicles, giving the exact size detail of a moving force. The principal use of this mode is for individual targetting, allowing the operator to precisely plot the position of a target for attack by aircraft. Intended kill-boxes can be superimposed on the screen image, and the predicted arrival time based on the target's previous movements can be calculated. In this way an attack aircraft can be vectored to its release position with a high chance of finding the target there at the precise time of its first pass. SSM allows the operator to direct attacks in geographic choke-points, the first attacks killing the first and last vehicles in a column and so halting its progress. Rapid post-strike intelligence can also be gleaned with this mode as stationary (i.e. successfully hit) targets disappear, and hard-copy images can be provided rapidly by a high-speed laser printer.

Synthetic Aperture Radar/Fixed Target Indicator (SAR/FTI): This creates near-photographic quality God's-eye images of ground terrain (known as patch maps), including bridges, airports and even stationary vehicles. The SAR images are combined in strips to build up a high-resolution 'mosaic' picture of the scene. This mode is of particular use in a reconnaissance function, and in detailing targets for aircraft such as the F-15E, which have a similar patch map capability.

Instant replay

As well as providing an instant picture of the battlefield, J-STARS has a history replay mode. This stores the images it has gathered, and can then run them 'fast-forward' to give the ability to spot overall trends that may not be obvious in real-time. Information is also provided concerning the regions of the surveillance area that are masked from the radar by terrain. In addition to the radar return images on the screen, the J-STARS system has the ability to overlay pre-stored cartography on the image, such details as roads, rivers and borders being of obvious value to the operator. The entire system operates in an interleaved mode, so that individual operators can provide their own 'customers' with the information they require. Information can be

Below: A classic example of the type of intelligence the J-STARS can provide is given by this WAS/MTI image taken in the last hours of the war with Iraq. Each cross is a vehicle, or small group of vehicles, and depicts the massive withdrawal from Kuwait City. The main central string of vehicles is heading along the Basra Highway.

Right: J-STARS at war. One of the E-8s of the 4411th Joint STARS Squadron begins its take-off roll at Riyadh Military Airport at the start of another long mission. The 49 combat missions undertaken by the two aircraft resulted in the system being aloft for the majority of the war period, a considerable feat for the team.

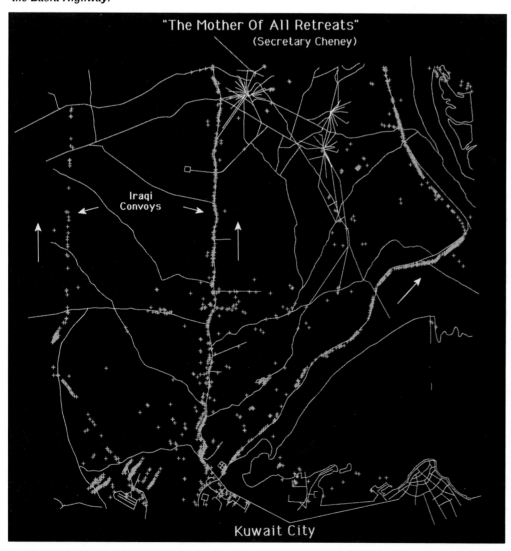

"The Mother Of All Retreats"
(Secretary Cheney)

Iraqi Convoys

Kuwait City

disseminated to air assets such as Air Force Command Centers, UAVs and suitably-equipped aircraft, via the Joint Tactical Information Distribution System (JTIDS) data link. A separate JTIDS link is maintained with the AWACS aircraft controlling the air battle.

Installed on the E-8A by way of test instrumentation, but worthy of mention, is the Completely Integrated Range Instrumentation System (CIRIS), used for testing new navigation equipment. Also, at the rear of the cabin are two terminals currently used to monitor the health of J-STARS powerful MIL-STD 1553-B databus. These will of course give way to operational stations in the E-8C. During Desert Storm, the ability of the diagnostic system to beam information via the Flight Test Data Link, over very long distances, meant that information could be received by the command modules back in Riyadh.

The Ground Station Modules, or GSMs, fall under the control of the US Army, and there is

no limit to the number which can be connected to the airborne observer. Six were sent to support Desert Storm operations, the type TSQ-132S-280 systems being deployed with the VII and XVIII Corps of the US Army, the Marine Corps, the British Army and with two central planning commands: army and air force.

The module is mounted on a standard Army flat-bed truck which also tows the generator needed to power the system. Later versions will be smaller. Information from the E-8 is received by a telescopic antenna which can be extended up to 30 m (100 ft). Inside the GSM are two consoles similar to those on the E-8 controlled by the Tac-

Right: A Gruman employee checks over the second E-8A prior to a sortie. The view serves to illustrate one of the principal design problems of the conversion: providing sufficient ground clearance for the radar fairing.

Boeing/Grumman E-8A

Built as a Boeing 707-323C for American Airlines, N8411 is the second of two E-8A development aircraft for the J-STARS programme. Delivered to Boeing Military Airplanes at Wichita, Kansas, for military conversion in June 1986, it was handed over to Grumman Systems Division at Melbourne, Florida, in the autumn of 1988 for systems integration. It made its first flight as an E-8A on 31 August 1989, following the first aircraft which took to the air on 22 December 1988. N8411 deployed to Europe in September 1990.

tical Surveillance Supervisor (TSS) and the Search Track Operator (STO). Either of these can access any of the previously-mentioned surveillance modes independently of the E-8 crew. They also have a printer to supply hard-copy information and a Global Positioning System (GPS) hooked into the military satellite navigation network for accurate positioning.

This easily-mobile system puts 'real-time' information directly into the hands of ground commanders who can watch a situation develop and plan their responses accordingly. Initial scepticism over the capability of the system during Desert Storm was quickly dispersed, notably by its role in the battle at Al-Khafji. Here the system detected the important fact that the initial Iraqi thrust was not a major attack, but rather a small-force recon intrusion. However, when a reinforcement column began to move towards the town, J-STARS was on hand to spot it before it became a threat to coalition forces engaging the initial Iraqi attackers.

Desert Storm operations

Throughout the build-up of allied forces in Saudi Arabia during Operation Desert Shield, Grumman technicians worked around the clock to prepare their aircraft for combat and to train those involved, on all sides, to utilise the system's potential to the full. Notification to deploy was issued on 17 December, and subsequently 770 tons of material to support operations were airlifted in by one C-141 StarLifter and five C-5 Galaxy transports. Under the aegis of the 4411th Joint STARS Squadron, the two E-8s arrived at Riyadh on the night of 11/12 January, and the aircraft were delivering intelligence on Iraqi actions, as promised, by the 14th. The air war commenced two days later. The two aircraft undertook 49 missions, resulting in a grand total of 535 combat hours. Most missions were of 11/12-hour duration, the longest lasting 14.6 hours. The air-to-air refuelling capability of the E-8 meant that one was aloft virtually full-time, throughout the whole of the hostilities.

The main mission became the location of SS-1 'Scud' missile sites, particularly the mobile launchers. For political reasons, the elimination of Iraq's medium-range missile capability became of paramount importance. In this task, the J-STARS operators worked closely with the F-15E Strike Eagle whose APG-70 radar shared imaging abilities similar to those on the E-8.

More typically, the J-STARS aircraft monitored the enemy in motion and in static positions. Working with Marine Corps and Army attack helicopters, Iraqi convoys and armoured formations were destroyed before ever coming near the front line. On 22 January, 58 out of a convoy of 60 tanks were destroyed after the formation was spotted by an E-8. Lastly, the aircraft were used to effectively deny the enemy the sanctuary of the night. Dramatic images from the J-STARS WAS/MTI showed the massive retreat from Kuwait in the last hours of the war.

No surprises

The key words for the J-STARS operation were 'no surprises'. While it was not an active weapon, it helped to position friendly forces to best advantage. Its surveillance capabilities allowed allied commanders to face the enemy knowing exactly where he was and where he was headed. Yet while the system does much to blow away the fog of war, it can still be affected by the mist. During the final advance into Kuwait, the E-8 operators spotted a major armoured battle formation closing on the flank of a US Marine Corps unit. For an anxious period all concerned waited while a reconnaissance team was sent out, until finally discovering that the unidentified force was the British Army's 1st Armoured Division completing its lightning pincer move into Kuwait.

Even the E-8 itself did not completely avoid trouble. One aircraft had to beat a hasty retreat when the approach of an unidentified aircraft was spotted by an orbiting E-3 Sentry. Ignominious as this 'retrograde' manoeuvre may seem, the E-8s were never alone in the sky: being classed as High Asset Value Aircraft, they were the charges of constant Combat Air Patrols (HAVCAP). Another aircraft, however, involved in a ''Scud' Hunt', lost its link with the AWACS and strayed into western Iraq. So intent on their task were the crew that they flew directly towards airfield H-3 and its heavy SAM defences. The aircraft did not come under fire, however, and executed a safe return to its normal patrol area.

The two Boeings and the 151 military and civilian personnel on whom the entire system

Left: Grumman continues to test the E-8, boosted by the results of the Gulf War deployment. Company technicians operated most of the sophisticated equipment during the war missions.

Radar

The Norden multi-mode radar offers an imaging range in SAR mode of up to 175 km (109 miles). In an 8-hour sortie 1 million km^2 (386,100 sq miles) can be surveyed.

Above: The radar antenna is housed in this long canoe fairing. The hatch into the former cargo hold of the airliner allows access to vital equipment.

Airframe

The Boeing 707-320C was the final and definitive civil variant, combining a quick-change interior for passenger or cargo operations, or a mixture of both. It is identified by the lack of ventral fin made possible by changes to the aerodynamics compared to previous variants.

Powerplant

The E-8As are powered by four Pratt & Whitney JT3D turbofans (military designation TF33). The option remains to re-engine the production E-8Cs with the more efficient and quieter CFM International F108 high bypass ratio turbofan.

'Fiddle'

The large teardrop fairing under the E-8A's centre-section houses the antenna for the Flight Test Data Link, fitted to the test aircraft only. This was used during Desert Storm for transmitting data over long distances back to central commands in Riyadh.

'Skittle'

Immediately aft of the 'Fiddle' radome is a small antenna for the Surveillance and Control Data Link, the primary means of transmitting data to the Ground Station Modules. Information is transmitted to other aircraft via the JTIDS link.

Consoles

As the E-8As carry so much test equipment, the number of operator consoles within the cabin is reduced to 10. The E-8C will have 17, plus one for defensive electronics.

Along with the Lockheed F-117, the E-8 programme emerged from the Gulf War as one of the technological 'stars' of the conflict, and it is one of the few high-cost defence systems under development that seems to have an assured future in an era of drastically cut defence budgets. The next airframe to be converted will be to full production E-8C standard, lacking much of the test equipment currently carried by the two E-8As.

depended came home to Grumman's plant at Melbourne, Florida, on 6 March 1991, as one of the biggest success stories of the war. J-STARS makes any modern concept of a constantly changing air-land battle possible. Lieutenant General Gordon E. Farrell, commander of the USAF's Electronic Systems Division, summed up the E-8's war-winning contribution thus: "It has proven its true value, on the battlefield; moving targets did not stay moving very long."

'FLANKER' Attack

A photo-essay by Sergei Skrynnikov/Avia Data

Above: 'Red 02' takes off. The aircraft carries a single AA-11 'Archer' practice round on the starboard outer pylon. The difference in colour between dielectric panels on the fin and the radome (which are dark green) and those on the wingtips (which are white) is noteworthy.

Right: The sharkmouth-intaked 'Red 10' dives on a ground target. The aircraft carries what appears to be a five-round rocket pod (perhaps housing 80-mm unguided rockets) under the starboard wing. The wingtip pods appear to house some kind of ESM/ECM equipment.

These photos show what may be a new multi-role variant of the Sukhoi Su–27 'Flanker', which appears to be based on the standard 'Flanker-B' interceptor used by Frontal Aviation and the IA-PVO. Distinguished by streamlined wingtip pods (with dielectric radomes at each end), this new variant dispenses with the usual wingtip anti-flutter weight/missile launch rails. Apparently in air force service (though perhaps with a trials unit), the three aircraft shown were photographed strafing ground targets with their 30-mm cannon and firing a new five-round rocket pod.

Below: A side view of 'Red 01' shows the new wingtip pods to advantage. The aircraft retains the long fairing between the engines of the 'Flanker-B', and not the shorter unit fitted to the carrierborne 'Flanker-D'. It houses a brake chute and chaff/flare dispensers.

Opposite page: Two views of 'Red 10', which is decorated with a gaudy sharkmouth on each engine intake (inset). In the main picture the aircraft is seen firing its GSh-301 30-mm cannon against a ground target. The muzzle flash is visible even in daylight.

F-15 Eagle
Air Superiority–guaranteed

Armed and extremely dangerous: Eagles on the hunt are the personification of the term 'air superiority'. Unrivalled performance and talons to match make the F-15 the world's No. 1 fighter, as proven several times in the Middle East.

Combat-proven in the skies over Iraq in both fighter and bomber roles, the F-15 Eagle reached maturity long ago, but has proved that it still rules the roost. An incomparable BVR interceptor, capable of killing with precision at extreme range, the F-15 is also an able dogfighter, bettered only by much newer lightweights. Master of the air superiority game, the Eagle is also becoming something of a jack of all trades. In its latest F-15E incarnation it is probably the world's greatest interdictor.

Fully able to carry air-to-ground stores (to great effect in the F-15E model), the Eagle was nevertheless designed as an out-and-out fighter. The large wing provides excellent agility at all altitudes, and two hugely powerful engines provide the muscle to turn what is a large and bulky machine on the ground into a sparkling performer in the air.

"We were running our intercept against the second group of MiG-23s. They were at low altitude, below 1,000 ft. Our radar, awesome as it is, is painting these guys, and we can see them at 80 miles range. At about 30 miles from the merge we punch our wing tanks off, but keep the centreline tank on. We now have better manoeuvrability if we get into an [close-in] engagement. If our missiles don't work and the man decides to engage us, we'll be able to turn more tightly without those tanks. We're descending out of the mid-twenties [thousands of feet altitude] doing about Mach 1.2. The weather is overcast; we couldn't see the ground.

"We're now thinking, 'We may never see these guys.' We can shoot them, obviously, but once the missiles go below the clouds, at best we'll see a glow. The critical decision as we get within 20 miles is: 'Okay, who's going to target who?'

"That's Captain Draeger's job as Number One to decide. His philosophy is that he will take the map-reader, the guy in the lead, first. If you kill the guy that's leading, everyone else will go, 'Oh shit! What do we do now?' So he targets the enemy leader. He targets me as Number Two on the north-western trailer. There's only one Iraqi left so he says, 'Okay, Three and Four, both of you take the southernmost guy.'

"We acknowledge. I say, 'Chevron Two, sorted. Two-seven-zero. Twenty-five miles.' It's just like William Tell [the annual USAF air defence competition]. So the flight lead has called the target plan and all we have to do is lock up the guy we're supposed to lock, then shoot.

"We take our shots. Captain Draeger shoots first; we're now inside 20 miles. I shoot next, just a couple of seconds later. At about 12 miles there's a hole [in the overcast] that just opens up. So we go diving through. So now we're in visual environment. As the missiles are flying towards the target we get the first tally-hos [visual sightings] at about 10 miles from the merge. We can see the 'Floggers' running across the desert, fast.

"Captain Draeger's missile hits his man right in the back. The airplane flies right through the fireball and comes out the other side. It hit him but it didn't knock him out of the sky. He's burning but he's not down. Captain Draeger goes to a heater [prepares to fire a 'Winder'] but before he can do this the fire reaches the wingroot and the 'Flogger' blows up in a huge fireball.

"Right about then my missile hits my guy. I call a second 'Splash'. There's another big fireball. Draeger comes off. He says, 'Let's come off North.' Once people start seeing fireballs, that gets their attention and you want to get the hell out of there, fast. A moment later I hear Rodriguez call the third 'Splash'. They were about three miles in front of us when they blew up, so we saw them pretty well . . ."

Captain Tony Schiavi, an F-15 pilot with the 58th TFS, 33rd TFW, describes his MiG-23 kill on 23 January 1991 during Operation Desert Storm. This engagement was a textbook example of the use of the F-15, four Eagles seeing three enemy aircraft at 80 miles, accelerating to engage them, then firing AIM-7 Sparrow missiles from well beyond visual range. Only a trick of the weather allowed the Eagle pilots to see their prey before they broke violently away, running for safety, and even then, they never closed to within AIM-9, let alone gun, range!

Swaggering across the ramp from his aircraft, the F-15 pilot is aware that he has the most glamorous job in aviation today, wearing designer sunglasses and clad in the distinctive apparel of the modern fast-jet pilot, with 'speed jeans' (more formally known as external anti-*g* trousers), life preserver and lightweight HGU-helmet. Publicly, he might describe himself as a latter-day knight, whose job is to engage in one-to-one combat in a chivalrous airborne joust. He sees himself as the rightful heir to the traditions of the great dogfighting aces of the past, from Richthofen to Jabara. In fact, this is largely harmless (if not entirely truthful) image building.

When being totally serious most Eagle drivers would liken the job to that of the assassin, whose aim is to sneak up on an opponent unseen, killing his victim even before he is aware of any danger. The F-15 is the ideal vehicle for such an airborne assassin, capable of destroying its targets at extreme range (the jargon calls it BVR, or Beyond Visual Range) using its sophisticated radar and guided missiles. And if any enemy survives the opening BVR onslaught? Then the F-15 pilot can engage in the classic one-on-one turning dogfight with confidence, though the element of chance inherent in all such engagements makes this very much a second choice. If the dogfight becomes a furball, involving multiple bogies, then close-in fighting is best avoided, even if you're flying an Eagle. "Once you get more than two versus two, the statistics become more and more unfavourable, and eventually the F-15 dies like anything else," warned one F-15 pilot. Such statements cannot detract from the fact that the F-15 is one of the most effective fighters ever built, and perhaps the most important aircraft in the US inventory today.

Forty eight F-15C Eagles from Langley AFB, Virginia, were the first Operation Desert Shield forces to land in Saudi Arabia. At the time, there was a real fear they might have to shoot their way in. Their arrival was timed for dusk, in the belief – later proven – that Iraqi pilots didn't like to fly at night. Even then, the temperature was 120° F. "Welcome to Saudi Arabia," crew chief M. P. Curphey said to several of the fighter pilots. "You're going to be hostages in three hours." No-one laughed. Some pilots flew protective CAP (combat air patrol) while others landed.

No-one has laughed, any time since, at the McDonnell F-15 Eagle – the US Air Force's front-line, air-to-air combatant of the 1990s.

To the contrary, it must be emphasised what a brave step the F-15 Eagle was – a new aircraft which was revolutionary in its structure (including no less than 26 per cent titanium, as compared with 10 per cent in the F-4E Phantom) and, in its aerodynamics, and with new engine and new radar, both radically advanced for their time. Given the number of innovations in this big, powerful, long-range, BVR, air-to-air

warplane, it is remarkable that it was developed with few serious impediments – its only important teething problems arose in the form of early problems with its engines.

Eagle awakenings

The F-15 Eagle emerged from tumult in the 1960s when the US Air Force was caught up in the wrong war at the wrong time and was unable to concentrate or reach consensus on what kind of fighter it wanted.

The USAF entered the 1960s planning on a mixed force of F-4s and F-111s as its top-of-the-line fighters. After the F-111 ceased to be a serious candidate as a fighter, a high-low mix was advocated by Lieutenant Colonel John W. Bohn in the paper 'Force Options for Tactical Air' (August 1964), which

Left: Of all the cockpits in aviation, few are more prized than that of the F-15. At his command the Eagle pilot has the most powerful fighter in the Western world, and one which has been proven in battle to be a winner.

Above: A tiger-striped F-15C MSIP of the 53rd TFS, 36th TFW, formates on a KC-135 tanker during Desert Storm. The two Iraqi flags under the cockpit stand testament to the Eagle's successes in this conflict – in the case of this aircraft a pair of Su-25s shot down while heading for sanctuary in Iran.

Left: Among the stipulations of the new fighter design was excellent visibility, that to the rear being a massive improvement over the Phantom. Demonstrating this is a Georgia ANG F-15A cavorting over Dobbins AFB.

called for a cost-effective combination of low-cost F-5s (or, as it turned out, A-7s) coupled with expensive fighters (the F-X-cum-F-15). As the decade went on, the Air Staff – blue-suited planners who make Air Force policy in D ring on the fourth floor of the Pentagon – approved a series of studies for a 'next generation' fighter under the label F-X.

The USAF funded several F-X conceptual studies for a new fighter at the very time American aircrews were caught up in combat near Hanoi in two-man, multi-role fighters (F-4s) which had been designed to shoot down enemy aircraft beyond visual range, using air-to-air radar and radar-guided missiles (AIM-7 Sparrow). The F-4 Phantom (which became the service's only real fighter, the F-111 'Aardvark' having evolved into a bomber) was tested, fielded and put into battle as if there would never again be any need to actually *fight* an adversary in the sky. "We expected to kill 'em before we would ever see 'em," says a one-time F-4 pilot. It was not true then, nor was it later, that blue-suiters in the Pentagon believed the dogfight was defunct. They simply failed, when making the F-4 operational, to give dog-fighting a high priority.

The USAF's Pentagon planners also abdicated. They forfeited what should have been mainstream thinking – advocacy of an aircraft designed for dogfighting – and, in so doing, they defaulted to renegades, a clique of rebels who became known, not only then but reactively in later years, as the 'fighter mafia'. At a time when Air Staff AOs (action officers) should have been cementing policy, the 'fighter mafia' bucked the system from within.

The 'mafia' upstarts included Major John R. Boyd, who defined much of today's thinking about energy manoeuvrability, and Thomas Christie, a mathematician who helped Boyd quantify his ideas. Although much of what Boyd preached was simple acknowledgement that air combat takes place in three dimensions, both men contributed valuable ideas about how to make the quantum leap from piles of paper about a hypothetical F-X to an actual aircraft capable of winning dogfights. Boyd also contributed substantially to

Above: The Eagle was the first fighter to adopt what has become the standard configuration for the genre with twin fins, twin engines and a large, relatively straight wing.

Right: Air superiority implies that the complete fighter must take on any opponent on more than equal terms. Not only was the Eagle given the power and manoeuvrability to handle hostile fighters and attackers, it was also given the dash speed and endurance to catch strategic bombers and maritime patrollers. The Iceland-based 57th Fighter Interceptor Squadron has probably more experience of 'Bear' catching than any other Western fighter outfit. For a long-range intercept of an aircraft such as this 'Bear-D' over the Atlantic, the Eagles are restricted to just a pair of Sparrows each.

the USAF's teaching of air combat tactics to new pilots.

But the 'fighter mafia's' Godfather was Pierre Spey, a Pentagon analyst who muddled issues. Spey advocated dogfighting capability for F-X (which the USAF needed) but reserved his most vocal arguments for a simple, lightweight fighter, which eventually resulted in the F-16. Spey claims to have helped the US Air Force get better fighters.

Air superiority fighter

The real beginning of today's F-15 Eagle came in February 1968 when Tactical Air Command chief General Gabriel P. Disosway signed off on an ROC (Required Operational Capability) statement holding that any F-4 replacement to emerge from the F-X studies must be an air superiority fighter. In May 1968, USAF Chief of Staff General John P. McConnell endorsed Disosway's package and allocated to the F-X effort – up to now, four years of conceptual work – his service's highest priority. In a departure from past practice, one which has since become more commonplace, the new fighter was assigned a designation (in late 1968) *before* an actual aircraft type had been chosen. It was to be the F-15.

A decision had been reached, it seemed. The future F-15 – whatever it looked like, whoever built it – would be optimised to engage and kill an adversary BVR, and would thus be designed explicitly for air-to-air combat. It would be able to dogfight. McConnell did not specify armament, but thought was well-advanced towards resurrecting a fighter weapon useful since World War I – a gun. The F-15 would *not* be (in the mould of the gunless F-4 Phantom) a 'multi-role' craft.

It is remarkable that Air Staff officers focused on air-to-air capability at the very time they were thumbing through reports from Vietnam which proclaimed that a multi-role fighter was 'the answer – a warplane which could not merely kill MiGs but also drop bombs, fly reconnaissance and maybe even do a little electronic snooping on the side. In 1968, fully two more years were yet to pass before Pentagon AOs would understand that in the narrow arena of air-to-air combat, Americans had fared dismally against Hanoi's

fighter force. The understanding was due, largely, to a report by US Navy Commander Frank Ault, himself a bomber pilot (AJ-2 Savage), who visited fighter units and submitted over 200 recommendations.

Since the North Vietnamese did not need to plan on overseas deployment, had a limited swath of geography to defend, and were fighting over home ground, it did not matter that their fighters – MiG-17s and MiG-21s – were flimsy and vulnerable. Had they possessed a sturdier fighter comparable to today's F-15 (though they had no need for the latter's range or endurance), they might have fared even better. Without a single multi-role aircraft in their air arm, without BVR capability, with fighters tailored for air-to-air dogfighting, Ho Chi Minh's minions did well enough.

In the 1950-53 Korean War, American pilots were widely touted as shooting down 15 MiG-15s for every F-86 Sabre lost. Both MiG and Sabre, not as originally designed but as they turned out, were optimised for close-quarters dogfighting. Revisionists have since adjusted the Korea ratio to 7-to-1, still second best in America's history – behind only

Above: The US Air Force's F-15 fleet is split between protecting overseas interests (in the Pacific and Europe), supporting rapid intervention forces for a multitude of contingencies (CONUS-based units), and for the dedicated defence of the United States. This machine is from the Oregon ANG, the premier unit primed with the task of defending the western seaboard.

Left: F-15s take shape in the McDonnell Aircraft Company factory at St Louis. This plant produced 5,057 F-4 Phantoms in its time, and is currently involved in the final stages of F-15 production, and continuing work on the AV-8 and F/A-18.

the American Volunteer Group, or 'Flying Tigers' in China during World War II. In 1965-68, this 7-to-1 'kill' ratio of the Korean War shrank to a dismal 1.5-to-1 ratio during Vietnam fighting.

The figure is worse than it sounds. All claims of damage inflicted to an enemy in combat are always exaggerated. It has since been verified that some of the warplanes shot down by Americans – thanks to the ever-present 'fog of war' and the persistent problems of identifying one's opponent – were F-4s rather than MiGs. In actual fighting near Hanoi, USAF jocks clearly shot down less than one MiG for every warplane they lost.

There were diverse reasons – among them poor training, missiles that didn't work, tactical restrictions. Commander Ault found that most American fighter pilots had never fired a live missile and that most fighter airframes had not recently fired one, either. The ROE (rules of engagement) often prevented the Americans from using their BVR capability. But the principal cause of the poor showing was that the F-4

Phantom was supposed to kill MiGs and be a multi-role performer, too. The USAF did not have a warplane dedicated to air-to-air combat.

Other issues, serious ones, kept the USAF in some confusion over what it wanted in its future F-15. Arguments persisted for a lightweight fighter, a stripped-down, no-frills flying machine with the simplicity of, say, the MiG-21. In a speculative paper given 'Specat' (special category) distribution in the Pentagon in 1968, Pierre Spey called for a 'hotrod of the skies'. The Northrop F-5A Freedom Fighter, as much as the MiG-21, was cited as the inspiration, although Spey's target weight for such an aircraft – 35,000 lb – is broadly equivalent to today's F/A-18 in air-to-air configuration, and is heavier than an air-defence configured F-16; hardly a simple lightweight.

F-15 decisions

The F-15, at this juncture, was still a military designation and not flyable hardware. Less important issues – less important, that is, than dogfight versus multi-role – remained unresolved and were vexing. Should a new fighter have one engine or two? Should it have one crewman or two? Should it be armed solely with missiles, as the F-4 Phantom had been, or should it also go into harm's way, as many now believed, packing a gun?

Here, lessons from Vietnam, although useful, produced mixed results. What Vietnam seemed to say to the Air Staff's AOs was that a multi-role fighter could fill USAF needs (which was dead wrong), that the ideal crew size for a fighter was two (still arguable, although the F-15 has since excelled as a single-seater), and that just as it was desirable to have a second set of eyeballs on board, so, too, was it a good idea to have a second engine (which was absolutely right). Most importantly, since the North Vietnamese had been so insensitive as to attack within visual range and to engage not just in hit-and-run tactics but – yes – the *dogfight*, the lesson which really mattered was the one which cried out 'yes, yes, yes' to the F-15 carrying a gun.

The decision to drop the gun on the F-4 had been made at an early design stage in the 1950s by those who knew the missile age had arrived and were preparing, next, to discard the pilot. A couple of years earlier, the F-104 Starfighter – a 'hot rod', to use Spey's term, but one which proved utterly useless for any military mission by a major power – had been billed as the 'missile with a man in it'. Vietnam, at least, re-

Left: The initial batch of 12 development aircraft included a pair of TF-15A two-seaters, this being the second of the two. The addition of the second seat was made behind the existing seat, necessitating a reduction in fuel capacity and a considerable increase in the size of the canopy, but with no penalty in combat capability.

Above: The first 10 YF-15A development aircraft were put through an intensive trials programme that involved all aspects of operations. The M61A1 Vulcan cannon was fired often to fully test the effects on the airframe and systems. The weapon was not fitted until aircraft No. 5.

versed the conventional wisdom that aerial warfare had no place for people or for shooting.

Debate persisted and the USAF really did not yet know with much precision what it wanted as late as 30 September 1968, when it issued an RFP (request for proposals) for a future F-15. The RFP was, however, quite specific on some points. The RFP specified that the new fighter should have: low wing loading with buffet-free performance at Mach 0.9; a high thrust-to-weight ratio; long-range pulse-Doppler radar with look-down/shoot-down capability; ferry range sufficient to permit self-deployment to Europe without midair refuelling; and a maximum speed of Mach 2.5.

The Mach 2.5 requirement was theoretically achieved, at the cost of great expense and complexity, although with missiles the F-15 is restricted to Mach 1.78.

The RFP spelled out other detailed requirements, by far the most important of which was a one-man cockpit. Other specifications related to fatigue life, maintainability, visibility, self-contained starting, and a maximum gross take-off weight of 40,000 lb (18144 kg) for the air superiority mission.

Three proposals

The F-X SPO (System Program Office; later the F-15 SPO) belonging to Air Force Systems Command (AFSC) at Wright-Patterson AFB, Ohio, under Colonel Benjamin N. Bellis, released the RFP to eight manufacturers. By 30 December 1968, the USAF had viable proposals from just three – McDonnell, North American and Fairchild-Republic. All were awarded $15.4-million contracts for the Contract Definition Phase.

The three designs for the F-X fighter – that is, the F-15 – were not remarkably dissimilar. North American's and Fairchild's had single tail fins. The Fairchild-Republic design, strongly backed by Congressmen from Long Island where it

would be built, had its engines hanging out from the fuselage beneath a blended lift surface. An exhaustive evaluation by AFSC led to the announcement on 23 December 1969 that McDonnell Aircraft Company had been chosen to build the new fighter. The firm's head, James P. McDonnell, had acquired Douglas Aircraft two years earlier but the two aerospace firms have retained distinct identities; no amount of advertising to the contrary could make the new fighter a McDonnell-Douglas aircraft. It was, and is, a McDonnell aeroplane.

Phantom experience

Much of the early work on it benefitted from McDonnell's Herman Barkey, who had led the F-4 design team. Principal engineering work on the McDonnell F-15 was overseen by George Graff, head of the design team, while programme manager Don Malvern dealt with the practical problems of organising the effort and moving it forward. Malvern had had a similar role with the F-4 Phantom. Morale was high at the St Louis facility, where key McDonnell people felt with some justification that they knew the design skills and the management techniques – as well as the needs of the customer, the US Air Force – to produce a first-rate fighter.

The initial contract called for 20 developmental aircraft, including a preliminary batch of 10 single-seat F-15As (71-0280/0289) and two two-seat TF-15As (71-0290/71-0291). The two-seaters were later redesignated F-15B. In addition to these Category I aircraft, the contract specified eight Category II FSD (full-scale development) aircraft, all F-15As (72-0113/0120).

Initial plans were to buy 749 F-15s. Twelve would be employed as Category I test aircraft, eight as Category II test ships (to be upgraded to operational configuration), and 143 as attrition reserves. One hundred and eight would have been employed for training (54 for command support). With 72 aircraft per wing, the total buy would give Tactical Air Command, USAFE (US Air Forces in Europe), and Pacific Air Forces three, two and one F-15 wings respectively. (As it turned out, the Category II Eagles did not become operational and, instead of a second USAFE wing, the USAF acquired four fighter-interceptor squadrons plus an Eagle squadron in Alaska.)

Before the new McDonnell fighter flew, it was preceded by flight tests with three RPRVs (remotely-piloted research vehicles), which were three-eighths scale replicas of the F-15 Eagle. The National Aeronautics and Space Administration's (NASA) Dryden facility at Edwards AFB, California, dropped these remote-control mini-Eagles from its much-used Boeing NB-52B Stratofortress mother ship (52-0008). The RPRVs were acquired by NASA on 4 December 1972. They weighed 2,425 lb (1099 kg), were 23 ft (7.01 m) long, and were made of aluminium, wood and fibreglass at a bargain-basement cost of $250,000 each. The use of flying replicas to gather data in advance of the maiden flight of a major aircraft type was a unique aspect of the Eagle's development and was considered a highly successful programme.

The F-15A prototype (71-0280) – sometimes referred to as a YF-15A with the Y prefix indicating service-test duties – was rolled out at St Louis on 26 June 1972. Dismantled and transported to Edwards AFB, California, aboard a C-5A Galaxy, the F-15A was flown a month later on 27 July 1972. At the controls was Irving Burrows, who had many years' experience as a company test pilot on the F-4 Phantom and other types. The maiden flight, in clear weather, was uneventful. Burrows has since spoken of the F-15's ease of handling. The TF-15A first flew on 7 July 1973.

Test programme

An ambitious programme was embarked upon with the first 12 Eagles built, the USAF's Category I test aircraft, known in shorthand as aeroplanes F-1 through F-10 and TF-1 and TF-2. Their assignments were as follows:

The No. 1 YF-15A, alias F-1 (71-0280), first flown 27 July 1972 as noted, opened the flight envelope and conducted handling and external stores trials.

The No. 2 YF-15A, or F-2 (71-0281), first flown on 26 September 1972, was the primary engine test aircraft.

The No. 3 YF-15A, or F-3 (71-0282), first flown on 4 November 1972, was the avionics test aircraft and the first to be equipped with APG-63 radar.

The No. 4 YF-15A, or F-4 (71-0283), first flown on 13 January 1973, was the programme's flying structural test aircraft.

The No. 5 YF-15A, or F-5 (71-0284), first flown on 7 March 1973, was the first Eagle with M61A1 Vulcan cannon and served as the armament development aircraft; later, it became the first GF-15A ground trainer for mechanics at the USAF's Sheppard Technical Training Center in Texas.

The No. 6 YF-15A, or F-6 (71-0285), nicknamed 'Killer', first flown on 23 May 1973, was the second avionics aircraft and tested the Eagle's flight control and missile fire control systems.

The No. 7 YF-15A, or F-7 (71-0286), first flown on 14 June 1973, tested armament and external fuel carriage.

The No. 8 YF-15A, or F-8 (71-0287), first flown 25 August 1973, was the programme's spin recovery aircraft and was also used for work at high angles of attack (high alpha) as well as fuel systems development.

The No. 9 YF-15A, or F-9 (71-0288), first flown on 20 October 1973, was used for aircraft and engine performance evaluations.

The No. 10 YF-15A, or F-10 (71-0289), first flown on 16 January 1974, did TEWS (tactical electronic warfare system), radar, and avionics work.

The first TF-15A, known as TF-1 (71-0290) and first flown on 7 July 1973, tested various systems. After this, every seventh Eagle produced was a two-seater.

The second TF-15A, or TF-2 (71-0291), began as the final Category I test ship. Subsequently, the first two TF-15As served as developmental ships in a variety of roles. TF-2 was only beginning many years of yeoman service as a Category I USAF test aircraft.

In 1976, an Eagle made a spectacular round-the-world tour covering some 34,000 miles (54716 km), attending air shows and showing itself to numerous potential buyers. The aircraft on tour was none other than TF-2.

The hard-working second TF-15A (soon redesignated F-15B) was given a striking Bicentennial colour scheme for 1976 and embarked on a long sales tour around the world. Included in the tour was a prestige display at the Farnborough air show.

At one juncture, McDonnell proposed an RF-15 reconnaissance version of the Eagle (not flown) with a new nose configuration accommodating cameras, SLAR (side-looking airborne radar), television, and a multi-spectral scanner. After this variant was rejected the company, as a private venture, conducted Project Peek Eagle in which a conformal centreline pod containing reconnaissance cameras, other imaging equipment, and data-link was test-flown. Not surprisingly, the test aircraft was TF-2 (71-0291).

In later years, TF-2 (71-0291) served as the F-15E Strike Eagle demonstrator and was also used to test the Eagle's proposed FAST pack conformal tanks. TF-1 became the F-15 S/MTD.

F-15 described

The actual aircraft which flew after years of study, design and development has a comfortingly conventional look today, but seemed a departure in 1972.

The pilot sits very high in this big fighter behind a one-piece windscreen and, though the canopy structure does not dispense with bows, has the excellent visibility so essential in any close-in fight. The pilot sits on a McDonnell Douglas ACES II zero-zero ejection seat and can fly and fight in the HOTAS (hands on throttle and stick) mode, getting key information from his HUD (head-up display) and cuing the aircraft with thumb and fingers.

The Eagle's all-metal, semi-monocoque fuselage, at 58 ft 3 in (17.76 m) long (nearly the length of a Dakota transport), supports a very large, low-loaded, cantilever, shoulder-mounted wing – *not* of variable geometry as in the Navy's F-14 Tomcat – swept at 45°. The wing, chosen after 100 designs were analysed in a year of wind-tunnel trials, is straightforward, having conventional outboard ailerons, conventional flaps and no other control surfaces. Remarkable, however, is the size of the wing with its area of 608

sq ft (56.51 m²) and, hence, the Eagle's low wing loading: the big-winged F-15 floats to earth so gently that it requires no braking parachute to retard its velocity on landing. The large area and low wing loading of the Eagle wing generate enormous amounts of lift and are a major factor in conferring air combat agility on the Eagle. It is worthy of note that the Eagle's wing is a multi-celled three-spar structure with multi-stiffened skins. Any of the three spars can be severed and the aircraft can still be flown.

Twin fins

At a late design stage, a single tail for the F-15 Eagle was rejected. The Eagle's tail unit is an all-metal structure of twin fins and rudders – remarkably thin, thanks to boron composite skin over honeycomb material – with all-moving horizontal tail surfaces outboard of the fins. (The experience with composites helped enormously with McDonnell's later AV-8B Harrier programme, as the Harrier has an all-composite wing and extensive use of composites in its fuselage.) Having twin fins sacrifices weight for good high-alpha performance and better survivability. The Eagle's stabilisers and rudders are interchangeable from side to side.

The Eagle's spine-mounted airbrake was an innovation. It could be deployed without pitch change and at any speed. Early in the Eagle's life, there were important modifications to its wingtip shape, tailplane, and dorsal 'barn door' speed brake. The builder removed some 3 sq ft of wingtip on each side beginning with the fourth aircraft to cure severe buffet experienced above 30,000 ft (9144 m) at speeds between Mach 0.85 and 0.95 and at 6g or more. The Eagle's tailplane leading edge was given a notch (dogtooth) to cure flutter problems. Buffet was produced when the huge speed brake was deployed, so the builder reduced the speed brake's extension angle and increased its area from 20 to 31.5 sq ft (1.9 to 2.9 m²).

Power in the early Eagle was provided by two 25,000-lb (11340-kg) thrust Pratt & Whitney F100-PW-100 turbofan engines with afterburners. Left and right engines of the Eagle are interchangeable and under ideal conditions can be re-

Above: Several of the development batch continue to provide sterling service in 1992. This aircraft (F-8) now flies with NASA from Edwards AFB under the HIDEC (Highly Integrated Digital Electronic Control) programme. This has a digital flight control system and digitally-controlled PW1128 engines, and investigates the performance gains of closely coupling the two.

Far left: A key component in the Eagle's success is the radar. This is the current standard unit, the AN/APG-70, as fitted to F-15Es and F-15C MSIP aircraft. It has excellent air-to-air capability, and remains unsurpassed in service aircraft for the interdiction mission.

Below: The continuing story of 291 saw the aircraft involved in weapons carriage trials which culminated in the F-15E variant. Here the FAST packs (now known as CFTs) are carried, with a full load of cluster bombs.

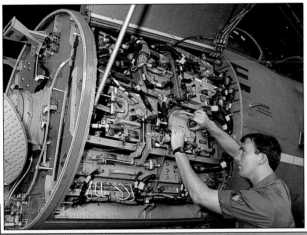

Above: The large wing (often derided by pilots of other aircraft as the 'tennis court') and upper surface blending are shown to advantage by this 33rd FW Eagle. The positioning of the engines close to the thrust line largely alleviates asymmetric handling problems should one be lost.

Right: A 32nd TFS F-15C displays the standard air-to-air load carried for most missions, consisting of four AIM-9M Sidewinders on the wing pylons, four AIM-7M Sparrows on the intake trunks and a centreline tank. If the engagement becomes a close-in fight, the Eagle still has the trusty M61A1 Vulcan cannon to fall back on.

placed by maintenance crews in as little as 20 minutes. The engines are fed by straight, two-dimensional external compression air intakes which embody the only use of variable geometry in the F-15: because the Eagle may have to fight at high angles of attack, the intakes can 'nod' up or down to keep the aperture facing directly into the airstream in order to maintain a smooth flow of air to the engines. The intake angle can also be adjusted to prevent more air than necessary being taken in.

Dating to August 1968 when the USAF awarded development contracts to Pratt & Whitney and General Electric for a next-generation fighter engine, the 15-ft 10-in (4.84-m), 3,070-lb (1,393-kg) F100 is an axial-flow turbofan with a bypass ratio of 0.7:1. It has two shafts, one carrying a three-stage fan driven by a two-stage turbine, the other carrying the 10-stage main compressor and its two-stage turbine. The F100 engine has had its share of teething troubles, compounded by labour disputes at two major subcontractors. Despite problems, the engine introduced numerous advanced features: the engine has a titanium keel, and a layer of titanium in the centre of the fuselage between the two powerplants to preclude a fire in one powerplant spreading to the other.

Eagle radar

The APG-63 radar in the F-15A is one of the Eagle's strongest assets, a quantum improvement over the F-4 Phantom radar, fully capable of BVR combat, and the first modern pulse-Doppler radar with genuine look-down/shoot-down capability.

In fact, the APG-63 – chosen after competition between Westinghouse and Hughes – is the first successful X-band coherent pulse-Doppler radar. Its display is a television-style scanned display rather than a conventional CRT (cathode ray terminal). In this display, aimed at easing the pilot's workload, clutter is filtered out automatically, giving very clean 'dots'. The radar has various air-to-air modes, employing different PRFs (Pulse Repetition Frequencies) depending on the type of search or engagement being undertaken. These include: long-range search: employing high and medium PRFs, this mode offers a compromise between the best air-to-air tracking of tail-on and nose-on targets, with the pilot selecting search ranges between 10 and 160 nm (18.5 and 296 km); velocity search: using high PRF, this mode is intended exclusively for head-on, high-closure-rate targets; short-range search: using medium PRF, this mode is optimised

for short-range manoeuvring for Sidewinder and gun engagements, and offers 10, 20 or 40-mile (16, 32 or 64 km) scale against multiple targets, with good discrimination against them.

To back up these three pulse-Doppler modes, the APG-63 has a non pulse-Doppler mode, using low PRF, good only as backup and useful only when 'looking up' since this mode offers no clutter rejection. There is also a beacon mode for interrogating other warplanes' IFF transponders, a manual tracking mode as backup for when the radar is not automatically tracking well, and a 'sniff' mode which detects jamming and emits tiny bursts of radar to minimise self-illumination of the Eagle. Finally, there is a radar mapping mode.

Talons of the Eagle

Given the importance of the far-reaching radar, armament of the F-15 Eagle obviously begins with BVR missiles, originally Vietnam-era AIM-7F Sparrows (today, AIM-7M) which require semi-active radar homing and make it difficult for the pilot of the launch aircraft to evade while, as Americans put it, "shooting somebody in the face." The Sparrow will gradually be supplanted by the AIM-120A AMRAAM (Advanced Medium-Range Air-to-Air Missile) which handles its own terminal homing onto target, but usually requires radar illumination from the fighter for a portion of its run-in. Four AIM-9J Sidewinder IR missiles (today, AIM-9M) also made up part of the fighter's arsenal, as well as a 20-mm M61A1 Vulcan ('Gatling') six-barrel cannon which became a fallback after efforts to develop a new 25-mm cannon for the Eagle foundered.

There were, in fact, two armament options for the Eagle which failed to materialise. One was the projected AIM-82 air-to-air missile with 50° off-boresight capability and wide-looking seeker head, a proposal which died early in the planning stages. The other was the 25-mm gun originally proposed: it was to have used caseless ammunition, which offers the advantages of higher velocity and flatter trajectory. After a competition between General Electric and Philco-Ford, the latter was awarded a contract for the 25-mm GAU-7 cannon. By September 1973, some $100 million had been spent on the GAU-7, but its feed system did not work properly and it could not be fired at high rates. Caseless ammunition, despite its advantages, also had serious drawbacks: it was difficult to handle and there was the danger of rounds cooking off, so every part of the gun system had to be lined, including the ammunition tank and the gun. In contrast, the 20-mm M61A1 Vulcan cannon was a proven item.

Below: The F100 engines of the F-15 have fully dilating nozzles to control the mass flow of air, as demonstrated here by this 32nd FS aircraft.

Bottom: Lightly-laden Eagles from Bitburg perform a spirited break after a pairs take-off. The large wing and powerful engine ensure excellent low-speed handling.

Production of an initial batch of 30 F-15A/B fighters was announced on 1 March 1973. The first Eagle delivered to an operational USAF unit was TF-15A 73-0108 (the 21st Eagle built), christened 'TAC 1'. This aircraft was accepted by President Gerald Ford in a ceremony on 4 November 1974 at Luke AFB, Arizona, for the 555th Tactical Fighter Training Squadron, the 'Triple Nickel'.

A TF-15A development aircraft was shown off to the world in the September 1974 Farnborough air show. The aircraft was ferried 3,063 miles (4930 km) non-stop and without air refuelling from Loring AFB, Maine, where it 'launched' at a weight of 67,000 lb (30390 kg), including 33,000 lb (14970 kg) of fuel. After 5.4 hours at an average speed of Mach 0.85, the Eagle had 4,300 lb (1950 kg) of fuel still in its tanks when it began its approach to a landing at RAF Bentwaters.

Long range had been one goal of the F-15 programme, achieved in part with two FAST (fuel and sensor tactical) packs – flush, low-drag fuel pallets developed for the F-15 and each able to carry 5,000 lb (2268 kg) of fuel. The original FAST packs attached to the side of either engine intake trunk (being made in bonded pairs) and were designed to the same load factors and airspeed limits as the aircraft itself. Today, these are referred to as CFTs (conformal fuel tanks) because

they carry fuel only, thereby admirably extending the Eagle's range – but the original plan was for these packs to carry sensors as well.

The FAST pack could be fitted to the F-15 Eagle using a standard bomb lift truck, with only two bolts: it needed just one electrical and two fluid connectors to make it operational. As originally planned, there were five options for FAST packs for different missions. All involved the carriage of fuel and AIM-7 Sparrow missiles on corners of the FAST pack. The five options included: interceptor: IRST (infra-red search and track), Northrop TISEO (target identification sight, electro-optical), and data-link; reconnaissance: cameras, LORAN, data-link, and photo flash; strike: laser designator, LLLTV (low light level television), FLIR (forward-looking infra-red), and LORAN; SAM suppression: ESM, ECM and chaff; thrust augmentation: a rocket booster.

In the early 1970s, US planners did not yet foresee a scenario in which F-15s might deploy on short notice to a spot as far away as Dhahran, Saudi Arabia – war plans for a fight in the Middle East would not be treated seriously until the 1978 Iranian revolution – and it was felt that the use of FAST packs, first test-flown on 27 July 1974, would permit global deployment of the Eagle without tanker support.

Streak Eagle

In 1974-75, McDonnell fielded a modified F-15A (72-0119) in an attempt to capture world-class time-to-climb records for jet-powered aircraft. Ostensibly, Project Streak Eagle was to boost *esprit* and provide data on F-15 capabilities, but the effort was also an unashamed effort to stress the fact that it was a very fast aircraft – a false impression, since as with many modern fighter airplanes, the F-15 will fly at over Mach 2.0 only when clean, with an operational load will fly at only Mach 1.7 and at low level will fly only at Mach 1.1 – as well as an unabashed bid for Congressional funding for production Eagles at a juncture when the fall of Vietnam made future

Stripped of all paint bar the logo and national insignia on the nose, the Streak Eagle was an unashamed attempt to demonstrate the power of the F-15. Most of its records fell much later to a specially-prepared Sukhoi Su-27.

military spending uncertain. Coincidentally, the effort was to demonstrate an important characteristic of a high-performance fighter designed to kill beyond visual range: acceleration, which imparts energy to an air-to-air missile before launch.

Under a $2.1-million contract of 1 April 1974, the aircraft was modified for the record attempts by deleting non-mission critical systems including flap and speed brake actuators, armament, radar, fire control system, a few minor items, and the 50 lb (22.67 kg) of 'Eagle gray' paint which, according to pilots, can increase drag and thus hamper air speed by as much as 15 mph (24 km/h). If function means beauty, the resulting Streak Eagle was the most splendiferous of the species *haliaeetus leucophalus*, the American Bald Eagle – a shiny, silvery aircraft, during part of its era tarnished by massive dosages of yellow-gold primer. It was also spritely, weighing some 1,800 lb (816.46 kg) less than comparable F-15A block 6 aeroplanes.

After obtaining sanction from the FAI (Fédération Aéronautique Internationale), the climb record attempts were mounted from Grand Forks AFB, Dakota, to seize the advantage of cold temperatures. Eight successful record attempts were made, the most dramatic being a climb to 98,425 ft (30000 m) in 207.80 seconds from brake release – the aircraft being secured by holdback cable at full afterburner before launch. This 1 February 1975 flight by Major Roger Smith overcame a previous record of 243.86 seconds by a Soviet MiG-25 'Foxbat'.

These high-altitude flights were carried out in much the same manner as firing a bullet upwards into the sky – the Streak Eagle simply kept going until it ran out of inertia and

went 'over the top', actually reaching about 103,000 ft (31394 m) in order to be in a climb at the requisite 98,425 ft. A high rate of climb was one reason the F-15A Eagle was later chosen as the US Air Force's ASAT (anti-satellite) platform.

At least the Streak Eagle enjoyed a brief moment of glory. Other hard-labouring testbed aeroplanes contributed much to aviation knowledge but never received much recognition for it. Based on a May 1971 contract, McDonnell developed a composite wing for the F-15 made up of boron and graphite filaments embedded in epoxy resin. The wing would have reduced radar signature, extended fatigue life, and saved 500 lb (227 kg) in weight. Much of the technology from this early attempt to use composites went into the manufacturer's AV-8B Harrier, which employs about 60 per cent composites in its fuselage structure. In a related project, the first TF-15A (71-0290, since redesignated F-15B) flew with aluminium-lithium wing panels stronger and lighter than the wing panels they replaced. Despite these tests, 'Au-Li' panels were not seriously pursued and an opportunity was lost for a technical lead, later attained by the Soviet MiG-29 'Fulcrum'. This was only one of several developmental projects in which the hard-working 71-0290 was employed before it became the F-15 STOL/MTD demonstrator.

While development work on the F-15 was hitting its stride, the US Navy was instructed in July 1971 to look at a possible navalised version of the Eagle. The sea service's much-preferred F-14 Tomcat had made its first flight on 21 December 1970; although the first airframe had been lost in a mishap and the Tomcat was having its own developmental problems, progress with the Grumman fighter was now well advanced and officers in the Pentagon's Op-05, the Navy's equivalent of the Air Staff, may have been less than fully enthusiastic about an aquatic Eagle.

A study by McDonnell showed that a tailhook-equipped Eagle for shipboard operations would weigh some 2,300 lb (1043 kg) more than the land-based F-15. This was without the ultimate BVR missile, the AIM-54A Phoenix, which was integral to the Tomcat and which Op-05 and NavAir (Naval Air Systems Command) planners now added to their Eagle study, increasing weight even further. For a time, the designation F-15N was bandied about. Company documents refer to the F-15(N) and the Phoenix-equipped F-15(N-PHX).

The idea of a carrier-based Eagle was resurrected, briefly, by Senate members in March 1973. In the end, the US Navy went ahead with what became a hi-lo cost mix of F-14 and F/A-18 Hornet fighters, and the F-15N was never ordered.

Below: Vortices stream from the wingtips as 36th TFW Eagles perform a textbook fighter break-to-land, pulling hard and high to unload energy for the downwind leg.

Eagle twice, in June and September 1975, and was considering 50 aircraft for North American air defence. Britain's Royal Air Force looked at the type in October 1975 and had a clear requirement for no fewer that 70 Eagles. At one time the RAF hoped to lease F-15s as a stopgap, pending delivery of the Tornado ADV. France evaluated the Eagle in April 1976 and Australia later that year during the worldwide tour made by the familiar TF-2 (71-0291).

In fact, it might be said that one colossal failure of the otherwise successful Eagle programme was the manufacturer's inability to wrest production orders from three nations which had a great need for a powerful, long-range, BVR interceptor – Australia, Canada and the United Kingdom.

The F-15 came along when the US Air Force was still pondering how to fight and win massive air battles, involving hundreds of aircraft, during a Soviet invasion of Western Europe, but it was the role of the F-15 in a Middle East balance of power which attracted the most visibility. The F-15 was so important to US policy in the Middle East that a State Department memorandum in the 1970s held that "the mere transfer of [F-15s] will alter the balance of US relations" in the region. Israel became the first foreign user in 1976, while a sale to Saudi Arabia, deemed 'pivotal' in the same document, took shape by 1977.

Four FSD F-15As reached the Jewish state as early as 10 December 1976. Israel has developed a mixed F-15A/B/C/D Eagle force ever since, and was still acquiring early US F-15As from inventory in November 1991. Saudi interest in vastly increasing its Eagle force was seen as a slim prospect of keeping production of the fighter alive well into the late 1990s.

Front-line US service

With its RTU (replacement training unit) gearing up at Luke AFB, Arizona, the USAF assigned its first F-15s in a combat role to the 1st Tactical Fighter Wing (FF tailcode, for 'First Fighter') at Langley Air Force Base, Virginia, the squadron converting to the new type from the F-4E Phantom beginning on 9 January 1976. The first aircraft were delivered in a light blue paint scheme, which was soon discarded.

The F-15 Eagle experienced some labour pains. At Luke, pilots were discovering that they could not mount the planned number of sorties. There were difficulties with parts and maintenance, and there persisted a more serious problem with the powerplant.

No one had foreseen that the F100 powerplant would encounter difficulties precisely because the F-15 Eagle enjoyed combat capabilities not found in earlier fighters. The USAF had underestimated the number of power cycles (movement from engine start to full power and afterburner, then back to lower power ratings used for approach and landing) undergone per sortie, and had not realised how much the Eagle's newfound air-manoeuvring capacity would result in frequent, abrupt changes of throttle setting. Key engine components such as first-stage turbine blades suffered greater wear and a higher failure rate than had been foreseen. Much of this was corrected with structural adjustments in the powerplant design, but a more serious problem continued to plague early Eagle engines – stagnation stalling.

When the air flow through the compressor was disturbed, as during high angle-of-attack manoeuvres, the engine core lost speed while its combustor section continued to pass hot gas to the turbine, causing the turbine to overheat. Under some conditions, as during a mild hard start, the engine could stall without the pilot immediately noticing. Unattended, this could result in damage, even crippling damage. Part of the solution was an audible warning system to alert the pilot to impending trouble.

Pressure on the afterburner resulting from a hard start could cause the engine to stall at high altitude and high Mach numbers. Emergency procedure for recovery was for the pilot to shut the engine and allow it to spool down, then re-

Above: Israel was the first foreign recipient of the Eagle. This classic photograph depicts a quartet of F-15As flying over the ancient fort at Masada.

Right: The Langley-based 1st TFW became the world's first front-line F-15 operator in January 1976. This early recipient carries AIM-9J Sidewinders.

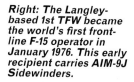

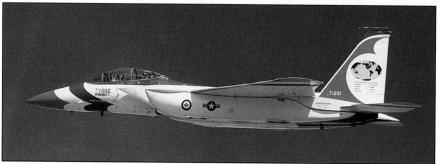

Above: Canada was one of the more serious potential customers for the Eagle, hence the maple leaf on the side of FAST pack-equipped 291. The flags on the nose highlighted the nations with specific interest (US, UK, Denmark, Norway, Iran, Israel, South Korea, Canada, the Netherlands, Belgium, West Germany, Saudi Arabia, Australia, France and Japan) while the tail recorded details of its world sales tour.

Non-American Eagles

While early problems were confronted, the F-15 Eagle programme moved ahead. Foreign interest was considerable. Israel, while it had little need for the Eagle's size or BVR capability, stood to gain enormous prestige and political clout by receiving a top-of-the-line American fighter at the start of its production run, concurrently with the US Air Force. Iran, too, saw the F-15 primarily as a high-ticket prestige item: when the Shah was given a TF-15A test flight, he made serious overtures for the aircraft not as a competitor to, but in addition to, the Grumman F-14 Tomcats which Tehran eventually purchased.

As early as July 1973, Iran evaluated the F-15 and enunciated a requirement for 53 aircraft. The Eagle was examined again in September 1974 and by West Germany in March 1975, the latter with a stated need for 200 aeroplanes. Japan evaluated the F-15 twice, in June and July 1975. Canada

open throttle. Modifications, including a quartz window in the side of the afterburner assembly to enable a flame sensor to monitor the pilot flame of the augmentor, provided an added solution but left the F100, even today, with a reputation as being temperamental under certain flying conditions. In the meanwhile, there were groundings and delivery delays. For a time in 1978-79, production of the F100 lagged to the extent that Eagles rolled off the St Louis production line without engines, and were mated with them later.

Technical 'glitches' aside, the F-15 programme was a model of success in meeting projected costs. Brigadier General Bellis (who added his star while overseeing the SPO office) and his successor Brigadier General Robert C. Mathis insisted on thorough accounting and documentation, and McDonnell, to its credit, performed untarnished by the contractor scandals which plagued Northrop and Grumman during this period. This squeaky-clean record was achieved in an era when one manufacturer was treating government procurement executives to weekends at hunting lodges stocked with wine, women and song.

The second wing to equip with Eagles was the 36th Tactical Fighter Wing (BT tailcode) at Bitburg, Germany, also an F-4E user, which became operational in 1977. In December 1977, a third wing, the 49th TFW at Holloman AFB, New Mexico, began to work up with the Eagle.

Tactical development

The 57th Fighter Weapons Wing (WA tailcode) at Nellis AFB, Nevada, also received its first F-15A/B Eagles in 1977. These went to the 433rd Fighter Weapons Squadron to train senior pilots, destined for new Eagle squadrons, in tactics. Instructors with the 57th FWW also developed and expanded on tactics while the wing carried out FOT&E (follow-on operational test and evaluation) for this aircraft type, working out minor 'fixes' in equipment and technique in actual flying situations. Tactics developed at Nellis, to an extent influenced by Boyd, became part of the syllabus at the base's Fighter Weapons School.

Deployment of the Eagle force was linked to US perception of the Soviet threat in Europe, so the next unit to pick up the F-15A/B was the 32nd TFS (CR tailcode) at Soesterberg, Netherlands, beginning 13 September 1978. The squadron, known as the 'Wolfhounds', uniquely comes under Allied (Dutch air force) control in its NATO mission.

In December 1978, the 33rd TFW, the 'Nomads' (EG tailcode), at Eglin AFB, Florida, joined the roster of F-15A/B

users. Soon thereafter, the Eglin wing briefly operated the first examples of the F-15C/D version of the Eagle, preparing these aircraft for onward delivery to the 18th TFW at Kadena, Okinawa, which began to receive them in September 1979.

The 21st Composite Wing (later Tactical Fighter Wing) at Elmendorf AFB, Alaska, began operating F-15A/B Eagles in the mid-1980s and later suffered an awkward incident: on 19 March 1990, the pilot of an F-15 accidentally fired an AIM-9M Sidewinder IR missile which struck and damaged another F-15. The inadvertent 'kill' received widespread attention within the Air Force (under similar circumstances, a Navy F-14 Tomcat had shot down a USAF RF-4C Phantom the previous year) and led to the relief of the 21st TFW commander Colonel H. S. Storer, Jr. What got overlooked, though the point had been made years earlier when an Israeli pilot landed a battle-damaged Eagle with its wing virtually blown off, was that the F-15 had enormous structural strength and survivability. The 21st Fighter Wing now operates the F-15C/D version and is forming an F-15E Strike Eagle squadron.

Three hundred and sixty F-15As and 58 F-15Bs were delivered to the USAF. The final units to receive the Eagle were

Below: The northern outpost of Alaska assumed greater strategic importance in the 1980s as Soviet forces increased in the Far East. F-15s were deployed to Elmendorf as part of the 21st Composite Wing, and began operations from that base and two forward alert locations. Intercepts of Soviet long-range 'Bear-H' bombers became commonplace.

Many years after it entered service, the F-15 remains a favourite air show performer, most displays opening with a maximum rate climb after a very short take-off run. Such performance is not just for show: the F-15 has constantly proven to be a very fast-reacting interceptor, capable of meeting intruders within a matter of minutes of their initial detection.

fighter-interceptor squadrons operated by Tactical Air Command for the air defence of the North American continent. Four TAC squadrons (5th, 48th, 57th and 318th FIS) under what is known today as the First Air Force, headquartered at Tyndall AFB, Florida, took the F-15A/B on charge in the interceptor role. The four F-15A/B Eagle interceptor squadrons, like today's Air National Guard squadrons which have the intercept mission, were often treated like a poor stepchild when it came to priorities, support, supplies, parts and logistics.

TAC had subsumed the one-time Air Defense Command years earlier and viewed its air defence of the United States with a split focus: there persisted a threat from the Soviet

Right and below: Much effort was expended on fitting the F-15 with a Vought anti-satellite missile for deployment with a Fighter Interceptor Squadron on each coast. The missile was launched from a zoom climb at about 80,000 ft, two rocket stages carrying it towards the satellite. Homing was by infrared. No warhead was fitted as the kinetic energy of the impact was more than sufficient to destroy the orbiting vehicle. The ASAT programme ended after one successful launch as it was felt to violate a space-testing treaty.

Union's long-range bomber force, and US warfighting plans included a limited capability to intercept 'Bears', 'Backfires' and cruise missiles during the first hours of a trans-polar conflict. However, it wasn't the traditional business of TAC, which is essentially a holding command for air-to-ground assets and has never had either an air defence or a combat role.

The bulk of air defence operations has since been taken up by the F-16A block 15 ADF (air defence fighter) Fighting Falcon (*World Air Power Journal,* Volume 5). The 48th Fighter-Interceptor Squadron, Langley AFB, Virginia, which disbanded on 1 October 1990, was the last CONUS-based active-duty interceptor squadron to fly the Eagle.

Anti-satellite mission

Closely related to air defence against bombers and cruise missiles was the ASAT (anti-satellite) mission which evolved in the late 1970s. The acronym ASAT refers not to any single weapon but to a range of anti-satellite weapons to have been launched from Earth or space. It was intended that ASAT weapons would neutralise Soviet military satellites, including low-orbiting photo-reconnaissance, electronic intelligence, and ocean surveillance spacecraft. At the time, it was understood that the Soviets had their own anti-satellite weapons. The ASAT programme came several years before the SDI (Strategic Defense Initiative).

To arm the F-15A/B Eagle for the ASAT mission, in 1979 a contract was issued to Vought for a two-stage, low Earth-orbit anti-satellite vehicle. First stage of the vehicle was derived from the AGM-69 SRAM-A (short-range attack missile), while the second stage was a derivative of the Altair III rocket. The ASAT weapon weighed 2,700 lb (1225 kg), was 18 ft (5.49 m) long, and was to be carried on the centre-line of the Eagle. To employ the ASAT weapon, the F-15A/B aircraft needed backup battery, microprocessor, and data-link for mid-course guidance.

Beginning in the early 1980s, numerous captive flights were made with the ASAT device, zoom-climbing to 80,000 ft (24384 m). The first launch from an F-15 was made in January 1984, when an ASAT missile was aimed at a pre-determined point in space. Later that year a second launch targetted the infra-red signature of a star. At least two subsequent launches also were aimed at celestial infra-red sources.

The first and only real launch at an actual satellite – fifth and final launch in the ASAT programme – came on 13 September 1985, when a 6512th Test Squadron F-15A (77-0084) stationed at Edwards AFB, California, took off from Vandenburg, zoom-climbed to 80,000 ft (24384 m) and launched its ASAT, seeking to destroy the Solwind P78-1 (also known as the gamma-ray spectrometer satellite, which the United

States had launched in February 1979). Travelling at 17,000 mph (27359 km/h) some 320 miles (514 km) above the Earth, the 2,000-lb (907-kg), 11-ft (3.35-m) satellite was in a circular polar orbit when the F-15, flying at Mach 0.98 in a 60-65° climb, made the launch. The first and second stages separated and the ASAT's miniature homing vehicle homed in on the satellite at almost 11,000 mph (17703 km/h), destroying it on impact. The USAF considered the test a success but it was criticised by both arms control advocates and solar scientists involved with the satellite: while the latter had officially outlived its useful life, it was still transmitting data.

Plans existed for ASAT to equip the 48th FIS at Langley and 318th FIS at MacChord AFB, Washington. These squadrons received three or four F-15A/B airframes which had been modified (wired) for ASAT operations, even though the ASAT programme was officially dropped in 1986. Congress banned testing of the weapon because it was perceived as violating a US-Soviet agreement on testing certain weapons in space.

To cite a final user of the F-15A Eagle, NASA operated two of the fighters at its Dryden facility at Edwards AFB, California. F-15A No. 2, also known as F-2 (71-0281), was acquired on 17 December 1975 and returned to the USAF on 28 October 1983 without ever being assigned a NASA aircraft number. (This machine is now on display on a pedestal at Langley AFB, Virginia). F-15A No. 8, also known as F-8

(71-0287, or NASA 835) was acquired 5 January 1976 and is still active with NASA.

C and D models

The F-15C/D versions of the Eagle – one- and two-seat improvements, respectively – introduced increased internal fuel and CFTs (the former FAST packs), and were intended for the Pratt & Whitney F100-PW-220 engine, although the first machines built retained the -100 powerplant. The F-15C/D also began operations with improved APG-63 radar and minor changes to the landing gear, increasing gross weight to 68,000 lb (30845 kg), as well as an overload warning which permits 9-*g* manoeuvres where the F-15A/B were formally limited to 7.33*g*.

A total of 408 F-15Cs and 62 F-15Ds was delivered to the USAF.

F-15E Strike Eagle

In the late 1970s, the USAF began studying possible ETF (Enhanced Tactical Fighter) concepts to replace the F-111 'Aardvark' in the low-level, night and bad-weather interdiction role. The F-15A/B/C/D series had originally been intended as dual-role aircraft but in 1975 the air-to-ground mission had been set aside – all early Eagles are still 'wired' for air-to-ground ordnance but lack software to accommodate it – making it the first USAF fighter since 1945 with no ground attack role.

The ETF studies led to today's F-15E Strike Eagle, a dual-role, two-seat fighter for long-range, deep interdiction missions in all weather, day or night – while retaining air-to-air combat capability. The USAF wanted an aircraft which could accomplish the strike mission alone, without need for fighter escort, electronic jamming aircraft or AWACS (Airborne Warning And Control System).

Above: The last remnants of the once-mighty Air Defense Command (now demoted to the 1st Air Force of Tactical Air Command) were issued with Eagles at the end of the F-15A/B production run, although all but the 57th FIS were subsequently deactivated. The first unit to go was the 5th FIS, based at Minot AFB, North Dakota, from where its beautifully-marked aircraft were charged with defence of the northern United States, a mission which had all but evaporated by the time the unit gained its F-15s.

Far left: The MacChord-based 318th FIS also posted Eagles on alert at Castle AFB, California, sharing the base with the 93rd Bomb Wing. B-52s from the latter unit played 'Bear' to give the Eagle pilots realistic strategic bomber targets for intercept practice.

Below: A new breed of Eagles was ushered in by 78-0468, the first of a long line of F-15Cs.

F-16F. The F-15E was chosen in 1984, partly on the basis of cost projections. Full-scale development of the F-15E began in 1984, followed by the first flight of an F-15E on 11 December 1986.

The F-15E is powered by the F-15C/D model's two 24,000-lb (10886-kg) thrust Pratt & Whitney F100-PW-220 low-bypass turbofans. Plans to deliver F-15Es with the 20-per cent more powerful 29,000-lb (13154-kg) thrust F100-PW-229 engine beginning in August 1991 were delayed slightly. The USAF had evaluated both the -229 and the General Electric F110-GE-129, both developed for the service's IPE (Increased Performance Engine) programme, and chose the Pratt & Whitney powerplant. IPE tests on the F-15E were led by Squadron Leader Rick Pope, a Royal Air Force officer on exchange duty with the 6512th Test Squadron at Edwards AFB, California.

State-of-the-art cockpit

In the production F-15E Strike Eagle, the pilot's front cockpit has redesigned controls, a wide field of vision HUD, and three CRTs which provide multi-purpose displays of navigation, weapons delivery, and systems operations. The rear-cockpit weapons systems officer (WSO) employs four multi-purpose CRT terminals for radar, weapon selection, and monitoring of enemy tracking systems. The WSO also operates AN/APG-70 synthetic aperture radar and Martin-Marietta LANTIRN (low-altitude navigation and targeting, infra-red, for night) weapons and targetting pods, and has minimal flight controls.

The AN/APG-70 radar display terminals provide bird's-eye views of ground targets that are of higher resolution and taken from further away than images produced by previous radars. Roads, bridges and airfields can be accurately identified from possibly 100 miles (161 km) away. As the F-15E nears the target, image resolution becomes sharper, enabling the crew to distinguish smaller individual targets such as aircraft, tanks and trucks, from possibly as far as 50 miles (80 km) away. A feature of the radar is its ability to create and freeze high-resolution ground maps during quick sweeps of the target area lasting only seconds.

The AN/APG-70, as integrated into the F-15E crew's very demanding duties, is intended to be used without eliciting detection by an enemy's air defences. While boring towards a target at low altitude an F-15E crew can turn on the radar to obtain an image of a target area located up to 45° to the side of the aircraft's flight path. Manufacturer's literature claims that the crew can then switch off the radar without emitting signals that can be detected by an enemy's ground defences. The quick-look, quick-processing capability of the radar, enabling it to pinpoint a target within seconds, does make it difficult for an enemy to track the F-15E's location and flight

The idea of replacing the F-111 arose prematurely – the Pave Tack-equipped F-111F remains a formidable system in the 1990s – and the Eagle was not an obvious candidate for the job. To the contrary, though the F-15A/B/C/D aeroplanes had all been built and tested with air-to-ground capability, the USAF had never factored this mission into its warfighting plans and has kept the Eagle tasked with air-to-air duties exclusively.

European competition

There were other obvious ETF candidates, including the Tornado. The prevailing view in the Air Staff has always been that the Tornado is short-ranged, to say nothing of the handicap imposed by its lack of a 'Made in USA' label. (Later, in a wholly different context, Rockwell teamed up to final-assemble the Tornado if the USAF would buy it as a 'Wild Weasel' aircraft, but this was not a factor in EFS decision-making.)

McDonnell and Hughes shared in privately funding the conversion of the second F-15B (71-0291) to serve as the prototype F-15E Strike Eagle. This aircraft first flew during August 1981.

The EFS studies led to a fly-off competition between the proposed F-15E Strike Eagle and the cranked arrow-wing F-16XL Fighting Falcon, referred to in the EFS context as the

path – but certainly not impossible. Furthermore, even without accurate detection, an enemy can defend against any low-flying strike aircraft simply by putting a lot of metal in its path: the 1991 Gulf War proved that any force using large amounts of conventional gunfire can 'kill' the most sophisticated warplane.

The F-15E's much-delayed and costly LANTIRN system has two pods. The navigation pod contains a FLIR (forward-looking infra-red) sensor that enables the crew to maintain high speeds at night and at low altitude, beneath bad weather. The FLIR produces daylight-quality video images that are projected onto the pilot's HUD.

The navigation pod also has its own terrain-following radar. The pilot can manually respond to cues from the

The first E models in service went to the 405th Tactical Training Wing at Luke AFB, where the Arizona sunshine and extensive desert ranges make for ideal training conditions.

F-15 Eagle

Above: The 4th Wing at Seymour Johnson is the primary F-15E user, with further aircraft based in Alaska with the 3rd Wing and England with the 48th.

Right: Little publicised is the F-15E's nuclear delivery capability, as demonstrated by this Eglin test aircraft carrying a pair of B61 tactical nuclear 'shapes'. The fuselage- and wing-mounted ciné cameras will record the separation of the bombs.

Below: Strike Eagles bask in the sun at Luke. The F-15E may be regarded as the world's best all-round warplane: not only can it deliver a huge array of air-to-ground weapons in all weathers and with great accuracy, its Eagle roots make it a superb air-to-air fighter.

LANTIRN system or can couple LANTIRN to the flight control system for 'hands off' terrain following at altitudes as low as 200 ft (61 m).

The targetting pod contains a high-resolution tracking FLIR, a missile boresight correlator, and a laser designator. Integration of the system, and of the targetting pod with the APG-70 radar's high-resolution ground-mapping mode, evolved only after considerable delay and extensive testing at Edwards AFB.

On 1 August 1987, the USAF activated its first F-15E training unit, the 461st Tactical Fighter Training Squadron ('Deadly Jesters'), part of the 405th Tactical Training Wing at Luke AFB, Arizona. This unit reached IOC (initial operating capability) in July 1988.

The 336th Tactical Fighter Squadron of the 4th Tactical Fighter Wing (now redesignated the 4th Wing) at Seymour Johnson AFB, North Carolina, attained limited operational capability with the F-15E in October 1989. IOC had been projected for approximately 1 August 1990, the day Saddam Hussein invaded Kuwait. In the meanwhile, on 14 June 1990, the F-15E experienced its first head-to-head competition with other aircraft types in the USAF's Long Rifle gunnery meet held at Davis-Monthan AFB, Arizona, and scored first and second in the contest.

Is the F-15E really the ideal replacement for the F-111F? Back-seaters acknowledge that the low-altitude ride in the F-15E is rougher than in the F-111 (or, for that matter, in the F-4 Phantom) due to lower wing loading and higher gust response. The F-15E is deemed by some as ideal for diving attacks and low-level dash but less than optimum for sustained low-level operation with its non-swinging and air-

combat-optimised wing planform. Weapons separation trials performed while putting the Strike Eagle through low-level paces over the Nevada desert, where vicious thermals abound, produced some crew discomfort. Later combat operations in Operation Desert Storm did little to prove or disprove low-level suitability, since these wartime sorties were flown mostly at medium altitudes. It is, however, indisputable that the F-15E's systems make it a more accurate bomb delivery platform.

Eagle operations

When the F-15A/B Eagle first entered service, it was flown by a rigorously selected cadre of pilots with strong experience in fighters, mostly in the F-4 Phantom, so that the 1st Tactical Fighter Wing at Langley AFB in 1976 may have amounted to the most competent collection of fighter pilots

Above: Although the capabilities of the F-15E are maximised when using precision-guided munitions, its superb attack radar and LANTIRN avionics make it a highly accurate free-fall bomber.

Left: In extensive tests at Edwards and Eglin the F-15E has been cleared to carry most stores. Here an AGM-65B Maverick precision anti-armour missile is fired.

'building block' techniques to bring them up to the mark of all-out combat capability. This involved practice with each of the separate weapons systems, frequent rehearsal of the aircraft's manoeuvrability, and the steady development of tactics.

Rigorous pilot training, itself affected by input from the pilots, was one factor in overcoming the sensitivity of the F100 engine to throttle slamming and violent use of afterburner in some envelopes. After completion of powerplant modifications already cited, emphasis in training on greater care with power settings brought about an 80-per cent reduction in inflight shutdowns.

During the early days of Eagle flying – and, to an extent, even today – pilots found themselves, in effect, undergoing additional training after they'd felt they were qualified in type. Most acknowledged that becoming proficient in the F-15 was not easy. Constant practice in simulators and on the ranges was viewed by many as a kind of graduate training scheme. Few denied that this was needed to bring them up to speed for the kind of mass air battles the Eagle might have to fight over Europe. After its huge investment in a new system and in new methods of training, the USAF was able to say, finally, that simulators, automation and a regimented approach to training made the Eagle more cost-effective than its predecessors.

Desert deployment

When the US launched Operation Desert Shield on 6 August 1990, days after the Iraqi invasion of Kuwait, the 1st Tactical Fighter Wing at Langley AFB, Virginia, under Colonel John M. 'Boomer' McBroom – earmarked for Middle East duty under US Central Command (CENTCOM) – began deploying F-15C/D Eagles of its 27th and 71st Tactical Fighter Squadrons on just hours' notice. Forty eight Eagles made the longest fighter deployment in history, flying 14 to 17 hours non-stop from Langley to Dhahran with six to eight air refuellings *en route*.

The fast-responding Langley Eagles were joined on 12 August by F-15E Strike Eagles from the 336th TFS, 4th TFW, at Seymour Johnson AFB, North Carolina. At this

assembled in many years. At the time, aircrews were saying that the Eagle was as close to ideal as they could want (focusing on its air-to-air potential only) and that they had hard work ahead to match their own capabilities with what the aircraft provided. By 1978, new pilots were entering the F-15A/B Eagle directly from flight training, and were working very hard to maximise the potential of the aircraft.

Langley pilots began a regimen of flying the Eagle in Red Flag exercises at Nellis AFB, Nevada, and on their computerised air combat range off the Virginia coast. The squadrons at Langley took newly type-converted pilots and used

juncture, because of delays in the programme, the F-15E had only begun to operate with the LANTIRN navigation pod and did not yet have the system's targetting pod, so the Strike Eagle was temporarily a low-tech purveyor of 'dumb' bombs. The early arrival of Eagle and Strike Eagle units – able to fit, readily, into facilities where Saudi Arabia, too, had F-15s – may have helped deter Iraqi forces from moving directly against Saudi oilfields.

While the build-up was underway, the USAF transferred 24 F-15C Eagles to the Saudi air force from its own inventory. F-15C Eagles of the 1st TFW immediately began flying combat air patrols, joined by Saudi F-15Cs and British and Saudi Tornado F.Mk 3s. The F-15Es began rehearsing the strike mission. Flying from their new home at Al Kharj air base, E model 87-0203 crashed on a low-level mission on 30 September 1990, killing two men aboard.

By November 1990, Desert Shield shifted from a defensive to an offensive posture with a second round of force build-ups. Almost unnoticed, in September the 33rd TFW from Eglin AFB, Florida, under Colonel Richard 'Rick' Parsons, deployed its 58th TFS with F-15C Eagles (but no two-seat F-15Ds) to Tabuk in western Saudi Arabia. In the second wave of the build-up, the 36th TFW at Bitburg, Germany, deployed F-15Cs of its 53rd TFS to join Parsons at Tabuk, and aircraft of its 525th TFS (since disbanded) to join the 7440th Composite Wing, poised to Iraq's west at Incirlik AB, Turkey. The 32nd TFS from Soesterberg, Netherlands, deployed to Incirlik as well. A second F-15E Strike Eagle squadron, the 335th, made the move from Seymour Johnson to Al Kharj after the conversion of this unit to the F-15E was rushed by unfolding events.

In the early hours of 17 January 1991, the US had five F-15C air-to-air and two F-15E strike squadrons included in its forces as Operation Desert Storm, the war against Iraq, began. F-15Cs escorted other warplanes on combat missions during Desert Storm, and most air-to-air engagements were fought by F-15Cs, the majority of these by the 58th TFS

'Gorillas', part of the 33rd TFW from Eglin, which ultimately scored 17 air-to-air victories.

The Mirage F1 kill scored by the 1st TFW's Captain Steven 'Tater' Tate in aircraft 83-0017 was credited as the first aerial victory of the war – as well as the Langley wing's only kill. Months later, a review confirmed that three 'Gorillas' preceded Tate in despatching Iraqi warplanes. Credit for the first kill of the war now belongs to Captain John 'J. B.' Kelk, 32, who shot down a MiG-29 'Fulcrum' at 3.10 a.m. on 17 January, closely followed by two other Eglin pilots who relegated Tate to number four in chronological sequence.

Above: Laden with cluster bombs, an F-15E from the 335th TFS makes an evening rendezvous with a tanker before heading into Iraq. Sidewinders were carried for self defence, but the E model's only kill (against a helicopter) was scored with a laser-guided bomb.

Left: McDonnell Douglas brothers in arms: a 1st TFW Eagle awaits take-off clearance with a Free Kuwait Air Force A-4KU Skyhawk at Dhahran.

Below: At first the 4th TFW F-15Es moved to Thumrait in Oman, but were moved forward to Al Kharj in Saudi Arabia.

Above: Ground crew use brute force to load an AIM-9M Sidewinder onto its wing pylon rail. By using the twin shoulder rails, the main pylon is left free for the carriage of a fuel tank, a major consideration for long endurance CAPs.

Below: Rarely seen on regular Eagles, the multiple ejector rack is the standard method of carrying air-to-ground stores. Six bombs can be carried on each rack, giving the F-15 a useful but limited attack capability if required.

Above: The F-15's cockpit was designed to minimise the amount of time the pilot had to spend with his 'head down' during combat. Consequently the cockpit is dominated by the large head-up display which presents vital combat information. Immediately below are the controls for the HUD and communications. To the left of this panel is the radar screen, below which is the armament panel and air speed indicator. The right-hand screen presents threat warning information, while below this are engine instruments and altimeter.

Right: Still wearing traces of its former service with the 94th TFS, this Eagle was used by the 3246th Test Wing for trials of the AIM-120 AMRAAM missile. This weapon is a direct replacement for the Sparrow, but introduces active radar homing for the terminal phase of the engagement.

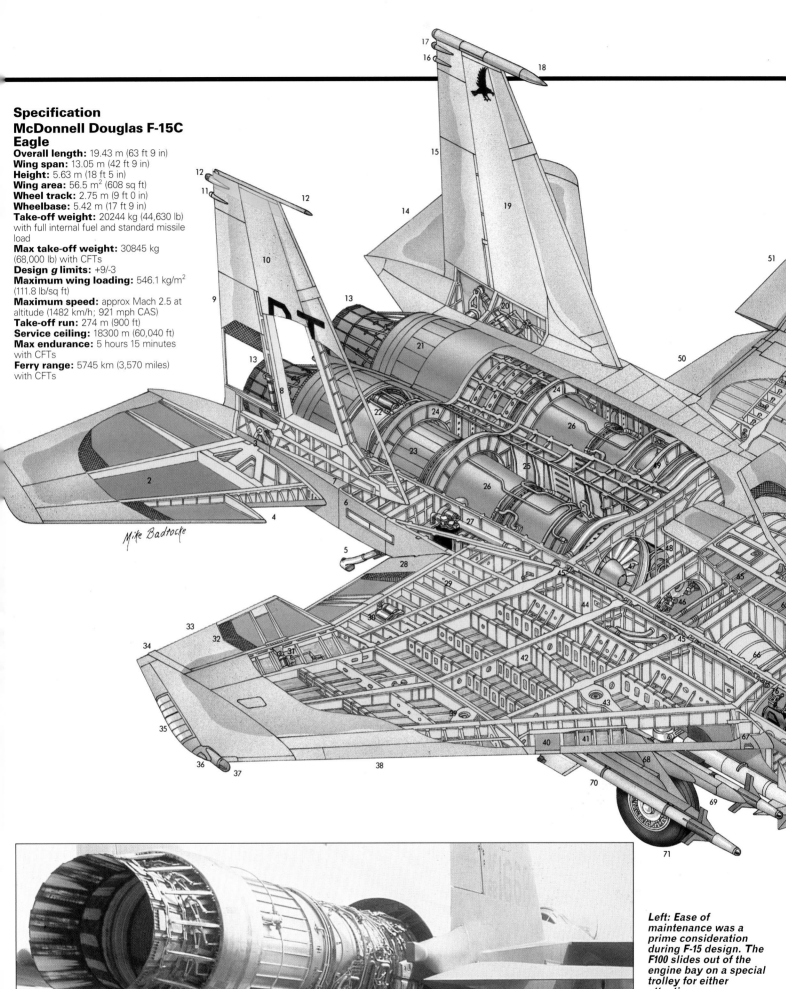

Specification
McDonnell Douglas F-15C Eagle

Overall length: 19.43 m (63 ft 9 in)
Wing span: 13.05 m (42 ft 9 in)
Height: 5.63 m (18 ft 5 in)
Wing area: 56.5 m² (608 sq ft)
Wheel track: 2.75 m (9 ft 0 in)
Wheelbase: 5.42 m (17 ft 9 in)
Take-off weight: 20244 kg (44,630 lb) with full internal fuel and standard missile load
Max take-off weight: 30845 kg (68,000 lb) with CFTs
Design g limits: +9/-3
Maximum wing loading: 546.1 kg/m² (111.8 lb/sq ft)
Maximum speed: approx Mach 2.5 at altitude (1482 km/h; 921 mph CAS)
Take-off run: 274 m (900 ft)
Service ceiling: 18300 m (60,040 ft)
Max endurance: 5 hours 15 minutes with CFTs
Ferry range: 5745 km (3,570 miles) with CFTs

Mike Badrocke

Left: Ease of maintenance was a prime consideration during F-15 design. The F100 slides out of the engine bay on a special trolley for either attention or substitution. This aircraft is an F-15E, seen during Gulf War operations, when the need for rapid maintenance was at its height.

Fuel system
The F-15C has eight individual Goodyear-built fuel tanks, located in the main inter-spar area, leading and trailing edges, and in the centre-section under the airbrake between the intakes. These provide 7836-litre (2,070-US gal) capacity. With Conformal Fuel Tanks (CFTs) adding 2839 litres (750 US gal) each and up to three 2309-litre (610-US gal) drop tanks available, total fuel capacity is 20441 litres (5,400 US gal). This is reduced in the two-seater versions in order to relocate avionics systems behind the cockpit. Inflight refuelling is accomplished via the boom/receptacle method.

Structure
The heart of the Eagle's sturdy structure are four carry-through frames which run across the central fuselage, each with holes to allow the intake ducts to pass through. At each end they form the main points to attach the wings, the three aft frames being attached to the three wing spars, and the forward point attaching to a leading-edge member. Machined titanium frames in the rear fuselage maintain structural integrity and provide the main mountings for the engine installation. The wings are jointed at the kink, the outer panels reducing to two central spars and the leading edge member. Both fins and tailplanes are formed around a central spar with an additional leading edge beam. The wing skins and ribs are integrally machined from light alloy and titanium, while the flaps, ailerons and wingtips are of aluminium honeycomb construction. The powerful airbrake is manufactured from a titanium/aluminium honeycomb, with a skin of graphite/epoxy composites.

Weapon options

Virtually all fighter Eagles have the same basic armament fit, consisting of four AIM-7 Sparrow missiles along the corners of the fuselage, and four AIM-9 Sidewinders on the wing shoulder rails. Local variations have seen the Israelis fitting the Python 3 in place of the AIM-9, and the USAF is beginning to carry the AIM-120 AMRAAM in place of the Sparrow. Air-to-ground stores can be carried on three (five if CFTs are fitted) stations, two on the wing pylons and one under the centreline, providing a maximum of 10705 kg (23,600 lb) of bombs. Stores management is handled by a Dynamic Controls system. The M61A1 cannon has 940 rounds, and can fire up to 6,000 rounds per minute. A General Electric lead-computing gyro is fitted for sighting.

Production

When F-15 fighter production ends with the completion of the last F-15C/Ds for Saudi Arabia, 1,034 aircraft will have been built by McAir, to which must be added 200 F-15E Strike Eagles and 177 F-15J/DJs by Mitsubishi for a grand total of 1,411. This may increase if Japanese procurement is extended, and if Saudi interest in an F-15F export version of the Strike Eagle is rekindled.

Aerodynamics

The wing has a NACA 64A aerofoil section with conical camber on the leading edge. Swept at 38° 42' at the quarter-chord, its thickness/chord ratio drops from 6.6 per cent at the root to 3 per cent at the tip. Set at zero incidence, it has a barely perceptible 1° of anhedral to reduce stability in the rolling plane. The tailplane has a large dogtooth notch close in to generate vortices and increase its effectiveness, while eliminating buffet, and the twin fins are positioned to make maximum use of vortices generated by the wing root. The height of the fins ensures that they maintain authority at high angles of attack. The all-moving tailplanes are mounted below the line of the wing to receive undisturbed airflow. Simple control surfaces include plain flaps, the large wing area of the Eagle generating more than enough lift to negate the need for slotting or blowing. Hydraulic actuation for the flaps and ailerons is by National Water Lift units, while the rudders have Ronson Hydraulic Units actuators. No spoilers or trim tabs are fitted. A Moog boost and pitch compensator is fitted to the control system to provide 'feel'. Airflow for the engines is admitted by two large wedge-shaped intakes, which 'nod' to cope with high angles of attack and control the amount of air being 'captured'. Downstream of the intake are moveable ramps which control the amount of air entering the duct. The intakes stand proud of the forward fuselage to separate the boundary layer.

McDonnell Douglas F-15C Eagle

1 Port all-moving tailplane
2 Boron-fibre tailplane skin panels
3 Tailplane pivot fitting
4 Leading edge dog-tooth
5 Runway arrester hook
6 Formation lighting strip
7 Fuselage side-body fairing construction
8 Rudder rotary actuator
9 Starboard rudder
10 Tailfin boron-fibre skin panels
11 Strobe light
12 ECM aerials
13 Variable area afterburner nozzles
14 Port all-moving tailplane
15 Port rudder
16 Tail navigation light
17 ECM aerial
18 Radar warning antennas
19 Port tailfin
20 Tailplane hydraulic actuator
21 Jet pipe shroud panels
22 Afterburner nozzle fueldraulic actuator
23 Afterburner duct
24 Engine bay machined titanium frames
25 Firewall
26 Pratt & Whitney F100-PW-220 turbofan engines
27 Bleed air system pre-cooler
28 Starboard plain flap
29 Trailing edge integral fuel tank bay
30 Flap hydraulic actuator
31 Aileron hydraulic actuator
32 Control surface honeycomb construction
33 Starboard aileron
34 Fuel jettison
35 Wingtip formation lighting strip
36 Starboard navigation light
37 Radar warning antennas
38 Cambered leading edge panel
39 Outboard pylon hardpoint
40 HF flush aerial
41 Leading edge fuel tank bay
42 Multi-spar and rib wing panel construction

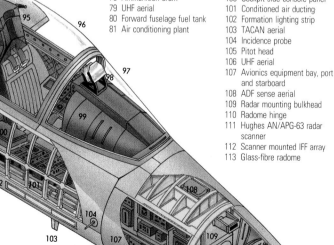

43 Inboard pylon hardpoint
44 Starboard wing integral fuel tank
45 Wing root fittings
46 Airframe-mounted accessory equipment gearbox
47 Engine compressor intake
48 Jet fuel starter/auxiliary power unit JFS/APU
49 Engine mounting main frames
50 Port flap
51 Port aileron
52 Fuel jettison
53 Wingtip formation light
54 Port navigation light
55 Radar warning antenna
56 HF flush aerial
57 Port wing integral fuel tank
58 Fuel tank reticulated foam lining
59 Port wing missile armament
60 Anti-collision light
61 Flight refuelling receptacle
62 Bleed air duct to air conditioning plant
63 Airbrake panel
64 Airbrake hydraulic jack
65 Centre fuselage fuel tanks
66 Intake ducting
67 Starboard anti-collision light
68 Wing stores pylon
69 Missile launch rails
70 AIM-9J Sidewinder air-to-air missiles
71 Starboard mainwheel, forward retracting
72 AIM-7F Sparrow air-to-air missile
73 Missile launcher unit
74 Cannon muzzle aperture
75 M61A1 Vulcan 20-mm cannon
76 Hydraulic gun drive
77 Ammunition feed chute
78 Ammunition drum
79 UHF aerial
80 Forward fuselage fuel tank
81 Air conditioning plant

82 Variable area intake ramp hydraulic actuators
83 Moveable intake ramps
84 Centreline external fuel tank
85 Variable capture area 'nodding' air intake
86 Nosewheel leg door
87 Nosewheel, forward retracting
88 Landing and taxiing lamps
89 Nose undercarriage leg and breaker struts
90 Tactical electronic warfare equipment [TEWS]
91 Canopy hydraulic jack
92 Rear pressure bulkhead
93 Structural space provision for second crew member [F-15D]
94 Canopy emergency jettison linkage
95 ACES II ejection seat
96 Upward-hinging cockpit canopy cover
97 Frameless windscreen panel
98 Pilot's head-up display
99 Instrument panel shroud
100 Cockpit side console panel
101 Conditioned air ducting
102 Formation lighting strip
103 TACAN aerial
104 Incidence probe
105 Pitot head
106 UHF aerial
107 Avionics equipment bay, port and starboard
108 ADF sense aerial
109 Radar mounting bulkhead
110 Radome hinge
111 Hughes AN/APG-63 radar scanner
112 Scanner mounted IFF array
113 Glass-fibre radome

The Eagle has closely-spaced engines to minimise asymmetric handling problems, the space between the jetpipes being occupied by a field arrester hook. This is used in emergency situations for stopping the aircraft when the brakes have failed.

*Georgia **ANG** F-15As take on fuel from a **Tennessee** Air National Guard **KC-135E**. Refuelling in the Eagle is easy due to the excellent visibility from the cockpit, although care has to be taken during the initial coupling so that the boom does not hit the canopy as the receiver moves forward from the pre-contact position.*

Powerplant
All F-15A/Bs (and some early F-15C/Ds) were powered by the Pratt & Whitney F100-PW-100 turbofan, nominally rated at 111.2 kN (25,000 lb) thrust with afterburning. Definitive F-15C/Ds have the F100-PW-220 engine of 105.7 kN (23,770 lb) thrust, the powerplant being retained for the early F-15Es. In 1991 F-15Es were being delivered with the F100-PW-229 of 129 kN (29,000 lb) thrust. A single F-15E was tested with General Electric engines in the shape of the F110-GE-129.

ECM
From the outset the Eagle was intended to carry a fully integrated internal countermeasures suite. This is the Northrop ALQ-135. Radar warning receivers are mounted on the port fin-tip and both wingtips.

Gun
Located in the starboard wing root, the 20-mm M61A1 six-barrelled cannon is supplied with 940 rounds in fighter versions. The ammunition is contained in a large drum in the central fuselage underneath the forward portion of the airbrake, and feeds ammunition through a chute which leads above the engine intake.

Camouflage
Most fighter Eagles wear this basic camouflage, which consists of two close shades of grey. The darker grey is applied to maximise the shadow effect of the bulged surfaces and to lessen the effect of sharp edges, particularly in plan view.

McDonnell Douglas F-15A Eagle

As F-15C/Ds completed the re-equipment of active-duty units, some A/B aircraft were 'cascaded' to Air National Guard units such as the 116th TFW, Georgia ANG. This aircraft is that assigned to the unit's commander, chosen for its appropriate serial number and painted in full colour markings. This unit, and the 159th Tactical Fighter Group of the Louisiana ANG and 131st Tactical Fighter Wing of the Missouri ANG, have battlefield air superiority as their primary mission, supporting the regular TAC Fighter Wings (1st, 33rd and 49th). Further ANG F-15 users (Oregon and Massachusetts) are part of the US air defence network, which is now largely reliant on the F-16 ADF serving with Guard units. Other early Eagles are being released from flying duties to act as gate-guards, ground instructional airframes and battle damage repair trainers.

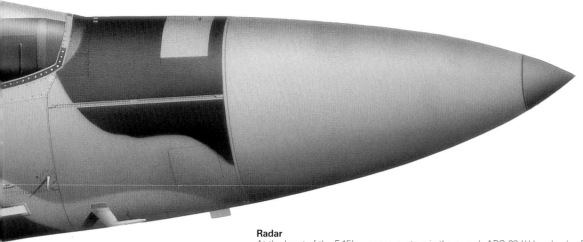

Radar

At the heart of the F-15's weapon system is the superb APG-63 I/J-band pulse-Doppler radar (or APG-70 in F-15E and MSIP aircraft). Built by Hughes, the APG-63 gives long-range detection and tracking of multiple small targets which can be travelling down to tree-top level. A gridded travelling-wave tube transmitter is employed, with digital Doppler signal processing and mode/data mangement. The antenna is a planar array, mounted on a three-axis gimbal. Behind this are three racks of associated equipment. The top rack has analog processor, power supply, data processor and digital processor, the centre rack has the main transmitter and antenna steering mechanism, while the lower rack mounts the receiver and exciter. The whole system is capable of operating across a wide spectrum of pulse repetition frequencies, processing modes and pulse widths. A programmable signals processor upgrade introduced in the 1980s allowed a Doppler beam-sharpened ground mapping mode to be added. The APG-70 is a much-improved version, with new line-replaceable units and other modifications such as doubled antenna drive rate.

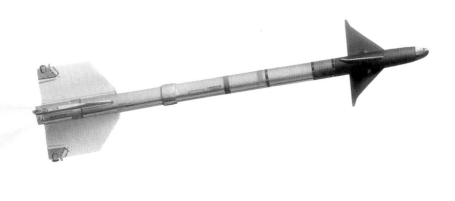

McDonnell Douglas/Mitsubishi F-15DJ Eagle
Hiko Kyodotai, Japan Air Self Defence Force
Nyutabaru, Japan

Japan is the only nation to have licence-built the Eagle, constructing the aircraft in F-15J (single-seat) and F-15DJ (two-seat) versions, basically equivalent to the early F-15C/D. Fourteen of the Japanese aircraft were built by McDonnell Douglas (two F-15J and 12 F-15DJ), and these were followed by eight F-15Js delivered in knock-down form for assembly by Mitsubishi. Subsequent production is expected to account for 177 aircraft, although a further batch of 15-20 may be ordered to cover the gap before the FS-X begins deliveries.

Mitsubishi is the prime contractor for the F-15J/DJ, and is responsible for building the forward and centre fuselage. Other important parts of the Japanese aerospace industry are heavily involved in the programme, including Kawasaki (which builds the wings and tail assembly), Fuji (landing gear doors), Nippi (pylons and missile rails), Sumitomo (undercarriage), Shin Meiwa (drop tanks) and IHI, which builds the F100-PW-100 engines. These are being upgraded fleet-wide to F100-PW-220 standard from 1991 onwards. Components are shipped back to Mitsubishi's Nagoya plant for final assembly, the main contractor also being responsible for flight testing.

In addition to employing the major constituents of the Japanese aerospace engineering industry, the F-15 programme involves local electronics experts. Both the ECM and radar warning systems are of indigenous design and manufacture, these being the J/ALQ-8 and XJ/APQ-1 respectively. A resultant minor difference between the F-15J and regular F-15Cs is the deletion of the port fin-tip bullet fairing.

Sufficient F-15s are in JASDF service to allow the diversion of a small number of aircraft to equip an air combat training unit, in whose striking markings this example is depicted. Other F-15DJs with the Hiko Kyodotai wear a green pattern over the regular Eagle camouflage. The F-15 is particularly useful for simulating the Su-27 'Flanker', which both the Commonwealth of Independent States and China have deployed in the Far East.

Avionics

The F-15 is extremely well-equipped with tactical, communications and navigation systems. Closely allied to the radar is a Hazeldyne APX-76 IFF interrogator with Litton reply evaluator, while the F-15 protects itself with a Teledyne APX-101 IFF transponder. For navigation the F-15 has a Litton ASN-109 inertial navigation system, backed up by a Honeywell ASN-108 AHRS. The INS not only presents positional data but also pitch, roll, heading, acceleration and speed information. Air data is handled by a Honeywell ASK-6 computer. Other navigation and communications equipment include an ARN-118 TACAN, ADF, ARN-112 ILS receivers and an HSI from Collins, the latter presenting navigation information on a symbolic pictorial display, ARC-164 UHF transceivers from Magnavox, Dorne and Margolin glideslope localiser antenna, and Teledyne angle-of-attack sensor. Defensive avionics on all but Japanese aircraft include the Northrop ALQ-135(V) internal countermeasures system, which acts on information from the Loral ALQ-56C radar warning receiver and Magnavox ALQ-128 electronic warfare warning suites (Japanese aircraft have indigenous equipment). Mechanical countermeasures are provided by Tracor ALE-45 chaff/flare dispensers.

Weapon system

Data from the APG-63 radar is processed digitally and tracking information is fed to the IBM CP-1075 central computer. Information is displayed to the pilot on either the Honeywell Vertical Situation Display or McDonnell Douglas Electronics AVQ-20 Head-Up Display. The VSD is a small CRT on the upper left dashboard, and is mainly used in the long-range phase of an engagement, presenting a cleaned-up radar picture and alphanumeric target data such as altitude, IFF return, ground speed, heading, range, aspect angle, closure rate and g-force. This information not only gives a tactical situation display, but gives the pilot a close idea of the type of aircraft he is tracking. At shorter range and in actual combat the HUD is used, which combines target information with vital aircraft performance figures. The main control panel for the radar is located in the left console at the pilot's side, although key functions can be controlled from switches on the throttles and stick. One control on the stick activates the automatic acquisition system at close ranges in one of three modes. First, a boresight mode locks the radar onto the first aircraft to enter the F-15's boresight, as designated by the gun reticle on the HUD; secondly, a 'super-search' mode locks onto the first target to enter the HUD field-of-view; and lastly, a vertical scan mode locks onto the first target into an elevation scan pattern. Steering and weapon information is then supplied to the pilot on the HUD.

Sidewinder

Throughout the F-15's career the AIM-9 Sidewinder has been the main short-range weapon of the type. Several versions have been standard, today's being the AIM-9M. This has all-aspect capability, and introduces a reduced-smoke motor and infra-red countermeasures capability to detect and reject decoy flares. The warhead is a 9.5-kg (21-lb) high explosive blast fragmentation unit, and fusing is by active laser.

Control surfaces

The Eagle has conventional control surfaces consisting of rudders on each of the fins, outboard ailerons, plain inboard flaps, all-moving tailplanes and a large airbrake.

Sparrow

Most Eagles carry the AIM-7M version of the Sparrow, which introduced a new seeker and improved ECCM to give a high capability against low-flying targets with cluttered backgrounds. Further development resulted in the AIM-7P, with better performance against sea-skimming missiles, although F-15 units have been the first to receive the all-new AIM-120 AMRAAM. The current Sparrow variants have a launch weight of 230 kg (507 lb), and an effective range of 45 km (28 miles). Fusing is by active radar, exploding a 39-kg (86-lb) HE blast fragmentation warhead.

GEORGIA

116 TFW

74116

Chris Davey

Right: The F-15E has a wealth of stores at its disposal, the most important of which are shown here. These range from the B61 tactical nuclear weapon (centre foreground), through Paveway laser-guided bombs and GBU-15 glide bombs, to cluster munitions, Mavericks and GP bombs. At far left is the Durandal runway penetrator.

Specification
McDonnell Douglas F-15E (1991) otherwise similar to
F-15C

Powerplant: two Pratt & Whitney F100-PW-229 turbofans, 129.0 kN (29,000 lb) thrust each
Maximum take-off weight: 36741 kg (81,000 lb)
Operating weight empty: 14379 kg (31,700 lb)
Maximum umrestricted landing weight: 20094 kg (44,300 lb)
Maximum internal fuel weight: 5952 kg (13,123 lb)
Maximum external fuel weight: 9818 kg (21,645 lb) (includes CFTs)
Maximum weapon load: 11113 kg (24,500 lb)
Maximum wing loading: 650.5 kg/m^2 (133.2 lb/sq ft)
Maximum combat radius: 1270 km (790 miles)
Maximum range: 4445 km (2,765 miles)
Gun armament: 20-mm M61A1 six-barrelled cannon with 512 rounds (F-15C has 940 rounds)

Above: Six stub pylons on each of the F-15E's CFTs cater for weapons carriage, plus storage on the wing pylons. LANTIRN pods are attached to the intakes.

Right: The F-15E's rear cockpit has four CRT displays for imagery and combat data, while the front has three. Advanced HOTAS technology is incorporated.

Forty eight F-15Es flew in the war. More than 2,200 missions totalling some 7,700 hours of combat time were logged by the 4th TFW's 335th and 336th Squadrons. F-15Es joined other allied aircraft in searching for and attacking 'Scud' ballistic missile launchers, on five- to six-hour sorties. Though only some of the F-15Es had LANTIRN targetting pods by war's end, pilots claimed that 80 per cent of laser-guided bombs dropped by F-15Es hit their targets.

As for the dogfight, its importance was temporarily sidetracked. F-15C air-to-air jocks feed upon the lore that their lot is to 'yank and bank' in a duel of wits and to defeat an adversary with bravado – like knights in a joust. Privately, most would admit the reality of their highly glamorous job is to smack the enemy in the teeth from the maximum possible range, preferably before the enemy knows he has been engaged. Had these pilots gone to war a few years earlier to defend Western Europe against an invasion by the Warsaw Pact, the Eagle's range and endurance (valuable against Iraq, because escort missions were flown to Baghdad and elsewhere) would have been of similar importance to its dogfighting ability, and air-to-air action would have raged furiously. The war with Iraq provided no occasion when skilled pilots on opposite sides could challenge each other in a contest of daring and, hence, no opportunity to validate the importance of dogfighting capability.

Many kills were racked up against Iraqi aircraft caught by chance or attempting to flee to Iran, rather than in serious air-to-air battles. F-15Cs scored 34 aerial kills (17 Eglin, 11 Bitburg, one Soesterberg, one Langley, two Saudi) of a total of 41 victories, plus two after the war's end. Of these, all but eight were achieved with the Eagle's BVR weapon, the Sparrow missile. Eight Eagle kills were racked up by AIM-9 Sidewinders and one by manoeuvring an opponent into the ground. The AIM-120A AMRAAM was not fired in anger, although more than 1,000 'captive carries' of the missile were racked up during combat missions in the final days of the war. The F-15 Eagle's 20-mm cannon was never fired against a hostile aircraft during Desert Storm.

One F-15C Eagle (Eglin's 85-0102, 'Spirit of the Gulf', a reference to the Gulf of Mexico) achieved three aerial victories during the war. One pilot is credited with three victories, including one on 22 March 1991.

To return to the F-15E Strike Eagle, wartime experience is being fed into work performed at Edwards AFB, California, by the F-15 CTF (Combined Test Force) under Lieutenant Colonel Richard A. Ferraioli on F-15E engine, software

Top: Both USAFE F-15 units were involved in war operations. Here a 32nd TFS aircraft departs Soesterberg for the journey to Turkey.

Above: One of the 36th TFW's 15 kills was a helicopter downed by Lt Col May in this aircraft, 80-0003.

Below: Operating from Tabuk in north-western Saudi Arabia, the Eagles of the 58th TFS, 33rd TFW, emerged as the war's top scorers with 17 kills to their credit. The squadron was given a free-ranging role over Iraq, enabling them to engage targets whenever possible.

No F-15C/D Eagle air-to-air fighters were lost during Desert Shield or Desert Storm – a remarkable achievement. Two F-15E Strike Eagles were shot down during the fighting with one crew killed, the other taken prisoner. The Strike Eagle scored one aerial kill, never acknowledged officially, of an Iraqi helicopter (apparently a Hughes 500) which it destroyed in an air-to-air engagement using a bomb. The F-15E crews received the full-up LANTIRN system near the end of the war, but acquisition of the targetting pod may have been premature and the system was not employed in combat to its intended capacity. Difficulties are still being encountered integrating LANTIRN fully with the operational F-15E.

'Maturing' warplane

The USAF had said all along that it was committing the F-15E to the Gulf even though the aircraft was 'still maturing'. To ease problems of supporting this new aircraft type in a remote combat zone, a special programme called Desert Eagle expedited contact between the 4th Tactical Wing (Provisional) at Al Kharj and the F-15 SPO at Wright-Patterson AFB, Ohio. The programme brought quick solutions to minor problems with parts and technical data for the Strike Eagle's BRU-46 bomb rack release mechanism, established new procedures for repairing or replacing windscreens damaged by sand, and accelerated weapon system certification for the Strike Eagle's varied ordnance load.

update, radar, weapons, specialised system evaluations, and LANTIRN development. Although P&FQ (performance and flying qualities) evaluations of the basic F-15E were completed during Desert Shield/Storm, work continues to clear the F-15E performance envelope for the full range of weapons it can carry, including Mk 20 Rockeye and CBU-87 cluster bombs, Mk 82 and Mk 84 250-lb (113-kg) and 1,000-lb (454-kg) bombs, AGM-65 Maverick missiles, and GBU-10 and GBU-15 guided weapons. F-15E performance is also being evaluated with an inert version of the SRAM-T (short-range air-to-ground missile, tactical).

It is now time to consider in greater detail the overseas users who made the F-15 Eagle not merely an American phenomenon but an international success.

Israeli Eagles

In the immediate aftermath of the 1973 October War, Israel was solidly established as a recipient of first-line US military aid and was an obvious customer for the F-15 Eagle. Israeli fliers looked over the manufacturer's TF-15A 'dog ship' (71-0290) in 1974. Despite a policy shift in the Carter years (1977-81) aimed at limiting overseas sale of advanced warplanes, Jerusalem began receiving Eagles with four F-15A FSD aircraft (72-0116/0118 and 72-0120), arriving in Israel beginning 10 December 1976 in the Peace Fox I programme.

These were followed by 19 F-15As (76-1505/1523) and two TF-15As (76-1524/1525) in Peace Fox II, offered at preferential financing to help offset sale of the same aircraft type to Saudi Arabia. Thereafter came 18 F-15Cs (80-0122/0130 and 83-0054/0062) and eight F-15Ds (80-0131/0136 and 83-0063/0064) in Peace Fox III.

Israel is receiving early F-15A (fiscal year 1973, 1974, 1975) aircraft which will not be upgraded in a MSIP (Multi-Stage Improvement Program) and which would probably otherwise be trashed. The aircraft will go to the Jewish state *gratis*, in essence as payment for heeding the US and not retaliating against Saddam Hussein during the Gulf War. Secretary of Defense Richard B. Cheney said in June 1991 that this batch consists of 10 F-15As and F-15Bs. Some of these early F-15As reportedly were operated briefly by the Missouri Air National Guard in St Louis in September 1991 before being turned over to Israel.

Israeli units which operate the F-15 are identified as Nos 106 and 133 Squadrons. Israeli Eagles saw action for the first time on 27 June 1977 when they shot down four Syrian MiG-21 'Fishbeds' over Lebanon. On 24 September 1979,

Until the Gulf War, virtually all the F-15's action had been provided by Israel, which had used the type to down over 50 (mostly Syrian) aircraft. It is believed that 40 of these kills were achieved during the hectic fighting over the Bekaa Valley in 1982. Most of the fodder were MiG-21s and -23s, but several of the high-flying MiG-25s were also destroyed.

Kill markings on the aircraft and stills from gun camera footage attest to the F-15's triumphs in Israeli hands. Although best-known for its exploits over Lebanon in 1982, the Eagle has been used in action by the IDF/AF on numerous other occasions, including the raid on the Iraqi nuclear reactor at Osirak.

Eagles shot down five Syrian fighters and on 27 June 1980 at least one more. In May 1982, two Syrian MiG-23 'Floggers' were claimed, the first of this type ever downed in battle.

On 7 June 1981, Israeli F-15s carrying FAST packs (now CFTs) flew a 1,000-mile (1610-km) combat mission to provide top cover for the F-16 attack on Iraq's Osirak (Tamuz) nuclear reactor near Baghdad. During Operation Peace for Galilee, the 1982 Israeli invasion of Lebanon, Eagles shot down a major portion of the 92 aircraft downed between 5 and 12 June 1982, including two Syrian MiG-23 'Floggers' near Beirut on 12 June 1982 and at least three high-flying Syrian MiG-25 'Foxbat' fighters using zoom climb (or 'snap-up') intercepts and AIM-7 Sparrow missiles. The 1982 campaign resulted in one Eagle, nicknamed 'Skyblazer', being credited with four kills.

Israeli F-15 Eagles differ from American aircraft in having the IC-7 ejection seat instead of the ACES II system employed on other F-15C/Ds. Israeli aircraft employ AN/ARC-109 radios instead of AN/ARC-164s, and their wiring for nuclear delivery capability has been deleted. Israeli Eagles can carry the indigenous AL/L-8202 ECM (electronic countermeasures) pod in addition to US-supplied AN/ALQ-119(V) and AN/ALQ-131 pods. All Israeli F-15s can carry FAST pack conformal fuel tanks which are manufactured locally by IAI (Israeli Aircraft Industries).

During 1982 operations in Lebanon, some F-15 Eagles reportedly employed the Python 3 all-aspect IR missile. The Python, developed by Rafael, was intended as a next-generation air-to-air missile with a cooled infra-red advanced seeker reportedly able to home on even faint IR targets, 30-g turning capability, and 10-mile (16-km) range.

Saudi F-15s

In the 1970s and 1980s, US arms sales to Saudi Arabia were controversial, because that Arab nation bankrolled adversaries of Israel. The equipping of the RSAF (Royal Saudi Air Force) with F-15 Eagles became a contentious domestic American issue.

Riyadh initially ordered 62 airframes, consisting of 47 F-15Cs and 15 F-15Ds under Project Peace Sun as a replacement for the Lightning fighter. Actual delivery consisted of 46 F-15Cs (80-0062/0106 and 81-0002) and 16 F-15Ds (80-0107/0121 and 81-0003). The total of 62 includes two attrition replacements, since the US imposed a limit (in 1980) of 60 Eagles which could be 'on board' in Saudi Arabia at any given time.

The RSAF began receiving its first F-15C/D aircraft in January 1981 and apparently reached IOC (initial operating capability) in August 1981. RSAF units are No. 5 Squadron at Taif, No. 6 Squadron at Khamis Mushait, and Nos 13 and 42 Squadrons at Dhahran.

Controversy over sale of this modern fighter was eased by Saudi assurance that the Eagles would be used solely in the air defence role. Still, restrictions were imposed which at first prevented delivery of CFTs to the RSAF. Because of political sensibilities a 1989 request for 12 attrition replacement F-15C/D Eagles was not at first accommodated.

During a period of border tensions, two Saudi F-15Cs shot down two Iranian F-4E Phantoms over the Persian Gulf on 5 June 1984, possibly the first time one McDonnell fighter scored an aerial victory over another.

The 2 August 1990 Iraqi invasion of Kuwait altered the Middle East equation and dramatised Saudi Arabia's status as a nation comparatively weak in military terms, with fewer than 60,000 personnel under arms. The constraint limit of 60 aeroplanes 'in country' was dropped. Twenty four F-15C/D Eagles were rushed to the Saudis from US Air Force stocks in Europe in September-October 1990. During Desert Shield and Desert Storm, Saudi F-15C Eagles shared combat air patrol with British Tornado F.Mk 3s and American F-15Cs.

Below: Equipped with a full missile load and three fuel tanks for maximum patrol endurance, a Saudi F-15C approaches a USAF KC-135 tanker during Desert Shield/ Storm operations. The Saudi F-15s took their place alongside USAF machines, French Mirage 2000s and Tornado ADVs of both the RAF and RSAF in providing a round-the-clock patrol to defend Saudi airspace.

Right: A No. 13 Squadron F-15C leaves Dhahran on a Desert Shield CAP. This unit provided the only non-USAF kills of the Gulf War by downing a pair of Iraqi Mirage F1s. In the previous 'Gulf War' Saudi F-15s were used to despatch a pair of Iranian F-4 Phantoms which had strayed towards Saudi Arabia.

For Saudi fighter pilots, the war's shining moment came when Captain Ayehid Salah al-Shamrani of the RSAF's No. 13 Squadron shot down two Iraqi Mirage F1s near the Persian Gulf after being directed to the Mirages by a Saudi AWACS.

In mid-1991, McDonnell began filling an order for 12 more F-15s (nine F-15Cs and three F-15Ds) which had been ordered by Saudi Arabia before the Gulf War, under a $333.5-million FMS (Foreign Military Sales) contract, by delivering the first two machines in this dozen. On 12 August 1991, McDonnell formally received the FMS for this purchase under the Peace Sun VI programme. The aircraft were to be delivered at the rate of two per month by February 1992. The first two were delivered by mid-August.

Saudi Arabia requested 24 additional single-seat F-15F airframes, based on the F-15E but without the second crew member and some advanced equipment. In December 1991, McDonnell surfaced a premature report that Saudi Arabia would seek no fewer than 72 additional Eagles (of unspecified type), then withdrew the report – criticised as a ploy for Congressional support – a week later.

Japanese service

Japan probably had several reasons for needing the new fighter: the archipelago nation has vast amounts of air space to defend, has both the Russians and Chinese as nearby neighbours, and was becoming concerned about the age of its F-4EJ Phantom force. Japanese fliers evaluated the F-15A/B Eagle at Edwards AFB in June-July 1975. Mitsubishi was selected in April 1978 as prime contractor for Japanese F-15J/DJ Eagles, which differ from American F-15A/B aircraft only in the deletion of a few sensitive items of ECM (electronic countermeasures), radar warning, and nuclear delivery equipment. Plans initially were to procure 123 aircraft for five squadrons of 18 each, the first two single-seaters and 12 two-seaters being built in St Louis by McDonnell under Project Peace Eagle. The first Japanese aircraft, a single-seater (02-8801), made its first flight at Lambert-St Louis Municipal Airport on 4 June 1980. Total planned procurement has risen to 191 aircraft.

The Eagle proved perfect for Japan's needs: fast-reacting to deter intruders that could launch from bases close to Japanese territory, long-legged to maintain patrols across the widely-spread archipelago during times of tension, and sufficiently capable to handle any aerial threat present in the region.

STOL/MTD demonstrator

When F-15B 71-0290 was modified to become the STOL/MTD (short take-off and landing/manoeuvre technology demonstrator), it was part of an ambitious programme by the USAF to improve ABO (air base operability) – the survival of its warplanes and fighting capability at airfields under attack. For years, the myth has been reiterated that fixed airfields are highly vulnerable. In fact, a variety of measures – point defences, construction teams, decoys and other deceptions – give airfields a high likelihood of remaining in use in the midst of a shooting war. The F-15 STOL/MTD would improve this situation by demonstrating the ability to land and take off from sections of wet, bomb-damaged runway no more than 50 ft by 1,500 ft (15 m by 457 m), at night, in bad weather, and in crosswinds up to 30 kt (34 mph; 55 km/h).

Below: Japanese plans for F-15 procurement are nearly complete, with two squadrons assigned to each of the three Air Defence Forces. 204 Hikotai's F-15Js share Hyakuri with the F-4EJ Phantoms of 305 Hikotai, scheduled to be the seventh and last Japanese Eagle squadron to form.

F-15 Eagle

Far right: High over the Mojave Desert, the F-15 S/MTD demonstrator displays the large canard foreplanes (actually modified F/A-18 tailplanes) that bestow outstanding short-field performance and agility. The thrust-vectoring nozzles were not added until later.

Opposite: Plans for the F-15 call for its gradual replacement in active-duty units by the Lockheed/Boeing/General Dynamics F-22, but service is assured for many years yet, notably with ANG units. Here the West Coast defenders of the Oregon Air National Guard strut their stuff over the surf of the Pacific shoreline.

Below: Providing a dramatic increase in field performance and manoeuvrability, the thrust-vectoring nozzles of the F-15 S/MTD also incorporate thrust reversers.

The F-15 STOL/MTD first flew on 7 September 1988. Objectives of the F-15 STOL/MTD programme were to investigate, develop, and validate advanced technology in four areas: two-dimensional thrust-vectoring, thrust-reversing engine nozzles; integrated flight/propulsion system; rough-field landing gear; and advanced pilot/vehicle interface.

At the time the programme began, the USAF's ABO effort was ambitious and well-funded. The F-15 STOL/MTD team had the advantage of Larry Walker being assigned as test pilot: he was a very experienced fast jet flier with Vietnam combat experience. The programme began tests in the four key areas, gradually increasing the level of difficulty, while the USAF cited STOL/MTD technology as one of a variety of ways an airfield could be kept in operation while under attack.

After a three-year flight test programme, the STOL/MTD Eagle made its 138th and final flight on the night of 12 August 1991, making a short landing under a simulated 200-ft (61-m) ceiling in total darkness. Using only 71-0290's ALG (Autonomous Landing Guidance) system, the aircraft made a perfect touchdown. Lieutenant Colonel Felix Sanchez later said that the difficult landing could have been accomplished "even if we'd had a 30-kt crosswind and a wet runway."

Improvement programme

As Eagles continue to serve around the world and to bulwark the USAF's fighter force, modifications and improvements will have to be taken for granted.

In an era of 'downsizing', the Pentagon's term for force reductions, Air Staff planners acknowledge that procurement of new-build F-15 Eagles will be limited by spending constraints, and have endeavoured to improve the fighter through an ambitious MSIP (Multi-Stage Improvement Program). Developed jointly by the manufacturer and the Warner Robins Logistics Center in Georgia, two separate MSIP programmes are under way for F-15A/B and F-15C/D models respectively. Both programmes replace Hughes APG-63 with APG-70 radar, improve avionics and replace central computers (F-15A/B analogue computers are replaced with digital computers, while F-15C/D digital computers are replaced with newer digital computers). MSIP improves the weapons panel and adds a CRT (cathode ray terminal) similar to that found on the F-15E Strike Eagle. All F-15C/D models are acquiring chaff/flare dispensers located behind the nosewheel door, also found on the F-15E.

Below: The culmination of the F-15 S/MTD programme saw 290 make a perfect fully automatic landing in a very short distance under the simulation of appalling conditions. The technology of S/MTD will play a large part in the design of future warplanes, notably in the field of ability to operate from badly damaged airfields.

Once an aircraft comes out of MSIP to return to combat service, as one insider puts it. "There are only three differences between an MSIP F-15A and an MSIP F-15C. The first, of course, is the number on the tail. The second is that C models have a new [radar] antenna located next to the horizontal stabiliser. And the third is that A models lack the 2,000 lb (907 kg) of extra fuel carried by the C model."

As MSIP progresses, the USAF plans to dispense with its very early F-15As (fiscal years 1973, 1974 and 1975) by making them available as gate guards or as load trainers. Some may be approved for FMS (Foreign Military Sales), and rumours persist that Israel will receive a significant number – *gratis* – as a payback for policy decisions made during the Gulf War.

The 36 F-15E Strike Eagles in the fiscal year 1991 budget (paid before 1 October 1991) were obtained after much wrangling and in-fighting. When the purchase was still in doubt, McDonnell temporarily dropped the Strike Eagle term and referred to the F-15E as the Eagle, feeling that emphasis on air-to-air capability would help 'sell' the only version of the fighter still being built for the USAF. The 36 airframes were approved, based upon USAF assurance to Capitol Hill legislators that these would be the very last American Eagles and that the Air Staff personnel would not return to the Hill a year later to ask for more. Any future request would focus, instead, on the planned Eagle replacement, the ATF (Advanced Tactical Fighter). Subsequently, the Lockheed F-22A Lightning II was selected as the ATF aircraft type.

Such was the situation on the eve of Desert Shield – and afterwards. The fiscal year 1992 budget request, still being debated at the time of writing, contained no F-15s, but Senate leaders expressed strong interest in adding 12 additional F-15E Strike Eagles to be paid for with funds obtained from Saudi Arabia for 24 F-15C/Ds obtained from US inventory in 1990. Also pending, although not part of budget deliberations, is a Saudi request for 24 F-15F Eagles, the F-15F being an export version of the Strike Eagle with sensitive equipment removed.

USAF Systems Command has long been evaluating a design proposal for an F-15XX, a simplified, or 'no frills' Eagle once suggested as a lower-cost alternative to the ATF. Since it must deal with the USAF daily, McDonnell must publicly take the position that it supports the ATF (though its own candidate was not chosen). Privately, the builder would be prudent to concentrate on the F-15XX with the goal of appealing to cost-cutting, at a time when the USAF itself is reducing from 36 combat wings to 26 and from 540,000 people to 450,000. If the F-22 Lightning II/ATF aircraft programme survives, it will be bad news for McDonnell in St Louis, but prospects are excellent that budgetary reality may overtake the F-22. Ironically, the new aircraft, which may not be able to outfight the budget-cutters, was designed from the outset to do battle at close quarters, at high or low speeds, at high angles of attack – in short, to dogfight. It must be clear, however, that the F-22 is a big, BVR aircraft designed for the same mission as the Eagle.

F-15 Operators

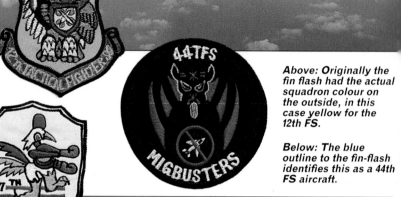

United States Air Force
Pacific Air Forces (PACAF)

18th Fighter Wing, Kadena AB, Japan
12th FS (yellow), 44th FS (blue), 67th FS (red)

The Okinawa-based 18th FW ('ZZ' tailcode) started with the F-15C/D version of the Eagle beginning on 26 September 1979. F-15C/D replacements for the wing's F-4D Phantoms were briefly operated, first, by the 33rd TFW at Eglin AFB, Florida, before reaching Kadena. The wing still has the Eagles supplied to it originally. Aircraft depot maintenance is carried out under contract with Korean Air Lines in Pusan.

With the drawdown of the USAF fighter force in Korea, the wing's proximity to the Korean peninsula has been increasingly important. The wing's F-15C fighters periodically stand alert duty in Korea.

Above: Originally the fin flash had the actual squadron colour on the outside, in this case yellow for the 12th FS.

Below: The blue outline to the fin-flash identifies this as a 44th FS aircraft.

Above: An unofficial 12th TFS patch. The others are the standard wing and squadron patches.

Above: 18th FW Eagles carry a Shogun warrior symbol on the inside of the tail surfaces. All three squadron colours are carried on the fin.

3rd Wing, Elmendorf AFB, Alaska
43rd FS (blue) bumblebee logo, 54th FS (yellow), 90th FS (red)

Formerly the 21st Composite Wing, the 3rd Wg ('AK' tailcode) at Elmendorf initially operated F-15A/B Eagles in a single squadron, 43rd TFS: these subsequently were transferred to the Air National Guard in Hawaii. The wing acquired early F-15C/D aircraft (transferred to it from the 1st TFW at Langley AFB, Virginia), and at the same time it added a second squadron, the 54th TFS, which has flown the F-15C from the start.

On 17 May 1990, the wing acquired its third squadron, the 90th TFS, transferred from Clark Field, Philippines (where it operated the F-4 Phantom), and equipped with the F-15E Strike Eagle. As late as September 1991, formation of the Strike Eagle squadron at Elmendorf was still under way with IOC (initial operating capability) not expected until late 1991.

The 21st CW was redesignated as a Tactical Fighter Wing, and subsequently on 26 September 1991 became just a Fighter Wing. On 19 December 1991 it adopted the 3rd Wing designation, following the disbandment of the Clark-based F-4 unit and absorption of the 90th TFS.

Above: In deference to the special nature of Alaskan operations, 3rd Wg Eagles are adopting this unusual scheme.

Left: A quartet of 43rd Tactical Fighter Squadron F-15As on patrol from Elmendorf. At the time, the 43rd was the only Eagle squadron assigned to the 21st Composite Wing, and the aircraft wore Alaskan Air Command badges on the fin.

Above: Until recently Alaskan units formed a command by themselves, but are now the 11th Air Force of PACAF, a fact reflected by the 21st TFW's fin badge. The 'Big Dipper' and North Star on the fin reflect the northern basing of the unit.

Right: What is now the 3rd Wing is represented by this 1991 21st Fighter Wing formation of three F-15Cs of the wing commander and the two fighter squadrons, together with an F-15E from the newly-acquired 90th TFS. Initially a pair of E-models was delivered to Elmendorf to allow for ground crew training on the new variant prior to the arrival of the full complement.

Tactical Air Command (TAC)

(Note: In September 1991, the USAF announced plans to merge TAC and the Strategic Air Command (SAC) into a new Air Combat Command by 1993, with numerous changes in wing designations and equipment to create an 'intervention', or composite, force. In late 1991 the suffix 'Tactical' was dropped from TAC Fighter Wing and Squadron designations.)

Right: Tactical Air Command has been the major F-15 user, all of its aircraft carrying the winged sword command badge on the fin. Soon this and Strategic Air Command will be merged.

1st Fighter Wing, Langley AFB, Virginia
27th FS (yellow), 71st FS (red), 94th FS (blue)

The 1st FW ('FF' tailcode, for 'First Fighter') was TAC's first operational F-15 Eagle unit. The wing operated the F-4E Phantom until it converted to the F-15A/B in 1975, and to F-15C/D models in the 1980s. It re-equipped with 1984 (MSIP/Multi-Stage Improvement Program) airplanes with upgraded APG-70 radars, chaff/flare dispensing system, glass screen, videotape HUD and AIM-120 (Sidewinder or fuselage Sparrow stations).

The wing's 27th FS claims to be the oldest flying squadron in the USAF, with a history dating to 15 June 1917. The 27th FS was the first operational squadron to fly the F-15, beginning 30 June 1975.

The 71st FS dates to World War II and also converted to the F-15 in 1975. The squadron scored the first American F-15 air-to-air kill on 17 January 1991 when Captain Steven Tate shot down an Iraqi Mirage F1 fighter during Operation Desert Storm.

The 94th FS is the 'Hat in the Ring' squadron associated with Captain Eddie Rickenbacker and other World War I aces, and is the second-oldest American fighter unit. It transitioned to the F-15 in 1977.

Below: A 1st FW F-15C is put through its paces, while at bottom is a wing commander's aircraft from 1984. Today the unit flies the F-15C MSIP aircraft, which it took to the Gulf. The wing badge forms the basis for the William Tell exercise patch.

Above: A 71st TFS F-15C launches from Dhahran at the start of a combat air patrol during Desert Shield. The wing was the first to send warplanes to the Gulf theatre following the invasion of Kuwait, the 71st TFS scoring the unit's only success during the subsequent fighting.

4th Wing, Seymour Johnson AFB, North Carolina ('Fourth but First')

334th FS 'Eagles' (blue), 335th FS 'Chiefs' (green), 336th FS 'Rocketeers' (yellow)

The 4th Tactical Fighter Wing ('SJ' tailcode) began converting from the F-4E Phantom II to the F-15E Strike Eagle in 1988. The wing's first F-15E, aircraft 87-0178, arrived 29 December 1988 and was named *Spirit of Goldsboro*, after the North Carolina city near the base.

The wing's three squadrons achieved IOC (initial operating capability) in the F-15E in reverse order of their numerical designations. IOC dates are 336th TFS, 1 October 1989; 335th TFS, 1 October 1990; and 334th TFS, 1 July 1991. Woven into this chronology was history's largest military build-up and the war with Iraq. The 336th TFS deployed in Operation Desert Shield before IOC, beginning on 12 August 1990, and remained in-theatre until the end of the Desert Storm conflict on 27 February 1991. The 335th TFS belatedly followed. The F-15Es went into combat before complete sets of LANTIRN targeting pods were received, dropping 'dumb' bombs until a laser-designating capability was added late in the Gulf War. During the conflict, two F-15Es flown by 336th TFS crews were shot down; one crew was killed and another was imprisoned until the war's end.

The 4th Wing's 334th FS 'Eagles' has a blue tailband with a white border, with EAGLES, a nickname which came long before the F-15E aircraft, in white script.

The wing's 335th FS 'Chiefs' has a green tailband with a white border with CHIEFS in white script.

The 336th FS 'Rocketeers' has yellow fin-cap trim.

In June 1991, the 4th TFW was redesignated the 4th Wing as part of the USAF's planned change to an 'intervention' force made up partly of composite wings with different aircraft types. At this time, the wing acquired additional resources at Seymour Johnson, including KC-10 Extender tankers.

Above: The 4th TFW's first F-15E accompanies a fully-marked 336th TFS aircraft on an early training mission.

Left: A new-looking F-15E of the 335th FS arrives after a ferry flight with a baggage pod under the wing. The aircraft has yet to have crew names painted under the cockpit.

Far left: The 4th was the first wing to redesignate when it picked up responsibility for the KC-10s co-located at Seymour Johnson, becoming simply the 4th Wing in the process.

Above: *The tail of the 4th Wing commander's aircraft reflects the new designation of the unit, while carrying the colours of all three F-15E squadrons assigned to the wing.*

Right: *The 'Chiefs' of the 335th TFS was the second of the 4th Wing's squadrons to get F-15Es.*

33rd Fighter Wing, Eglin AFB, Florida
58th FS 'Gorillas' (blue), 59th FS 'Golden Pride' (yellow), 60th FS 'Crows' (red)

The 33rd FW ('EG' tailcode), known as the 'Nomads', converted to the F-15A/B Eagle from F-4E Phantoms in 1978, with its last Phantom (68-0466) departing on 25 May 1979. The first Eagle received was an F-15B (77-0156) for maintenance training on 21 September 1978. An F-15 arrival ceremony followed on 15 December 1978. The wing's final F-15A/B aircraft for its initial period at full strength was another F-15B (77-0168) delivered on 21 June 1979.

The wing converted to later-model Eagles beginning with receipt on 3 July 1979 of the first F-15C (78-0470) to be turned over to an operational unit. At this juncture, however, the wing was merely 'staging' aeroplanes intended for the 18th TFW at Kadena AB, Okinawa. The wing's 60th TFS, between 15 June 1979 and 16 April 1980, trained 55 pilots and transferred 54 F-15C/Ds to the Okinawa wing, beginning on 26 September 1979 with the 'Ready Eagle III' deployment of 18 F-15C/Ds to Kadena.

With the 16 April 1980 completion of the 'Ready Eagle III' effort, the Eglin-based 33rd TFW 'Nomads' reverted to earlier fighter aircraft. On 5 June 1980, the 33rd TFW began converting from the F-15C/D back to the older F-15A/B, receiving F-15A/Bs from the 32nd TFS, Soesterberg, Holland.

Subsequently, the wing again adopted F-15C/D models. The first of these was an F-15D delivered on 23 February 1983.

More recently, the wing has converted to MSIP (Multi-Stage Improvement Program) F-15C/D aircraft. On 23 June 1987, the wing received its first APG-70 radar-equipped MSIP F-15C. On 3 November 1989, the wing received its last MSIP F-15C (86-0166).

Officials at the 33rd FW say that the wing began 'captive carry' tests of the AIM-120 AMRAAM (Advanced Medium-Range Air-to-Air Missile) in January 1989, although an F-15C Eagle from the wing was observed carrying AMRAAMs at least three months earlier. The wing's 58th TFS became operational with AMRAAM in February 1991, right in the middle of Operation Desert Storm.

The 33rd TFW's 58th TFS 'Gorillas' became the wing's first F-15 squadron on 1 January 1979 and received its first F-15A (77-0130) on 15 March 1979. The squadron reached initial operating capability in the F-15A on 23 May 1979. Subsequently becoming an F-15C operator, the squadron deployed to Tabuk, Saudi Arabia, during Operation Desert Shield and scored 17 of the 41 aerial victories of the Gulf War. Beginning in February 1991, the squadron became operational with the AMRAAM missile and made several hundred combat sorties with it, although none was fired in combat.

The 59th FS 'Golden Pride', alias Proud Lion, has a patch which shows a lion positioned to strike with clouds and stars in the background to suggest day and night capability.

The 60th FS 'Crows' uses an insignia of a crow carrying a tommy gun. Both the 59th and 60th squadrons provided pilots who flew with the 58th in the Persian Gulf.

Above: *The 33rd TFW became the leading air-to-air unit in the Gulf War, flying its Eagles from Tabuk in north-western Saudi Arabia.*

Below and right: *Two views of 60th FS F-15Cs. The 33rd Fighter Wing operates the MSIP F-15C, this featuring the APG-70 radar originally developed for the F-15E.*

Above and below: The 33rd Fighter Wing regularly practises out-of-area operations, deploying at short notice overseas. Its aircraft are regularly seen in Europe on exercises.

Above: Flight suit patches of the 33rd Fighter Wing's three flying squadrons.

Above: The tail of one of the 33rd's original F-15Cs reveals a usage of the aircraft's serial to highlight the wing number. Note the Eagle motif on the inside of the vertical fin.

49th Fighter Wing, Holloman AFB, New Mexico

7th FS 'Bunyabs' (blue), 8th FS 'Black Sheep' (yellow), 9th FS 'Ironheads' (red)

The 49th TFW ('HO' tailcode) became a user of late-production F-15A/B Eagles in 1977, replacing the F-4E Phantom, the last example of which was given up on 20 December 1977. The wing is the last regular Air Force unit to operate the F-15A/B model. Its 9th TFS was deployed to the Persian Gulf region (apparently to Tabuk, Saudi Arabia) to relieve an Eglin squadron following the end of hostilities in Operation Desert Storm. The wing is scheduled to be disbanded as part of the force reduction of the 1990s.

The wing's 7th TFS 'Bunyabs', a unit with a 50-year history which traces its nickname to World War II campaigns in New Guinea, was deactivated 30 September 1991, its final F-15A sortie being flown by 49th TFW commander Colonel Frank Campbell on 13 September 1991. The wing's remaining two squadrons will be deactivated 30 September 1992. The wing's 8th FS uses a sheep motif, while its 9th FS has a distinctive knight's mask insignia.

Below: This Holloman Eagle had nose art specially applied to honour the city to which the air base is closely situated.

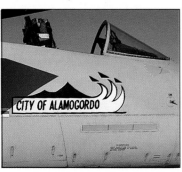

Above: An F-15A of the 7th TFS launches on a training mission, carrying two wing tanks instead of the more common centreline tank.

Left: The yellow fin-stripe denotes the 8th FS, confusingly called the 'Black Sheep'. The airbrake is deployed to slow the F-15's approach.

Left: *Although it has now been around for many years, the F-15 is still a star air display attraction. For maximum effect display aircraft are flown without missiles, tanks or pylons.*

Above: *The 49th Fighter Wing is the last active-duty unit with the F-15A, but is in the process of deactivating. The 49th number-plate may transfer to the F-117 unit when it moves to Holloman.*

57th Fighter Weapons Wing, Nellis AFB, Nevada

422nd TEWS 'Vampires' (black/yellow checkerboard), 433rd FWS 'Satan's Angels' (red)

The 57th FWW ('WA' tailcode, reportedly for 'Weapons Acquisition') is Tactical Air Command's test and evaluation unit for fighter weapons and tactics. The wing received its first F-15A/B Eagles in 1977. These first ships were assigned to the 433rd FWS. The 57th FWW gave up its F-4E Phantoms soon after but has continued to operate a variety of USAF tactical aircraft. The F-15C/D Eagle reached the wing in the early 1980s.

The wing's 422nd TEWS (ex-422nd FWS) insignia is a vampire with pistol in one hand and dagger in the other. The squadron has a black and yellow checkerboard tail design. The squadron operates the F-15C and provides aircraft for the Fighter Weapons School's F-15 syllabus.

The 433rd FWS 'Satan's Angels' is reportedly being constituted after a period of inactivation and may operate F-15E Strike Eagles assigned to the wing.

Above: *As TAC's main tactical evaluation unit, the 57th FWW has been heavily involved in the F-15 programme. Today, F-15Es are much in evidence at Nellis.*

Left: *The regular F-15 fighter versions are used for both test and fighter school purposes. This is an F-15A seen in 1981.*

Below: *F-15As of the 433rd FWS. Far left are the wing badge and two badges associated with the F-15 Fighter Weapons School.*

58th Tactical Training Wing, Luke AFB, Arizona

461st TFTS 'Deadly Jesters' (black/yellow), 550th TFTS 'Silver Eagles' (silver/black), 555th TFTS 'Triple Nickel' (green/white)

The 58th Tactical Training Wing (designated a Tactical Fighter Training Wing, or TFTW, until a 1 April 1977 name change), with its tailcode 'LA', enjoys superb flying weather in the Arizona sun near Glendale. In this ideal climate, the wing became the RTU (replacement training unit) for F-15 Eagle operations at the outset of the Eagle's service career.

The first Eagle delivered to an operational unit in the US Air Force was TF-15A 73-0108, christened 'TAC 1', accepted by President Gerald Ford in 14 November 1974 ceremonies at Luke for the wing's only F-15 squadron, the 555th Tactical Fighter Training Squadron, or 'Triple Nickel'. The wing's 461st TFTS 'Deadly Jesters', with black and yellow colours, received its first F-15 on 1 July 1977. The 550th TFTS 'Silver Eagles', silver and black, received its first F-15 on 25 August 1977.

On 29 August 1979, the 58th TTW terminated F-15 training and transferred its F-15s to the 405th TTW, activated at Luke on that date. Today's 58th Fighter Wing (tailcode 'LF') has become an RTU for the F-16 Fighting Falcon but may again pick up Eagles when the 405th runs down.

Below: The 58th TFTW was the first TAC recipient of the Eagle, using its aircraft to establish a training unit at Luke AFB.

Above: Luke's first Eagle squadron was the famous 'Triple Nickel' (555th TFTS), a natural for the honour, as shortly before it had been responsible for 38 MiG kills during the air fighting over Vietnam.

325th Fighter Wing, Tyndall AFB, Florida

1st FS 'Griffins' (red), 2nd FS 'Unicorns' (yellow), 95th FS 'Bones' (blue)

The 325th Fighter Wing, formerly designated a Tactical Training Wing, or TTW ('TY' tailcode) was activated on 1 July 1981 as part of the Air Defense Weapons Center (ADWC) and serves as the RTU (replacement training unit) for Tactical Air Command's and the Air National Guard's F-15 air-to-air community. In late 1991, it was expected that an Air National Guard (ANG) unit would also be assigned the RTU function but early plans to assign this duty to the Missouri Air National Guard at St Louis were cancelled and a decision on a Guard RTU is still awaited.

The Tyndall wing's first F-15A (74-0103) was received on 7 December 1983 and training of the first F-15A/B class by this wing was begun in August 1984. The wing is also responsible for all F-15 maintenance training for Tactical Air Command and for training of air weapons controllers. Tyndall and its wing is also the home of the William Tell air-to-air weapons meet, usually held every two years although the scheduled 1990 event was pre-empted by Operation Desert Shield.

With the RTU at Luke AFB, Arizona, giving up all Eagles except F-15E models, the 325th FW, now responsible for training in the F-15A/B, will assume the RTU mission for the F-15C/D as well. With force reductions in the 1990s, the role of early F-15A/B Eagles in the air defence of North America is gradually being reduced.

The wing's 1st TFTS 'Griffins' was activated on 1 January 1984 and employed the F-15A/B from the beginning.

The 2nd TFTS, officially 'Second to None' or 'Unicorns', and unofficially the 'Horny Horses' because of the unicorn insignia, converted beginning in January 1984 from the F-106A Delta Dart to the F-15A/B.

The 95th TFTS with its 'Mr Bones', top-hatted skull insignia, was the wing's last squadron to acquire the McDonnell-built fighter. Known as the 95th FITS (Fighter

Above: As one would expect of a unit with a training mission, the 325th FW has a large proportion of two-seat aircraft in its inventory.

Above: This 325th aircraft displays the abbreviation for the Air Defense Weapons Center, highlighting Tyndall's central place in the air defence organisation.

Right: A 95th TFTS F-15A in classic Eagle landing pose.

A variation of *Tyndall* tail markings shows the 325th *FW*'s commander's aircraft, with multi-coloured fin stripe.

Interceptor Training Squadron) when it flew the T-33A Shooting Stars, the squadron underwent a name change when it began flying F-15A/B Eagles on 1 April 1988.

The 325th was redesignated the 325th Fighter Wing (*without* the modifier 'Tactical') in August 1991 as part of continuing USAF structural changes.

Above: The 2nd *TFTS* flew F-106s before it picked up the Eagle training mission in 1974. These are F-15As – the 325th is now also involved in all F-15C training. At right is the 'Mr Bones' patch of the 95th *FS*.

405th Tactical Training Wing, Luke AFB, Arizona

461st TFTS 'Deadly Jesters' (black/yellow), 550th TFTS 'Silver Eagles' (silver/black), 555th TFTS 'Triple Nickel' (green/white)

Activated at Luke AFB near Glendale, Arizona, on 29 August 1979, the 405th Tactical Training Wing became Tactical Air Command's RTU (replacement training unit) for the F-15A/B Eagle. In 1988, the wing began transitioning to all F-15E Strike Eagle aircraft to act as RTU for the E model only. Curiously, no F-15C aircraft has ever been assigned to Luke, although F-15A, B, D and E variants have all been assigned at one time or another. The 405th TTW took over three squadrons formerly assigned to the 58th TTW:

The 461st TFTS 'Deadly Jesters' (black/yellow) received its first F-15E Strike Eagle on 1 August 1987, converting from F-15A/B/D. The squadron's tail marking is a black tailband with three yellow stripes centred horizontally and a yellow jester's face rearmost. This squadron is scheduled to be disestablished in 1992;

The 550th TFTS 'Silver Eagles' (silver and black) received its first F-15E on 12 May 1989, converting from F-15A/B;

The 555th TFTS 'Triple Nickel' (green and white) is currently equipping with the F-15E, replacing the F-15A/B.

On 1 January 1981, the 426th TFTS 'Killer Claws', blue and yellow, an F-4 Phantom unit, was assigned to the 405th TTW as an F-15 squadron. The 426th TFTS was deactivated 29 November 1990. Remaining F-15E squadrons may return to 58th Fighter Wing control as the 405th is run down.

The 405th TTW took over as an F-15 training unit in 1979.

The 405th TTW is now responsible for all F-15E training, having discarded the pure fighter models and disbanded one squadron in the process. This quartet contains aircraft from both the 461st and 550th TFTS, the first two E-equipped units.

Left: The 426th TFTS (left) was the casualty when the 405th ditched its fighter F-15 training commitments, its fin colour being predominantly red. The fins of the F-15Es (above) show the wing commander's aircraft.

Left: Luke is now Strike Eagle country, the excellent flying weather and proximity to large weapons ranges proving ideal for the attack training mission.

Above: The 'Triple Nickel' squadron continued their training role with the F-15, being the last unit to convert to the 'E'. This aircraft is an F-15D.

Tactical Air Warfare Center (TAWC), Eglin AFB, Florida

The Tactical Air Warfare Center ('OT' tailcode) oversees the 4485th Test Squadron, which flies several tactical combat aircraft types. In 1982, the squadron operated an F-15C (78-0542) with an unofficial OT&E tailcode (for operational test and evaluation). The TAWC has flown F-15A/B Eagles and now has F-15C/D models. Its aircraft have a black and white checkerboard tail design.

Below: An F-15B of the TAWC lands with Sidewinder missiles and dummy Sparrows. The 'OT' tailcode stands for Operational Test, highlighting the unit's role.

Right: The 4485th Test Squadron has a number of Eagles for trials work, including this F-15A (seen carrying a baggage pod for an air show visit).

First Air Force, Langley AFB, Virginia

Tactical Air Command's First Air Force maintains responsibility for the air defence of the United States. This formation is a descendant of the long-defunct Air Defense Command, known in its final years as Aerospace Defense Command, which on 1 October 1979 transferred its resources to Tactical Air Command. On that date, TAC then formed ADTAC (Air Defense Tactical Air Command) at Colorado Springs, subsequently transferring ADTAC to Langley AFB on 1 June 1981. A further organisational change (after the onset of the F-15 Eagle era) saw ADTAC become First Air Force, activated on 6 December 1985.

First Air Force at its inception operated four

squadrons (5th, 48th, 57th and 318th FIS) equipped with the F-15A/B model in the interceptor role. Each of these squadrons had three or four airframes which had been modified (wired) for ASAT (anti-satellite) operations, even though the ASAT programme was officially dropped in the early 1980s. The bulk of air defence operations is now being carried by the F-16A ADF (air defense fighter) Fighting Falcon (*World Air Power Journal*, Volume 5) and the 57th FIS is the last F-15 interceptor squadron.

Right: Carried between 1981 and 1985, the badge of ADTAC graced the Eagles of four fighter interceptor squadrons which operated as part of the organisation.

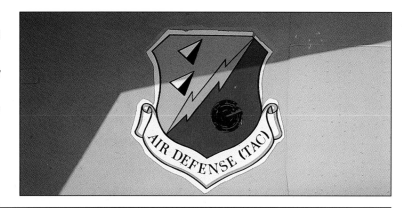

5th Fighter Interceptor Squadron, Minot AFB, North Dakota

The 5th FIS 'Spittin' Kittens' had a brief life in very colourful F-15A/B Eagle fighters until being disbanded in the late 1980s. The squadron received its first aircraft in April 1985, replacing the F-106A Delta Dart, the last of which departed on 5 April 1985. Inactivated 1 July 1988, the squadron's aircraft went to the Massachusetts Air National Guard.

Right: The three CONUS-based First Air Force units had the most colourful markings applied to regular squadron Eagles in USAF service, the 5th Fighter Interceptor Squadron wearing these striking markings. Based at Minot AFB, the 5th FIS was placed to provide air defence to the north, but the unit flew the type for barely three years before disbandment. Today the defence in this part of the nation is handled by the F-16 ADFs of the 119th FIG at Fargo.

48th Fighter Interceptor Squadron, Langley AFB, Virginia

The 48th FIS (which belatedly adopted an 'LY' tailcode, after operating for some time with none) was the final First Air Force unit to retain F-15s. The 48th received its first F-15A (76-0087) on 14 August 1981. Tail marking for the squadron was a medium-blue tailband with four white stars. The squadron officially converted to the F-15A/B on 5 April 1982, replacing the F-106A Delta Dart, the last of which had departed on 9 March 1982. The 48th FIS was deactivated on 30 September 1991 and its Eagles were transferred to the Missouri Air National Guard in St Louis.

Above right: When ADTAC was demoted to being just First Air Force, the F-15 Eagles picked up TAC badges and standard tailcodes.

Right: The 48th FIS in happier days when it had full colour ADTAC markings. Today the unit does not even exist.

85

Eagle Operators

57th Fighter Interceptor Squadron, Keflavik NS, Iceland

The 57th FIS ('IS' tailcode) flies the F-15C/D Eagle to intercept Soviet long-range bombers and reconnaissance aircraft in and around the vulnerable region known as the GIUK (Greenland, Iceland, United Kingdom) 'gap'. The squadron converted from early F-4E Phantoms to F-15C/D Eagles in November 1985, without ever operating F-15A/B models. Its aircraft wear a black and white checkerboard design on the vertical fin cap. The squadron is part of Air Forces Iceland.

Right: The last First Air Force flying unit is the 57th FIS, which flies as part of Air Forces Iceland, as demonstrated by the 'IS' tailcode and the map of the island on the fin.

Below: The 'Black Knights' of the 57th FIS has a long history of intercepting Soviet maritime reconnaissance aircraft, flying F-102s, F-4Es and now the F-15C/D Eagle.

318th Fighter Interceptor Squadron, McChord AFB, Washington

The 318th FIS (which operated without a tailcode before adopting 'TC', roughly for Tacoma) converted to F-15As on 30 December 1983, employing its early Eagles as interceptor replacements for the F-106A Delta Dart. The squadron was deactivated on 7 December 1989 and its aircraft were transferred to the 142nd FIG at Portland, Oregon's Air National Guard unit.

Right: The 318th FIS at McChord AFB was entrusted with the defence of the western seaboard, and regularly maintained an air defence alert at Castle AFB in California in addition to one at its home base. The star emblem was a striking feature, which sadly disappeared.

Above: With the adoption of TAC-style markings, the 318th FIS had to struggle to retain a vestige of its former glory. The tailcode stands for the local city of Tacoma.

Right: Although the unit has gone, the 318th's aircraft are still on the West Coast with the 142nd FIG.

Air Force Logistics Command

(To be merged with Air Force Systems Command to form a new Air Force Materiel Command on 1 July 1992.)

Warner Robins Air Logistics Center (WRALC), Warner Robins AFB, Georgia

The Warner Robins Air Logistics Center handles depot maintenance for Tactical Air Command F-15A/B/C/D/E Eagles, as well as providing battle damage repair training. Some of the depot work is also performed at Sacramento, California, although the latter location has no F-15 aircraft of its own. The 2875th Test Squadron at Warner Robins performs FCFs (functional check flights) on all F-15s emerging from the depot.

At one time, the Center was in possession of an F-15A (77-0068) with an unofficial 'WR' tailcode. Today, the Center has two F-15A airframes (76-0116 and the aforementioned 77-0068) which wear the 'RG' tailcode officially assigned to its aircraft (and also worn on C-130B 57-0527).

Right: 77-0068 was the first F-15A Eagle picked up by the Warner Robins ALC, for use by the F-15 maintenance depot. The unit generates enough of its own test work to justify the possession of two airframes. The 'RG' tailcode stands for Robins, Georgia.

Below: Before adopting the current (and official) 'RG' codes, 77-0068 wore the 'WR' code for Warner Robins. The smart fin stripe incorporated the badge of Air Force Logistics Command.

Above: The F-15s assigned to Warner Robins ALC wear this smart badge depicting the national bird modified to the shape of the McDonnell version of the Eagle.

Air Force Systems Command

(To be merged with Air Force Logistics Command to form a new Air Force Materiel Command on 1 July 1992.)

3246th Test Wing, Eglin AFB, Florida

The 3246th TW, part of the Armament Division, USAF Systems Command (formerly with an 'AD' tailcode, now with 'ET' for 'Eglin Test'), operates the 3247th Test Squadron which uses a variety of current USAF aircraft types and currently has some F-15C/D Eagles. The squadron recently acquired two F-15E Strike Eagles.

Above: The 3246th TW's main work is involved with ordnance applications to service types. This aircraft was the first F-15C, seen at Eglin while involved in air-to-ground drops of ordnance (cluster bombs carried here). The former 'AD' tailcode stood for Armament Division.

Below: Fighter Eagles are still on 3246th TW strength in the shape of F-15Cs and Ds (illustrated). All aircraft now wear the 'ET' Eglin Test tailcode.

Left: F-15Es are undergoing extensive weapons tests at Eglin, this example carrying a suite of TV cameras to record the intimate nature of stores separation during bomb drops.

Below: The Eagle has always had the ability to carry external ECM pods, but they are very rarely seen. Here an Eglin F-15A carries an AN/ALQ-131.

6510th Test Wing, Edwards AFB, California

The 6510th TW ('ED' tailcode) supports the 6512th Test Squadron, which operates a broad mix of operational USAF aircraft types for test missions, including most types of fighters now in service. The F-15A/B/C/D Eagles operated by the test unit have a blue tailband with white Xs and a white border. The unit once operated the ASAT (anti-satellite) F-15A. The unit also carried out tests with the first F-15E Strike Eagle.

Right: Every USAF service type passes through the 6510th TW's hands at one point or another, and with a major type such as the F-15 many airframes are involved. Tests continue long after the aircraft enters service, working on new equipment, new variants or other programmes unrelated to the aircraft type. Among the 6512th TS aircraft is this F-15D.

Above: Aircrew from the 6512th Test Squadron who are assigned to Eagle flying wear this Combined Test Force patch.

Left: Before delivery to the 3246th Test Wing at Eglin, the first F-15C was at Edwards for air-to-ground trials. This view shows the CFTs and tangential weapons carriage to advantage.

Above: Edwards' best-known Eagle is the F-15 S/MTD, fitted with canards and thrust-vectoring nozzles for short field and manoeuvre research. Note the attractive colour scheme.

Right: F-15s of the CTF reveal different tail badges. The 6510th TW fin contains cacti to signify the desert location of Edwards.

Left: One of the hardest-working Eagles is 71-0291, used for a long string of test programmes. Under programme 'Peek Eagle' it is still on 6512th TS strength.

Above: The F-15E has been a major Edwards programme in recent times, particularly the integration of both targetting and navigation pods of the LANTIRN system.

United States Air Force in Europe

32nd Fighter Squadron, Soesterberg, Netherlands

The 32nd FS ('CR' tailcode), known as the 'Wolfhounds', operates F-15C/D Eagles from Camp New Amsterdam, Soesterberg, Netherlands, where it comes directly under Allied NATO control. The 32nd TFS received its first F-15A/B Eagles beginning on 13 December 1978 (replacing the F-4E Phantom). The squadron has since equipped with F-15C/Ds. All aircraft wear an orange fin stripe outlined in green. During Operation Desert Storm, the 32nd TFS was deployed to Incirlik AB, Turkey, and attained four air-to-air kills. It has supplied some airframes which were taken from US inventory for Saudi Arabia's air force in 1990.

In late 1991, the 32nd FS was scheduled to revert to MSIP F-15A/B Eagles from the current F-15C/D models.

Above: The 32nd FS comes under operational control of the Royal Netherlands Air Force, hence the royal-style squadron crest, and this addition proclaiming some allegiance to the monarchy!

Above: The 32nd TFS complement was depleted during Desert Shield/Storm when some of its aircraft were supplied to the RSAF. Others were on hand in Turkey to provide air cover over northern Iraq from Turkey.

Left: Wear it loud and proud! The 32nd TFS commander's aircraft is adorned with the squadron nickname.

36th Fighter Wing, Bitburg AB, Germany

22nd FS 'Stingers' (red), 53rd FS 'Tigers' (yellow), 525th TFS 'Bulldogs' (blue)

The 36th FW ('BT' tailcode) is equipped with F-15C/D Eagles, which replaced the F-4E Phantom in 1977, reaching full strength by 30 September 1977. The wing is assigned the air defence mission for NATO's central front. The wing expected that its aircraft would be the first in combat if war had come in the theatre, an increasingly unlikely event now that the Warsaw Pact has dissolved.

During Operation Desert Storm, the wing deployed its 53rd TFS to Tabuk, Saudi Arabia, and its 525th TFS to Incirlik, Turkey. The wing's 53rd FS 'Tigers' (yellow fin stripe containing black tiger stripes) has new-build (Fiscal Year 1984) aircraft. Its 525th TFS 'Bulldogs', similarly equipped, had as its insignia a bulldog with bandages. Following success in Desert Storm, the 525th TFS has been deactivated and the wing reduced to two squadrons.

The 22nd FS with its 'Stinger' insignia is one of the two 36th Fighter Wing squadrons escaping the recent axe. It was the only squadron of the 36th not to deploy during Desert Shield, although aircrew were assigned to the other two squadrons.

Above: The 53rd TFS and its F-15C MSIP aircraft were deployed to Saudi Arabia. This aircraft, 84-0019, was flown by Lieutenant Robert W. 'Gigs' Hehemann when he shot down two Sukhoi Su-25s on 6 February 1991.

Above: *Tiger stripes adorn the fin-stripe of this 53rd TFS F-15D. The 'Bulldogs' added pawprints to their blue stripe.*

Left: *Aircraft from the three squadrons fly over Germany. For many years the 36th TFW was the principal air defence unit in southern West Germany, providing an alert facility and patrolling the Air Defense Identification Zone.*

Below: *Among the many specially-marked 36th TFW aircraft over the years was this patriotic commander's machine.*

Below: *For the 1991 Tiger Meet, the 53rd TFS produced this handsome scheme.*

48th Fighter Wing, RAF Lakenheath

The 48th FW ('LN' tailcode) is scheduled to convert from the F-111F Aardvark to the F-15E Strike Eagle during 1992. The wing's 492nd FS will be first to make the conversion, and a second squadron (either the 493rd or 494th FS) will follow. Principal reason for the change is the USAF decision to consolidate its F-111 assets.

Right: *Pictured over the Eglin ranges, this F-15E already wore 48th Fighter Wing marks long before the unit officially received the type. Replacing the F-111F, the F-15E provides greater flexibility in the face of reduced forces in Europe.*

United States Air National Guard

102nd Fighter Interceptor Group, Otis ANGB, Massachusetts

This group's 101st Fighter Interceptor Squadron, Massachusetts Air National Guard, operates the F-15A/B Eagle in the interceptor role as a replacement for the F-106A Delta Dart. The first pair of F-15As joined the unit in September 1987, having been transferred from the 5th FIS at Minot AFB, SD. Massachusetts Guardsmen have on several occasions intercepted and escorted Soviet long-range reconnaissance aircraft, usually Tupolev Tu-95 'Bear' types, over the Atlantic.

Right: Massachusetts aircraft wear the state name on the tail, and the inscription 'Cape Cod' on the tank.

116th Tactical Fighter Wing, Dobbins AFB, Georgia

The 116th TFW operates the 128th Tactical Fighter Squadron of Georgia Air National Guard at Dobbins AFB just outside Marietta. Georgia Guardsmen received their first Eagle (F-15A 74-0128) on 28 March 1986, replacing the F-4D Phantom. The Georgia unit employs early F-15A/B Eagle aircraft in the battlefield air defence role.

Below: Georgia's F-15s include the 'Boss Bird', resplendent in full-colour fin-stripe and unit number presented in dropped shadows.

Right: Initially flying with black fin-stripes, Georgia's aircraft today now fly with low-visibility markings. The wing has a tactical air defence role.

150th Tactical Fighter Group, Kirtland AFB, New Mexico

In late 1991, it had not been confirmed but was widely reported that this group's 188th Tactical Fighter Squadron, of the New Mexico Air National Guard, was scheduled to transition to the F-15A/B. The change, if it takes place, will leave an F-15 presence in New Mexico after the 49th FW at Holloman AFB shuts down.

159th Tactical Fighter Group, New Orleans, Louisiana

The 159th TFG's 122nd Tactical Fighter Squadron, Louisiana Air National Guard, known as the 'Coonass Militia', was the first Air Guard unit to equip with the F-15, receiving airframes which had served previously at Luke AFB, Arizona. In mid-1991, the Louisiana Air National Guard was converting from early (Fiscal Year 1973) to later (Fiscal Year 1977) F-15A/B models, the latter being transferred from the 49th FW at Holloman AFB, New Mexico. Louisiana Guardsmen have an air-to-air battlefield mission.

Flying the tactical air-to-air mission, the 'Coonass Militia' of the Louisiana ANG utilise late-FY F-15As. The 122nd TFS is arranged in four flights, with red, yellow, green and blue fin-stripes.

Right: Aircraft from the four 122nd TFS flights in formation. Above are two patches, one bearing a legend in Creole.

131st Tactical Fighter Wing, Lambert-St Louis International Airport, Missouri

The 131st TFW is parent unit for the 110th Tactical Fighter Squadron, Missouri Air National Guard ('SL' tailcode). The squadron is assigned the battlefield air superiority mission and will provide DACT (dissimilar air combat training) to Guard units equipped with F-16s. Reports that Missouri will become an RTU (replacement training unit) are not accurate.

Missouri's wing and squadron occupy a unique, if very cramped, location. Situated across Lambert-St Louis Airport from the McDonnell Aircraft Company plant (with McDonnell Douglas corporate headquarters also nearby), the Missouri Guard has long counted among its members countless employees of 'McAir', including some of the manufacturer's senior officials. No written rule has ever been put on paper that the unit must operate McDonnell equipment, but tentative plans in the late 1980s to equip with the F-16 Fighting Falcon were abandoned, almost certainly because 'McAir' shares the neighbourhood.

The Missouri ANG began converting to the F-15A/B Eagle from the F-4E Phantom in May 1991, with the receipt of its first F-15A Eagle (76-0030), transferred from the Tactical Air Warfare Center (TAWC) at Eglin AFB, Florida. In June 1991, the unit received its first F-15B (76-0129) from the same previous 'owner'. A ceremony took place on 15 September 1991 to mark the departure of the unit's final Phantom and IOC (initial operating capability) in the F-15A/B.

Below: Missouri Guard Eagles carry a representation of the famous St Louis arch on the fin.

Above: Two generations of McDonnell airpower in flight over 'McDonnell City' – St Louis. Missouri was an obvious recipient for the F-15 due to its heavy company connections, the Guard unit occupying the same airport as the factory.

Right: An early F-15 for the Missouri ANG. It does not carry the 'Lindbergh's Own' intake badge shown far right.

142nd Fighter Interceptor Group, Portland, Oregon

The 142nd FIG's 123rd Fighter Interceptor Squadron, Oregon Air National Guard, received its first Eagle (F-15B 76-0139) on 1 October 1989 and was fully operational by early 1990, having previously been the final user of the F-4C Phantom. The unit had flown the F-4C for 8½ years and, before that, the F-101B/F Voodoo for 10 years. Most of the unit's F-15 aircraft came from the 318th FIS at McChord AFB, Washington, which was being disbanded. As an interceptor group, the Portland unit has had occasion to intercept and escort Soviet aircraft, including 'friendlies' coming to participate in US air shows.

Right: The Oregon Air National Guard's Eagle unit has largely assumed the West Coast air defence commitment previously assigned to the 318th FIS, whose aircraft it largely adopted. At top right is the unit's first Eagle, an ex-318th F-15B in full colour squadron markings.

Below: The 142nd FIG's F-15B is seen in the hangar at Portland.

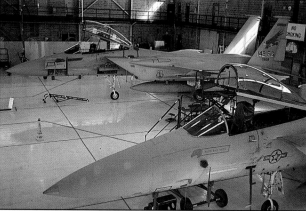

154th Composite Group, Hickam AFB, Hawaii

The 154th TFG's 199th Fighter Interceptor Squadron was one of the last users of the F-4C Phantom before receiving its first F-15A/B Eagles. In the summer of 1987, the transition took place during which time Eagles from the Georgia Air National Guard travelled to Hickam to stand the air defence alert commitment until the Hawaii Guard could become fully operational. Hawaii's Guardsmen acquired their F-15A Eagles – examples being 74-0086 and 74-0088 – from the USAF's 21st Tactical Fighter Wing at Elmendorf AFB, Alaska, during which time the latter fighter wing began converting from A to C models and acquired a second squadron.

In mid-1991, the Hawaii Air National Guard was preparing to convert from its early F-15A Eagles to early F-15C models.

The 199th FIS represents the air defence of the Hawaiian islands, flying from Hickam AFB.

NASA

NASA has had two F-15As assigned to its Dryden Facility at Edwards AFB. 71-0281 was acquired on 17 December 1975 and returned to USAF use on 28 October 1983 (it is now on display at Langley). 71-0287 was taken on charge on 5 January 1976, and is still active at Dryden under the 'HIDEC' programme.

Below: NASA's current Eagle is 71-0287, which flies under the HIDEC programme from Edwards AFB, California.

Above: NASA had two scale models for testing in the early 1970s. These were radio-controlled and released from the Boeing NB-52B.

Israeli Defense Force/Air Force (IDF/AF) (Heyl Ha'Avir)

Israeli air crews evaluated the manufacturer's TF-15A 'dog ship' (71-0290) in 1974. Despite an effort during the Carter years (1977-81) to limit US transfers of advanced warplanes to foreign users, the Jewish state has received Eagle deliveries taking place in instalments.

Four F-15A FSD (full-scale development) aircraft (72-0116/0118 and 72-0120) arrived in Israel beginning 10 December 1976, apparently for developmental work, in the Peace Fox I programme. It has been reported by an Israeli source that the government later fell because their arrival violated the Sabbath. These were followed by 19 F-15As (76-1505/1523) and two TF-15As (76-1524/1525) in Peace Fox II, offered at preferential financing to help offset sale of the same aircraft type to Saudi Arabia. Thereafter came 18 F-15Cs (80-0122/0130 and 83-0054/0062) and eight F-15Ds (80-0131/0136 and 83-0063/0064) in Peace Fox III. No. 106 Sqn formed specifically to operate the F-15C.

Israel is rumoured to be the intended recipient of early F-15A (Fiscal Year 1973, 1974, 1975) aircraft which will not be upgraded in an MSIP (Multi-Stage Improvement Program) and which would probably otherwise be scrapped, that will go to the Jewish state *gratis* as a *quid pro quo* for policy decisions made during the Gulf War.

More than any other nation, Israel has closely guarded the names of its fighter squadrons, their insignia, and their lineage and locations. The units which operate the F-15 are identified as Nos 106 and 133 Squadrons at Tel Nov.

Israeli Eagles saw action for the first time on 27 June 1977 when they shot down four Syrian MiG-21 'Fishbeds' over Lebanon. On 24 September 1979, Eagles shot down five Syrian fighters and on 27 June 1980 at least one more. In May 1982, two Syrian MiG-23 'Floggers' were claimed, the first of this type ever downed in battle. On 7 June 1981, Israeli F-15s carrying FAST packs (conformal fuel tanks) flew a 1,000-mile (1610-km) combat mission to provide top cover for the F-16 attack on Iraq's Osirak (Tamuz) nuclear reactor near Baghdad. During Operation Peace for Galilee, the 1982 Israeli invasion of Lebanon, Eagles shot down a major portion of the 92 aircraft downed between 5 and 12 June, including two Syrian MiG-23 'Floggers' near Beirut on 12 June and at least three high-flying Syrian MiG-25 'Foxbat' fighters using zoom climb (or 'snap-up') intercepts and AIM-7 Sparrow missiles. The 1982 campaign resulted in one Eagle, nicknamed 'Skyblazer', being credited with four kills.

Above: Defender of the Promised Land: an F-15A of No. 133 Squadron flies over Tel Aviv, proudly carrying four Syrian kill marks on its nose.

Below: No. 133 Squadron was the first Heyl Ha'Avir Eagle unit, and today flies the A-model. The eagle's head badge is a fairly recent addition to the fin.

Right: No. 133 carries a small buzzard badge on the starboard fin. The unit is based at Tel Nov alongside No. 106.

Below: The red/white chevron inside the fin identifies No. 106 Squadron at Tel Nov. This unit operates the F-15C/D aircraft delivered to Israel.

Right: With two large Eagle squadrons, and more aircraft being delivered, the IDF/AF seems certain to form a third F-15 unit. This F-15A is from No. 133 Sqn.

Japan Air Self Defence Force (JASDF) (Nihon Koku Jietai)

Japanese officers carried out two flight evaluations of the F-15A/B Eagle at Edwards AFB, California, in June-July 1975. Mitsubishi was selected in April 1978 as prime contractor for Japanese F-15J/DJ Eagles, which differ from American F-15A/B aircraft only in the deletion of a few sensitive items of ECM (electronic countermeasures), radar warning and nuclear delivery equipment. Plans initially were to procure 123 aircraft for five squadrons of 18 each, the first two single-seaters and 12 two-seaters being built in St Louis by McDonnell under Project Peace Eagle. The first Japanese aircraft, a single-seater (02-8801), made its first flight at Lambert-St Louis Municipal Airport on 4 June 1980. Total planned procurement has risen to 177 aircraft built locally, for a combined total of 191.

The Japanese F-15 force is divided between the three Air Defence Forces as follows:

Northern Air Defence Force – Hokbu Koku Homentai

2 Kokudan (Air Wing) Chitose
201 Hikotai – fourth unit to get the F-15, beginning in March 1986 following the retirement of 207 Hikotai's F-104s.
203 Hikotai – second JASDF F-15 unit, this squadron received the first of its 18 aircraft on 13 April 1983, replacing the F-104J.

Central Air Defence Force – Chubu Koku Homentai

6 Kokudan (Air Wing) Komatsu
303 Hikotai – fifth in the list of JASDF units, 303 Hikotai was the first ex-Phantom unit to form, beginning in November 1986. Official re-formation occurred in April 1987.

7 Kokudan (Air Wing) Hyakuri
204 Hokotai – as the third JASDF F-15 unit, 204 Hikotai began its transition from the F-104J Starfighter on 16 April 1984.
305 Hikotai – this is expected to be the last F-15J squadron to form, sometime in 1993. At present it flies F-4EJs.

Western Air Defence Force – Seibu Koku Homentai

5 Kokudan (Air Wing) Nyutabaru
202 Hikotai – the first recipient of the F-15 was the Rinji F-15 Hikotai (temporary F-15 squadron), which formed in December 1981 to act as the F-15 OCU. During 1982 the squadron was re-formed as 202 Hikotai, ex-F-104J Starfighter, continuing in the OCU role.

Hiko Kyodotai – problems with the Mitsubishi T-2 poor accident record and lack of power led to the JASDF adopting the F-15DJ for an aggressor squadron at Nyutabaru. Six aircraft are assigned, wearing special camouflage schemes for dissimilar air combat training.

8 Kokudan (Air Wing) Tsuiki
304 Hikotai – the sixth and latest unit, 304 Hikotai disposed of its F-4EJs in favour of the F-15J in April 1990.

Right: A pair of 201 Hikotai F-15s accompany two 432nd TFW F-16s from Misawa in a show of northern Japanese air power. 201's base is at Chitose on the island of Hokkaido, only a short flight from Soviet territory. The squadron badge depicts a wolf's head.

Below: 202 Hikotai was the first Japanese F-15 recipient, and has acted as the OCU since. It operates a fair proportion of the F-15DJ two-seaters.

Original squadron complement was set at 18 aircraft per Hikotai, but recent production has seen this number swelled to 22. 203 Hikotai was the first unit to receive an increase, the other squadrons following from 1987 onwards.

Above and left: 204 Hikotai was the first Central Air Defence Force F-15 operator, forming at Hyakuri in 1984. The eagle badge is carried on both inner and outer fins.

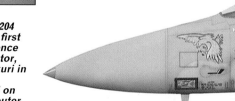

Camouflage
Japanese Eagles wear this standard camouflage consisting of two tones of air superiority grey. National insignia and squadron badges are carried in full colour.

Above: At present each Air Defence Force has two Eagle squadrons, although an extra unit (305 Hikotai) is planned for the central region. This aircraft is from 303 Hikotai at Komatsu.

Above: The JASDF's most recent squadron to form is 304 Hikotai at Tsuiki, the second unit to convert from the F-4EJ Phantom. The first four F-15 users had all previously flown the Starfighter.

Left and below: A specialist unit within the JASDF structure is the Hiko Kyodotai, based at Nyutabaru on the southern island of Kyushu. From here the unit flies F-15DJs on dedicated aggressor duties, for which its aircraft wear special schemes, including this green and grey aircraft. The unit badge is a cobra, worn on the outside of the fins only.

McDonnell Douglas/ Mitsubishi F-15J

Japan has been the only country to build the F-15 under licence, using the early F-15C/D as the baseline model, although with some local differences. The first two single-seaters and 12 two-seaters were completed in St Louis, these followed by eight single-seaters supplied in knock-down form for final assembly by Mitsubishi. Other Japanese companies are also involved in the programme.

Right: 203 Hikotai became the first front-line Japanese Eagle squadron in 1983, following the establishment of 202 Hikotai as the OCU.

ECM
Among the indigenous equipment fitted to the JASDF aircraft is the J/ALQ-8 ECM suite and XJ/APQ-1 radar warning system.

Serial
The JASDF has a complicated six-digit serial system. The first corresponds to the procurement year (7=1987), the second the basic class of aircraft (2=multi-engined), the third the basic role (8=all-weather fighter) and the last three the individual aircraft number in sequence (898).

Powerplant
JASDF Eagles are currently powered by a pair of Pratt & Whitney F100-PW-100 turbofan. From 1991 these are being replaced by F100-PW-220s, offering 105.7 kN (23,770 lb) thrust each with afterburning.

97

Saudi Arabia

In the 1970s and 1980s, US arms sales to Saudi Arabia were controversial – because of that Arab nation's position towards Israel – and the equipping of the RSAF (Royal Saudi Air Force) with F-15 Eagles became an especially contentious domestic American issue.

Riyadh initially ordered 62 airframes, consisting of 47 F-15Cs and 15 F-15Ds, under Project Peace Sun as a replacement for the Lightning fighter. Actual delivery consisted of 46 F-15Cs (80-0062/0106 and 81-0002) and 16 F-15Ds (80-0107/0121 and 81-0003). The total of 62 includes two attrition replacements, since the US imposed a limit (in 1980) of 60 Eagles which could be 'on board' in Saudi Arabia at any given time.

The RSAF began receiving its first F-15C/D aircraft in January 1981 and apparently reached IOC (initial operating capability) in August 1981. Saudi units are: No. 5 Squadron at Taif, No. 6 Squadron at Khamis Mushait and No. 13 Squadron at Dhahran.

The controversial sale of this modern fighter aircraft was eased by Saudi assurance that the Eagles would be used solely in the air defence role. Still, restrictions were imposed which at first prevented delivery of CFT (conformal fuel tanks) to the RSAF, and because of political sensibilities a 1989 request for 12 more attrition replacement F-15C/D Eagles was not accommodated.

During a period of border tensions, two Saudi F-15Cs shot down two Iranian F-4E Phantoms over the Persian Gulf on 5 June 1984, possibly the first time one McDonnell product scored an aerial victory over another.

The 2 August 1990 Iraqi invasion of Kuwait altered the Middle East equation and dramatised Saudi Arabia's status as a nation comparatively weak in military terms, with fewer than 60,000 personnel under arms. The constraint limit of 60 aeroplanes 'in country' was dropped. Twenty four F-15C/D Eagles were rushed to the Saudis from US Air Force stocks in Europe in September-October 1990. During Desert Shield and Desert Storm, Saudi F-15C Eagles shared combat air patrol duties with British Tornado F.Mk 3s and American F-15Cs.

For Saudi fighter pilots, the war's shining moment came when Captain Ayehid Salah al-Shamrani of the RSAF's No. 13 Squadron shot down two Iraqi Mirage F1s near the Persian Gulf after being directed to the Mirages by a Saudi AWACS.

In mid-1991, McDonnell began filling an order for 12 more F-15s which had been ordered by Saudi Arabia before the Gulf War under a $333.5-million FMS (Foreign Military Sales) contract by delivering the first two machines in this dozen (nine F-15C, three F-15D). On 12 August 1991, McDonnell formally received the FMS for this purchase under the Peace Sun VI programme. The aircraft were to be delivered at the rate of two per month by February 1992. The first two were delivered by mid-August.

Saudi Arabia requested 24 additional single-seat F-15F airframes, based on the F-15E but without the second crew member and some advanced equipment.

Above: No. 13 Squadron is the Dhahran-based RSAF F-15 unit. These machines carry AIM-9P Sidewinders.

Left: A No. 13 Sqn aircraft undergoes maintenance during Desert Shield, when the unit shared its facilities with the F-15s of the 1st TFW from Langley.

Below: Saudi F-15 at war: a No. 13 Sqn aircraft formates on a USAF KC-10 during a Desert Storm CAP.

McDonnell Douglas F-15C Eagle

In an effort to maintain the peace in the Middle East, and to continue its considerable and vital influence in both Jewish and Arab camps, the United States elected to supply F-15s to Saudi Arabia following the sale of the fighter to Israel. However, considerable restrictions were placed on the force, which were only lifted when the Iraqi invasion of Kuwait revealed the vulnerability of the world's largest oil-producing nation. The arrival of the F-15 and the replacement of the Lightning in the interceptor role dramatically improved the Saudi ability to defend its own airspace, a fact illustrated in 1984 when two Iranian Phantoms were shot down.

Fuel
This F-15 is shown in maximum endurance combat air patrol configuration, carrying three 2309-litre (610-US gal) drop tanks. The RSAF has Boeing KE-3A tankers to extend the endurance of its interceptors and AWACS aircraft.

Procurement
The US imposed a limit of 60 F-15s on Saudi Arabia, although attrition has accounted for two further aircraft, the total comprising 46 F-15Cs and 16 F-15Ds. Twenty-four aircraft were rushed from USAFE stocks in late 1990 to meet the demands of Desert Shield.

Weapons
Saudi F-15s were originally supplied with AIM-9P Sidewinders, but the all-aspect AIM-9L/M series became available later in the aircraft's career. Four AIM-7M Sparrows are also carried for longer-range work.

Saudi service
The Royal Saudi Air Force has formed four F-15 squadrons, No. 5 at Taif, No. 6 at Khamis Mushait, No. 13 at Dhahran, and No. 42. This latter squadron was hastily formed at Dhahran in 1990 to operate the Eagles supplied directly from the 32nd TFS and 36th TFW in Europe, one of which is depicted here.

Desert Storm
When Saddam Hussein's forces invaded Kuwait on 2 August 1990 and immediately threatened the rich oilfields of Saudi Arabia, the F-15s and Tornado ADVs of the RSAF were on full alert as the primary counter to any further Iraqi ambitions. Soon joined by USAF F-15s and RAF Tornado F.Mk 3s, the three forces pooled their resources at the base at Dhahran to provide continuous combat air patrols to protect Saudi airspace, a task which continued throughout the entire Desert Shield/Storm period. These CAPs made few engagements, but one which was successful resulted in Captain Al-Shamrani of No. 13 Squadron downing a brace of Mirage F1EQs which were believed to have been attempting an Exocet launch against coalition shipping in the Persian Gulf.

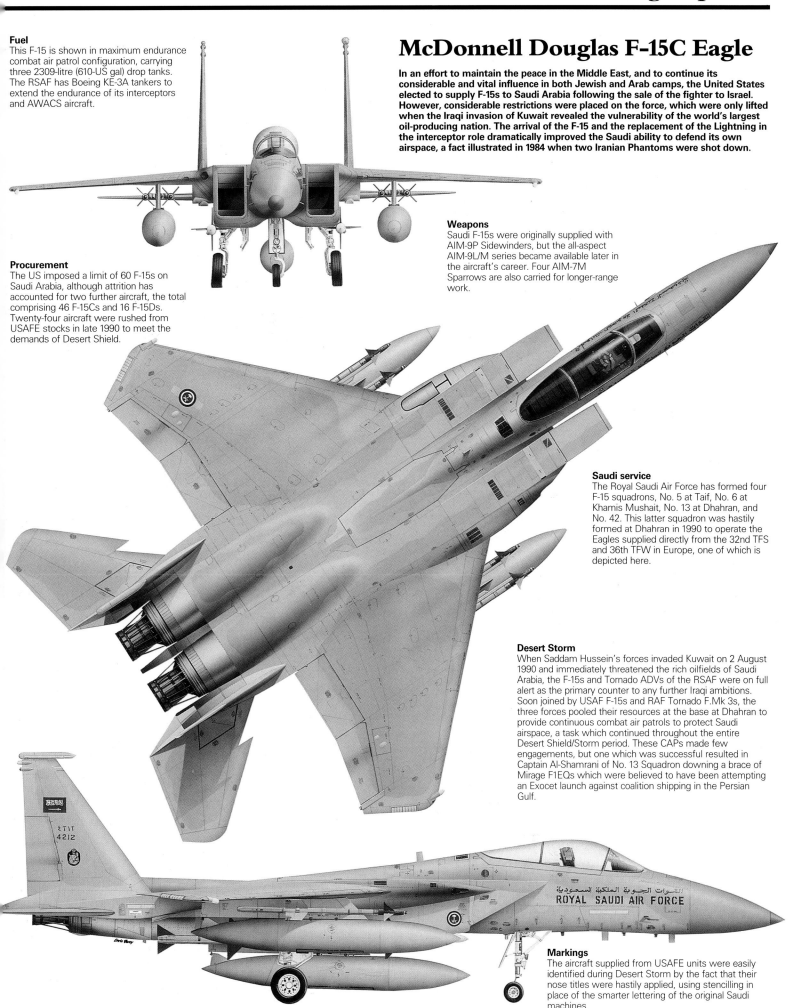

Markings
The aircraft supplied from USAFE units were easily identified during Desert Storm by the fact that their nose titles were hastily applied, using stencilling in place of the smarter lettering of the original Saudi machines.

INDIA'S FABULOUS 'FISHBEDS'

Above: Wearing the traditional Eagle's head and star badge of No. 8 Squadron on their noses, and an '8' and lightning flash on their rudders, three MiG-21FLs maintain a tight formation en route to an *ACT* engagement, probably along the lines of 'stripes' versus 'spots'.

Right: A No. 8 Squadron pilot climbs aboard his MiG-21FL. It retains the original one-piece forward-hinging canopy, which also acts as a blast shield in the event of an ejection. The mix of RAF-style ranks, uniforms and organisation with Soviet equipment is unique.

The MiG-21 'Fishbed' has played a major role in Indian military aviation for almost three decades. Blooded in two major wars with neighbouring Pakistan, the MiG-21 has been procured in huge numbers, and has been manufactured indigenously under licence. The total number of MiG-21s received by India stands at 830, including 580 licence-built models. The 250 Soviet-built MiG-21s included all 70 two-seaters. Even today, the MiG-21 is the most numerous fighter type in IAF service, equipping some 18 front-line squadrons and a plethora of support units. The original MiG-21F-13 has now disappeared from Indian skies, but large numbers of MiG-21FLs, PFMAs, MFs, Ms and bis remain in use.

Above: A single MiG-21 leads a formation of one each MiG-23MF, MiG-25R, MiG-27 and five MiG-29s. The ageing 'Fishbed' lacks the glamour and capability of its newer stable-mates, but still has excellent performance and is numerically the most important type in service. The small size of the MiG-21 is particularly noteworthy.

Below: Single examples of all the MiG types in Indian Air Force service. Leading the formation is a No. 102 Squadron 'Trisonics' MiG-25R, followed by a No. 9 Squadron 'Wolfpack' MiG-27L, a No. 223 Squadron 'Tridents' MiG-29, and a No. 224 Squadron 'Warlords' MiG-23MF, with a No. 101 Squadron 'Falcons' MiG-21M bringing up the rear.

Above: Bedecked with yellow stars on its fin and rear fuselage, this MiG-21bis wears the distinctive black and yellow squadron badge of No. 24 Squadron, 'The Hunting Hawks'. Pilots often choose their own ACT colour scheme.

Below: Most of India's MiG-21bis aircraft wear an overall air superiority grey colour scheme, though its effectiveness is somewhat marred by the various squadron badges, high-vis national insignia and ACT markings.

Left: Scramble! Members of the 'Hunting Hawks' practise a rapid-reaction take-off. Even the fuel bowser wears the unit's black hawk insignia. Primary weapons for the MiG-21bis are the R-60 (AA-8 'Aphid') IR homing missile and the underfuselage cannon pod.

Right: The star in No. 8 Squadron's badge, as well as its 'Eighth Pursoot' nickname, commemorate early links with the USAAF during World War II. Most Indian MiG-21FLs wear an overall silver colour scheme.

Below: Two MiG-21bis of No. 37 Squadron, the 'Black Panthers', break away from the camera ship. The nearest aircraft carries a yellow lightning bolt along the length of its fuselage. A twin-barrelled GSh-23 cannon is carried under the forward fuselage.

Right: Three No. 101 Squadron 'Falcons' MiG-21Ms on patrol carry the sleek supersonic external fuel tanks designed for the aircraft. The various dots and stripes extend to the upper and lower surfaces of the wings. The MiG-21 remains a potent short-range interceptor and air superiority aircraft, and is also in service with India's neighbour Pakistan in its Chinese-built F-7P form.

Below: Based at Adampur alongside a MiG-23MF and a MiG-29 squadron, No. 101 Squadron includes this ageing MiG-21U 'Mongol', used for conversion and continuation training, and as a unit hack. The tiny nose intake of the original MiG-21 series is particularly evident here. The light weight of the 'Mongol' gives it sparkling performance, but it lacks range and endurance.

Right: No. 23 Squadron is known as the 'Cheetahs', and operates the MiG-21bis. A cheetah's head decorates the nose of the squadron's aircraft. The blue tail applied to this MiG-21bis for ACM training is showing some signs of wear and tear.

Above: A No. 4 Squadron MiG-21 with a camel-riding soldier in ceremonial dress. "What's the difference? The camel has greater range," joked one pilot. The Indian MiG-21bis production line produced the very last 'Fishbeds' built, while engines were also manufactured locally. The aircraft seems set to remain in service for many years, since replacement by the MiG-29 would be prohibitively expensive, and the future of the indigenous LCA is uncertain.

Below: Two 'Fishbeds' fly a tight echelon starboard at medium level. This pair of No. 4 Squadron MiG-21bis from Jaisalmer each wears a slightly different squadron badge. The squadron is known as the 'Orioles', a type of plumed tropical song bird, and this features in the unit marking. The MiG-21bis is reportedly a pleasant aircraft to fly, with relatively vice-free handling.

India's Fabulous 'Fishbeds'

Above: A MiG-21bis of No. 4 Squadron arms up prior to a sortie over the range. The cautionary sign and red flag warn people not to walk in front of the aircraft, whose Soviet UB-16-57 rocket pod is fully loaded with 16 unguided 57-mm rocket projectiles. Indian MiG-21s can carry a wide variety of bombs, rockets and missiles for use in the ground attack role, although they are used mainly for air defence duties. In the latter role, the 23-mm cannon is usually augmented by AA-2 'Atoll' air-to-air missiles.

Below: A No. 4 Squadron 'Orioles' MiG-21 lets fly with a full pod of 57-mm rockets over the range. While primarily tasked with air defence duties, India's MiG-21 squadrons frequently practise a secondary ground attack role, for which the 57-mm rocket is an ideal weapon. Firing a full rocket pod is an exhilarating experience, but the expense makes it a relatively rare event. It is more normal to fire single rockets, rather than salvos, during training. Live weapons training exercises are therefore extremely popular.

Right: Some of India's MiG-21bis fighters are camouflaged, like this aircraft, which wears the unit badge of No. 26 Squadron, 'The Warriors'. Some of the unit's aircraft are finished in an air defence grey colour scheme, and these have the word 'Warriors' along the fin leading edge. This aircraft's temporary camouflage paint is already beginning to flake away, especially on the rim of the nose intake and around the canopy frame.

Above: Camouflaged MiG-21bis aircraft are also operated by No. 3 Squadron 'Rattlers', based at Pathankot alongside the similarly equipped No. 15 Squadron. This aircraft carries the unit's distinctive rattlesnake and winged sword badge ahead of the fuselage, with another, larger snake ahead of the AoA sensor. The name 'Rattler' on the forward fuselage is applied to the individual aircraft, which here may be the squadron commander's. The black and yellow lightning flash tail decoration is for ACM training.

Above: Parked in front of its dispersed hardened aircraft shelter, this No. 3 Squadron MiG-21bis is nicknamed 'Mamba'. The camouflage paint scheme may indicate that the squadron has a primary close support or ground attack role, or may merely indicate a low-level air defence assignment. Little is known about the deployment of Indian Air Force squadrons, which can be (and often are) switched to a number of fully-equipped forward airfields.

Bell's AH-1

Cobra Family

Above: Laden with two seven-shot rocket pods and eight **TOW** missiles, a production **AH-1S** presents its ultra-slim frontal aspect to the camera.

Developed specifically as a helicopter gunship for use in Vietnam, the HueyCobra has demonstrated remarkable versatility and such tremendous growth potential that the aircraft is still in production more than 26 years after the first prototype made its maiden flight. Blooded in Vietnam, the Cobra went on to fight in Israel's various wars, and with the US Army and Marines in Grenada, Lebanon, Panama and, most recently, in the Gulf. An ongoing programme of modifications and upgrades seems certain to ensure that this remarkable helicopter will remain in service into the next century.

Below: The Bell Sioux Scout, Cobra progenitor.

L
ike many successful military aircraft the AH-1 Cobra, still fulfilling a vital front-line role after 24 years of front-line service, began life as a company-funded private venture. Less commonly, this private-venture type was originally seen purely as an interim type, and was ordered as such. As is so often the case, the more-sophisticated, more-capable definitive machine which the US Army thought it needed proved to be a spectacular failure, and the 'interim' helicopter was left to fill the gap. The AH-1 HueyCobra has done so admirably.

US Army experiments with armed helicopters, and the development of tactics and doctrine, began some years before the long and costly involvement in Vietnam. The French use of armed helicopters in Algeria was particularly influential. In 1960, the Army Tactical Mobility Requirements Board recommended the formation of an 'Air Assault Division', in which the helicopter completely replaced vehicles for transport, and which would include a number of armed escort helicopters. This led directly to the formation of the 1st Cavalry Division (Air-

mobile) and its early deployment to South East Asia to test the new concept. Thus, from the very beginning of the Vietnam War, the use of armed helicopters (mainly to escort troop-carriers) became routine. The then-new Bell UH-1 Iroquois was the most commonly used transport (or 'Slick') and 'gunship' type, armed with four M60 machine-guns, rocket pods, and sometimes heavier guns when used in the latter role. Rocket-armed UH-1s quickly became known as 'Hogs', while mixed gun- and rocket-armed aircraft earned the soubriquet 'Cobra'.

Above: An early AH-1G, complete with tinted transparencies, ripples off a pod of unguided 2.75-in rockets. It was not until the introduction of the AH-1Q that the Cobra gained a dedicated guided anti-armour weapon in the shape of the TOW missile. The tandem stepped cockpits gave both pilot and gunner an excellent view forward.

One of the earliest lessons to come out from early operations in Vietnam was that the heavily armed 'Hogs' and 'Cobras' were considerably slower than the troop-carrying 'Slicks' which they escorted – a far from ideal state of affairs since it increased the formation's exposure time to enemy fire. Bell's answer was a dedicated armed helicopter (the first in the world) which would have greater speed and manoeuvrability than the helicopters it was to escort, and which would carry a heavy weapon load. It revealed a mock-up of the D-225 'Iroquois Warrior' in June 1962. This was recognisably similar to the AH-1 we know today, with a tandem stepped cockpit housing pilot (rear) and gunner, and with weapons pylons on a stub wing and a nose-mounted weapons turret. (It also seemed to use UH-1 transmission and other components, making it popular at a time when commonality was becoming a powerful buzz-word.)

Proof of concept

The D-225 mock-up generated a great deal of interest, which Bell nurtured with a lightweight proof-of-concept helicopter, the Model 207 Sioux Scout, which was based on the airframe of an OH-13. This was underpowered and could not carry a worthwhile load, but it proved a useful demonstrator. When it was turned over to the 11th Air Assault Division for evaluation in January 1964, they were enthusiastic in their

Above: Possibly the first hover. The first prototype Cobra seen in its original configuration with retractable landing gear and ventral fin. The starboard side transparency over the rear cockpit has been left off. The production AH-1G differed only in small details.

Left: The Bell D-225 'Iroquois Warrior' mock-up, complete with gunner's pantograph-mounted sight. French AS11 anti-tank missiles were later fitted to the mock-up, which also carried a streamlined 20-mm cannon pod below the fuselage. The nose turret was designed to accommodate a grenade launcher.

recommendations that a scaled-up version should be developed.

Meanwhile, the US Army had become convinced of the need for a dedicated armed helicopter, and in August 1964 issued a request for proposals to tender for the Advanced Aerial Fire Support System requirement. This specified a very advanced, long-range, high-performance, highly capable aircraft, which would inevitably require an extended development period. Bell responded to the AAFSS requirement with the D262, but when Bell realised they were not going to win the competition they pressed on, from March 1965, with building a prototype of their private-venture Iroquois Warrior (by now known as the Model 209), since they knew that the US Army desperately needed an effective aircraft quickly, accurately forecasting that an interim type might be necessary.

Simultaneously, the Army decided that it did need an interim type to fill the gap until the projected 1970 in-service date of the AAFSS. To meet an early in-service date, the Army decided that it needed an adaptation of an existing design, and therefore considered armed versions of the Sea King, the Chinook and the Sea Sprite, as well as Bell's Model 209, which was disingenuously described as a 'modified UH-1'. Bell backed up this description with a promise that the Model 209 could be procured quickly, perhaps even being substituted for UH-1 gunships already ordered.

The Model 209 was formally presented as an interim type in August 1965, and within one month the prototype was flying. The Model 209 was formally selected on 7 April 1966, when the US Army placed a $2.7-million contract for two prototypes, with a $20.5-million production contract for 110 aircraft following six days later. The success of Bell's fiction that the 'new' type was merely a modified UH-1 can be gauged by the fact that the new aircraft was referred to as the UH-1H in the initial contract.

New names

The Army traditionally named its helicopters after American Indian tribes, and might initially have wanted the new attack helicopter to follow this tradition. At the time, the Army was engaged in litigation with Piper, who were also naming their aircraft after Indian tribes, leaving the way clear for a new name. The UH-1 (originally designated HU-1) was universally, if unofficially, known as the Huey, while the gunship versions were already known as Cobras. Bell felt that the name HueyCobra had a good ring to it, as well as providing a link with the wartime Airacobra and Kingcobra. A dictionary definition of the Cobra as a 'snake which resides in Far Eastern climes, detecting its enemy visually or by sensing body heat, striking quickly, spitting venom with deadly accuracy' sold Bell on the name, which was formally adopted in July 1966, along with the new

Above: An AH-1W lets fly with an AIM-9 Sidewinder air-to-air missile. This weapon gives the nimble little Cobra a useful self-defence or anti-helicopter capability. An anti-radar Sidearm can be carried in the same position.

Right: Competitor to the equally unsuccessful Sikorsky S-67 Blackhawk, the stillborn Model 309 KingCobra flew as single- (seen here) and twin-engined prototypes, but was not adopted for production in either form. Many of the advanced features developed for the Model 309 were subsequently adopted for later production Cobra variants, however.

Bell's AH-1 Cobra Family

Left: The Cobra's final sunset lies many years away. The type proved that it is still a viable front-line tool during the war in the Gulf, and in both US and foreign hands the AH-1 will continue to have an important part to play.

Below: Both the US Army and the US Marine Corps deployed Cobras to the Gulf for participation in Desert Storm, and most were painted in appropriate desert camouflage schemes. US Army units operated the AH-1F (seen here) while the Marines deployed both AH-1Ws and AH-1Js. The trusty TOW missile and the M197 cannon were the main weapons used.

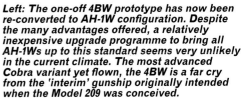

Left: The one-off 4BW prototype has now been re-converted to AH-1W configuration. Despite the many advantages offered, a relatively inexpensive upgrade programme to bring all AH-1Ws up to this standard seems very unlikely in the current climate. The most advanced Cobra variant yet flown, the 4BW is a far cry from the 'interim' gunship originally intended when the Model 209 was conceived.

designation AH-1.

The production AH-1G retained the 27-in chord main rotor and dynamic components of the UH-1C, with a new 3-ft wide fuselage incorporating a tandem cockpit and a nose weapons turret. Stub wings were used as attachment points for the weapons pylons. The twin-bladed main rotor of the UH-1C had already proved to be tough, durable and fairly resistant to battle damage, as well as being cheap and simple to manufacture and service. The stabilisor bar fitted to Hueys was deleted, however, necessitating the provision of an electronic stability-augmentation system.

The Cobra reached Vietnam in August 1967, and quickly began operations. Often operating in conjunction with OH-6 scout helicopters, the AH-1s built up an impressive record, but the basic aircraft seemed to have little application to the European environment once the Vietnam War ground to a close. Such was the versatility of the Cobra, however, that new versions had already been developed, with new sensors and new weapons, which quite literally transformed the aircraft. The design and development of new Cobras have continued almost unabated ever since, and the AH-1's origins as an 'interim' type have been largely forgotten.

Bell's AH-1 Cobra Variants

Bell AH-1 Cobra single-engined variants

The US Army's Cobras have constantly been modified and refined to meet changing requirements and to deal with ever more capable threats. This has resulted in a steady stream of ever more capable variants, sharing only the same basic configuration, and with improved avionics, systems, engine and armament. The bigger twin-engined variants designed to meet the needs of the Marines represent almost a different family of aircraft; related, but with many different features.

Model 209 prototype

The Model 209 prototype was designed and built as a private venture, but its superiority over the armed versions of the Chinook, Huey, Sea King and Sea Sprite quickly won it official backing and a production order. Rolled out on 5 September 1965, and flown two days later, the aircraft quickly demonstrated a record-breaking speed of 175 kt.

This superb achievement was due entirely to the alliance of a powerful and proven dynamic system with a minimal-drag fuselage. Indeed, the Model 209 was the first design to ever really tackle the problem of aerodynamic drag in a rotary-wing craft, at a stroke introducing a new configuration that would be copied by designers of attack helicopters to the present day.

With its broad twin-blade rotor, the overall impression of the Model 209 demonstrated some parentage from the UH-1, but the very slim fuselage and purposeful lines suggested a far more ferocious animal. Bell called the aircraft the HueyCobra to suggest both sides of its creation, but only the latter half stuck with the aircraft. In Vietnam the venomous nature of the beast often resulted in it being referred to as simply the 'Snake'.

The first prototype was flown with a retractable skid landing gear, since it was initially thought that this would give better streamlining and a better turret arc. These factors were initially felt to outweigh the disadvantages of complexity and higher weight.

The aircraft served for nearly six years, undertaking a variety of marketing and experimental tasks. During this time it was brought up to virtually stock AH-1G configuration, but was modified back to its original configuration for retirement to the George Patton Museum at Fort Knox.

It has been stated (by Charlie Siebel, one of the Cobra's joint designers) that there was also a second Model 209, with a fixed undercarriage from the start, and with a stronger wing to allow heavier weapons to be carried.

Above: An early production standard AH-1G, with clear nose cone accommodating twin landing lights.

Below left: The Model 209 prototype, seen during an early test flight with landing gear retracted. The retractable skids allowed the nose-mounted gun a greater arc of fire.

Below: The Model 209 prototype in later configuration, with M197 cannon, enlarged ammunition bay, TOW missiles, and landing gear fixed in the extended position. The ventral fin was removed early on.

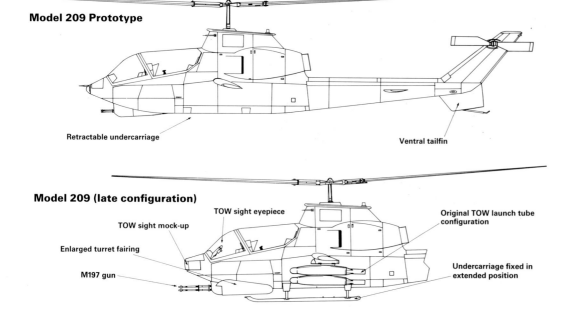

Model 209 Prototype

Retractable undercarriage

Ventral tailfin

Model 209 (late configuration)

TOW sight eyepiece

TOW sight mock-up

Enlarged turret fairing

M197 gun

Original TOW launch tube configuration

Undercarriage fixed in extended position

Above: The prototype (nearest) and first two production AH-1s. The prototype has already lost its ventral fin, and the landing gear is fixed, with non-standard fairings. It also carries a test instrumentation boom.

AH-1G

During flight tests of the Model 209 prototype, it had been found that stores could be jettisoned throughout the flight envelope with the skids extended, and that their retraction gave no useful increase in turret travel or drag reduction. Accordingly, simple fixed skids were used on the production AH-1G, which also dispensed with the ventral tailfin initially fitted to the Model 209.

Other things omitted from the production AH-1G included the armoured glass windscreen, which was felt to impose an unacceptable weight penalty.

On 7 April 1965, following the success of the Model 209, the US Army placed a $2.7-million contract for two more Cobras for qualification and testing, while a production order for 110 more followed days later. Deployment of the new aircraft was accorded a very high priority, and the NETT (New Equipment Training Team) formed at Fort Hood was sent to Bien Hoa in late August 1967.

The AH-1G proved extremely successful in Vietnam, even operating at night in conjunction with searchlight-equipped Hueys. One hundred and fifty seven were lost to AAA and small-arms fire, four to SAMs and 12 during VC attacks on airfields. A further 109 were lost in non-combat-related accidents in Vietnam. This represented a relatively low attrition rate for a front-line combat helicopter during that conflict. Exact loss figures are uncertain, since many aircraft were rebuilt several times.

During its production life, the AH-1G was constantly refined. Early aircraft had tinted canopies in an effort to reduce the greenhouse effect of the large canopy, but on later aircraft these were replaced by a more efficient air conditioning system. The landing lights were also relocated from their original position set into the nose to a retractable housing behind the gun turret.

Early AH-1Gs were fitted with an Emerson Electric TAT-102A turret, containing a single GAU-2B (formerly known as the XM-134) six-barrelled 7.62-mm Minigun, with 8,000 rounds of ammunition. This turret was used due to the initial availability problems which afflicted the intended turret, the dual weapon XM28.

The TAT-102A was soon replaced by the XM28 turret, and this could mount two weapons, either the GAU-2B/A Minigun (with 4,000 rounds per gun) or the XM129 40-mm grenade launcher (with 300 rounds per launcher), or a mixed pair. The turret could be trained through a 230° arc, and could be elevated to 25° or depressed to 60°.

Although effective, the 7.62-mm Minigun was always felt to lack range and stopping power, and carriage of further 7.62-mm weapons in M18 pods did nothing to overcome these shortcomings. One solution to the problem was 2.75-in rockets, but these never proved very accurate in the hands of squadron pilots, although their shortcomings were camouflaged by the fact that the very skilled, highly experienced instructors who inevitably performed firepower demonstrations could put an FFAR in a pickle barrel. Accordingly, in late 1969, six AH-1Gs were fitted with a single M35 20-mm cannon on the port underwing pylon, fed with 950 rounds of ammunition carried in streamlined boxes mounted on the skids. This weapon had a rate of fire of 750 rpm, compared with 4,000 rpm for the Minigun or 400 rpm for the grenade launcher. The US Army ordered 350 conversion kits.

This weapon had a range in the order of 3,000 yd, but vibration and muzzle blast

were considerable. Aircraft therefore had to have strengthened panels fitted, and co-pilots had to hold the canopy shut when the weapon was fired! Development of a new, turret-mounted, large-calibre gun was very slow, and was not completed in time to be applied to the AH-1G.

All but the earliest AH-1Gs featured a new tail rotor location, on the starboard side of the fin. Switching from the left-hand side of the fin to the right-hand side finally cured the yaw stability problem which had afflicted the prototype and early production AH-1Gs. Some early aircraft were modified to receive the new tail rotor configuration in Vietnam, using field modification kits.

The AH-1G always remained a relatively simple daylight-only weapon in front-line service, although there were two attempts to give the aircraft a degree of night/all-weather capability. The SMASH (South-east Asia Multi-sensor Armament Sub-system for HueyCobra) system consisted of an Aerojet Electro Systems AN/AAQ-5 nose-mounted SSPI (Sighting System Passive Infra-red), similar to a modern FLIR and an Emerson Electric AN/APQ-137B moving-target indicator high-resolution radar, mounted in a pod under the starboard wing. The SMASH trials aircraft retained its M28 turret, M35 20-mm cannon and seven-shot M158 rocket launchers. The system was not considered a success. The CONFICS (CObra Night FIre Control System) used low-light television to control the gun turret, but proved no more successful than SMASH.

The AH-1G was evaluated by a number of countries, including Britain, Australia and New Zealand, but the only export customers have been the Spanish navy, which took delivery of eight M35-equipped aircraft (designated Z.14) as shore-based aircraft to support coastal fast patrol boats in 1972, retiring them in 1985, and Israel, which took 12. Thirty eight US Army AH-1Gs were transferred to the US Marine

Corps, which used them operationally in Vietnam prior to receiving the AH-1J.

A handful of AH-1G Cobras were used by the US Customs Service between December 1981 and May 1986 for night interceptions of drug-running aircraft and boats, often guided by a FLIR-equipped OV-10D. The aircraft, known as Snakes, were stripped of armour and armament and carried a powerful searchlight in the redundant turret. They were replaced by modified UH-60 Black Hawks. A number of AH-1Gs relegated to the training role were redesignated TAH-1G. All surviving AH-1Gs in front-line US Army and National Guard service (of 1,119 delivered) have been re-worked to AH-1S, AH-1E or AH-1F standards.

Left: This gaudy AH-1G was used to support a military research programme in the Arctic. It has the early landing light configuraton (below) and port-mounted tail rotor.

Left: The pointed fairing above the landing skids identifies this aircraft as an AH-1G/M35. Armed with rockets and fitted with the sugar scoop exhaust suppressor, this AH-1G was one of those deployed to Vietnam, where it is seen here hover-taxiing at its base.

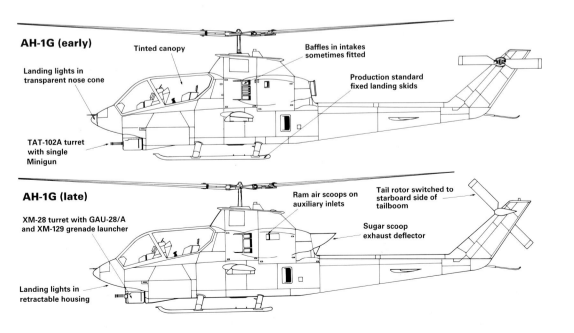

AH-1G (early)

Tinted canopy

Baffles in intakes sometimes fitted

Landing lights in transparent nose cone

Production standard fixed landing skids

TAT-102A turret with single Minigun

AH-1G (late)

Ram air scoops on auxiliary inlets

Tail rotor switched to starboard side of tailboom

XM-28 turret with GAU-28/A and XM-129 grenade launcher

Sugar scoop exhaust deflector

Landing lights in retractable housing

AH-1G continued

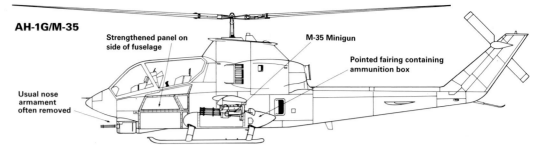

AH-1G/M-35

Strengthened panel on side of fuselage

Usual nose armament often removed

M-35 Minigun

Pointed fairing containing ammunition box

Above: The strengthening anti-blast panels fitted to the port forward fuselage of M35-armed Cobras is clearly visible here. This aircraft has had the weapons removed from its undernose turret, lessening the effect of the weight penalty imposed by the M35 cannon.

Right: The M35 was a six-barrelled Gatling-type rotary cannon. A single such weapon was installed under the port wing of some 35 AH-1Gs, some of which served until well into the 1980s. Ammunition was carried in two streamlined sponsons mounted above the landing gear skid supports, with a cross feed below the fuselage.

Left and far left: Two views of the M35 mounted on an AH-1G. The whole M35 system weighed almost 544 kg (1,200 lb), but proved devastatingly effective. The installation was limited to the AH-1G, later variants gaining a much greater increase in killing range by using the TOW missile. Spanish AH-1Gs carry the M35 cannon.

Below: During the 1960s, when the US military went in for contrived acronyms, one AH-1G/M35 was modified under the ENSURE (Expedite Non-Standard Urgent Requirement for Equipment) programme as the SMASH (Southeast Asia Multi-sensor Armament Sub-system for HueyCobra) testbed. This consisted of an AN/AAQ-5 FLIR/SSPI (Sighting Station Passive Infra-red) in the nose, with a podded AN/APQ-137 moving target indicator radar in a pod on the starboard wing.

Right: The sole AH-1G delivered to NASA initially flew from the Langley Research Center as NASA 541, and was engaged in many trials, including attempts to reduce rotor and engine noise. During its use by NASA the aircraft gained a distinctive white colour scheme. Moving to Ames, where it served mainly as a chase aircraft, the helicopter became NASA 736, before finally returning to the US Army and a rebuild to AH-1S standards.

Original left-hand tail rotor

Emerson Electric AN/APQ-137B moving target indicator and high resolution radar pod

AH-1G SMASH

Aerojet Electrosystems AN/AAQ-5 nose-mounted SSPI

Nose landing light deleted

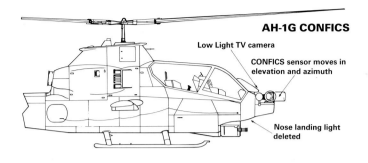

AH-1G CONFICS

Low Light TV camera

CONFICS sensor moves in elevation and azimuth

Nose landing light deleted

Above: A close-up view of the Low Light Level TV sensor mounted in the nose of the CONFICS (CObra Night FIre Control System) testbed.

Left and right: Port and starboard side views of the CONFICS AH-1G. The equipment proved singularly unsuccessful, and the Army went back to using flares and searchlights while it waited for better technology!

JAH-1G

The single JAH-1G (71-20985) was an armament testbed converted to fire and guide the AGM-114 Hellfire ATM. The first Hellfire firing from the JAH-1G took place on 21 October 1978. This followed exhaustive trials at the Hunter Liggett Military Reservation in 1974, during the AH-64 development programme, when a number of Cobras fitted with the Rockwell AAD-2 Airborne Laser Tracker were used to launch Hellfire, while two others designated targets. The latter aircraft were fitted with the Ford Aerospace Airborne Laser Locator Designator (ALLD, later re-designated ATAFCS – Airborne Target Acquisition Fire Control System). One of these ATAFCS-equipped aircraft was the YAH-1R. While the US Marines have chosen to modify their Cobras to be able to use Hellfire, the US Army have not, leaving their Cobras with the less useful TOW system while AH-64 Apaches carry AGM-114. The JAH-1G was later used as the test aircraft for the XM197 gun turret.

AH-1G ALLD

Ford Aerospace Airborne Laser Locator Designator (ALLD) pod

Inactivated nose turret

AH-1G ATAFCS

Re-packaged nose-mounted ATAFCS sensor

Inactivated nose turret

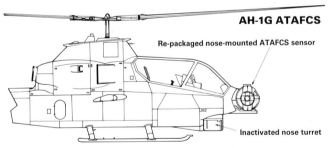

Above: During trials of the AGM-114 Hellfire missile, a number of Cobras were used as launch and designation platforms. This AH-1G carried a Ford Aerospace ATAFCS designator in the nose.

Left: ATAFCS/ALLD is carried on the starboard wing of an AH-1G Hellfire designator aircraft.

Left: The ALLD (later re-designated ATAFCS) pod contained an Aeronautic precision stabilised sight, an International Laser Systems designator, a Rockwell spot tracker, a Texas Instruments FLIR and a Lear Siegler TV.

Above: Two AH-1Gs were used to launch Hellfires, and one of these was later given full AGM-114 capability to become the JAH-1G. For a time a 'Hellfire Cobra' seemed a realistic production option.

YAH-1Q

The helicopter's potential as an anti-tank weapon was obvious from quite an early stage, and it was widely accepted that a well-armed attack helicopter could come close to being a flying tank, since it would be mobile, manoeuvrable and pack a heavy punch. The first dedicated anti-armour weapon applied to a helicopter was the French AS11, an adaptation of a wire-guided infantry anti-tank missile. This missile proved disappointing when used operationally, and in Vietnam 115 firings

resulted in only two tank kills. Unguided rockets proved similarly ineffective against armoured targets.

The TOW (Tube-launched, Optically-tracked, Wire-guided) missile was similarly adapted from a ground-launched weapon, but its longer range and heavy warhead made it deadlier than the AS11. Under development for the ambitious AH-56 Cheyenne, TOW was sent to Vietnam for operational testing, carried by UH-1s, and quickly notched up 26 tank and 33 other

kills, including bunkers and barges, in 81 firings.

Bell quickly realised that a TOW-armed AH-1 would be a potent anti-armour weapon, and a cheap alternative to the troubled AH-56, and began development of the TOW-armed Model 309 as a private venture. The Kingcobra did not attract a production order, though, and the Army issued their AAH Requirement that led to the AH-64 Apache. In the interim, in March 1972, Bell were instructed to

investigate the integration of the TOW missile with the existing AH-1 Cobra under the Improved Cobra Armament Programme (ICAP). Eight AH-1Gs were therefore fitted with the XM26 TSU (Telescopic Sighting Unit) launch and guidance system jointly developed by Bell and the Hughes Corporation for service trials under the designation YAH-1Q. Three hundred and forty seven TOW missiles were fired by these aircraft between February 1973 and January 1975.

AH-1Q

Even before the TOW/YAH-1Q trials were complete, Bell received an order to convert 101 AH-1Gs to AH-1Q configuration, with the M65 TSU (the production designation of the XM26), Sperry Univac helmet-mounted sights for both crew members, and provision for up to eight TOW missiles. The helmet-mounted sights were used to guide both the gun turret and the M65 TSU, giving much improved acquisition time. Only 92 AH-1Q conversions were actually produced by Bell, and the first was delivered on 10 January 1975.

Some sources suggest that some of Israel's Cobras were delivered in AH-1Q configuration. With the increased weight of armament and TSU, the AH-1Q was dramatically underpowered, and the 'sugar scoop' exhaust outlet and associated auxiliary inlet scoops, fitted to some late AH-1Gs, were therefore deleted.

Right: An early AH-1Q launches a TOW missile.

YAH-1R/YAH-1S

During the YAH-1Q trials, the TOW missile proved extremely successful, but the aircraft itself was felt to be severely underpowered, especially for the kind of Nap-Of-Earth (NOE) tactics being developed for TOW. These fears were confirmed by service experience with the production AH-1Q. In 1975, a high-level report had recommended updating the whole Cobra force pending the service entry of the AAH, and this was accepted. Accordingly, in an effort to provide more power, the ICAM (Improved Cobra Agility and Manoeuvrability) programme was instituted. Under this programme the 1,800-shp Lycoming T53-L-703 was flight tested in a rebuilt AH-1G (70-15936), redesignated as the YAH-1R, and in a

converted AH-1Q (70-16019), which was redesignated YAH-1S. Both aircraft also incorporated the proven drivetrain developed for the 'Huey Tug' and used on the Model 309 and AH-1J International.

Right: The YAH-1S was a converted AH-1Q used to test the 1,800-shp T53-L-703 engine under the ICAM (Improved Cobra Agility and Manoeuvrability) programme.

Below: The similar YAH-1R was a converted AH-1G, and thus lacked TOW equipment. It is seen here with prominent photographic calibration marks on the fuselage.

Improved AH-1S

In December 1975, the Army published a report which suggested updating the AH-1 pending the service entry of the new AAH (Advanced Attack Helicopter). This led directly to the ICAM (Improved Cobra Agility and Manoeuvrability) programme, under which all 92 surviving AH-1Qs and 198 AH-1Gs were modified to a new standard. Bell and the US Army agreed on a whole series of modifications for the AH-1 and these were incorporated in several stages, both by modification and retrofit, and on the production line.

Right: The Improved AH-1S was basically an AH-1Q with the uprated T53-L-703 engine, or an AH-1G with that and TOW equipment. This aircraft has been fitted with Kaman K-747 blades.

The first and most important features of the upgrade were the provision of TOW capability and the use of the more powerful T53-L-703 engine tested in the YAH-1R and YAH-1S. This used improved materials and could run at higher

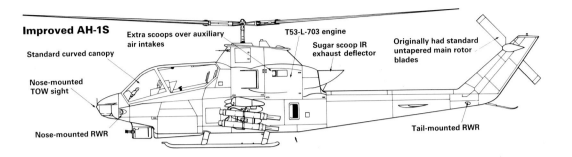

Improved AH-1S

Standard curved canopy

Nose-mounted TOW sight

Nose-mounted RWR

Extra scoops over auxiliary air intakes

T53-L-703 engine

Sugar scoop IR exhaust deflector

Originally had standard untapered main rotor blades

Tail-mounted RWR

Below: An AH-1S dashes for cover during exercises over the North German Plain. TOW launchers are carried, but missile tubes are not fitted, giving them a curiously empty appearance. The T53-L-703 engine gave sufficient power for the TOW-armed Cobra to manoeuvre at low level, and also allowed the sugar scoop exhaust suppressor (omitted from the critically underpowered AH-1Q) to be reintroduced.

temperatures, as well as being fitted with an upgraded fuel control system. Output was increased from a theoretical maximum of 1,400 shp to 1,800 shp, which translated into a take-off rating of 1,290 shp, compared with the AH-1G's 1,100 shp. All 92 AH-1Qs were re-engined to bring them up to this baseline standard, as were 198 AH-1Gs, which also received TOW compatibility. Sixty one were Germany-based US Army AH-1Qs and these were brought up to Improved AH-1S standard by Dornier at Oberpfaffenhofen between May 1978 and February 1979. The Improved AH-1S has been known simply as the AH-1S since 1988.

Production AH-1S (redesignated AH-1P in 1988)

Production of the TOW-equipped, up-engined Cobra has been in three basic stages (known to Bell as Steps), and the resulting variants have been distinguished by three prefixes, and later by three new designations. Under Step 1, 100 new-build AH-1Ss were delivered to the US Army between March 1977 and September 1978. These aircraft differed from the Improved AH-1S in having a new 'flat plate' canopy, an improved instrument panel for Nap-of-Earth operation, CONUS navigational equipment, a radar altimeter, an APR-39 radar-warning receiver, and a further uprated engine and transmission system. From the 67th aircraft all were fitted with the tapered Kaman K-747 composite main rotor blades. These have

Production AH-1S/AH-1P

Improved instrument panel layout

Flat pane canopy

CONUS nav equipment

Radar altimeter

Kaman K-747 tapered composite blades on 67th and subsequent aircraft

Uprated engine and transmission

also been retro-fitted to all surviving S (and possibly even late G) airframes. The older blades were temporarily re-fitted to some aircraft (including the AH-1Es and AH-1Fs)

in the mid-1980s, when the K-747 blades started losing tips through bonding failures. This problem was quickly resolved.

Below: The Production AH-1S (now AH-1P) was the first Cobra variant to feature the new low-glint 'flat plate' canopy. Most were fitted with tapered Kaman K-747 blades.

Up-Gun AH-1S

(redesignated AH-1E in 1988)

Step 2 of the AH-1S production programme covered 98 new-build aircraft. These received all the same modifications as had been applied to Step 1 aircraft, and also received the Universal gun turret and M197 20-mm three-barrelled cannon, a lightweight derivative of the M61, with a rate of fire of 730 rpm. This has a field of fire of up to 110° on each side of the nose, and can be elevated to 20.5° and depressed to 50°. It carries 750 rounds of ammunition. A new Baldwin Electronics XM138 wing stores management sub-system was also fitted, allowing rockets to be selected and fired singly or salvoed. The whole modernised armament package was given the acronym ECAS (Enhanced Cobra Armament System). This generated a need for extra electrical power, so a 10-KVA alternator was fitted, in a bulged housing on the port side, ahead of the engine intake. Two ECAS-standard AH-1Ss were supplied to Japan for evaluation, where they were subsequently brought up to AH-1F standards.

Up-Gun AH-1S/AH-1E

Bulge housing 10-KVA alternator (port side only)

Universal gun turret with M197 20-mm cannon

Right: Down in the weeds. The Up-Gun AH-1S (now known as the AH-1E) was the first single-engined Cobra with the M197 20-mm cannon, a lightweight three-barrelled derivative of the M61.

Modernized AH-1S/AH-1S (MC)

(redesignated AH-1F in 1988)

Step 3 of the AH-1S production programme, and representing the current production single-engined Cobra, was the Modernized AH-1S. Ninety nine were built for the US Army between 1979 and 1986, with an additional 50 for the National Guard, while 378 AH-1Gs were rebuilt to the same standard between November 1979 and June 1982 (this total includes 42 TAH-1S trainers). This variant remains in production (at the rate of 3 per month) for

export, while Fuji in Japan continues to produce the aircraft under licence (70 have been funded for the JGSDF). Customers for the AH-1F include Israel (30), Jordan (24), Pakistan (20 plus 10 options), South Korea (42 plus 28 options) and Thailand (4). All AH-1P and AH-1E improvements are incorporated, to which are added an exhaust IR suppressor, an AN/ALQ-144 active IRCM jammer, closed-circuit refuelling, new secure voice

Below: The gunner's cockpit of the Modernized AH-1S (now AH-1F) is dominated by the eyepiece for the TSU for the TOW missile. Dual controls are not fitted, so if the pilot in the back seat takes a hit . . .

Below: The rear cockpit of the AH-1F incorporates a Kaiser Head-Up Display for the pilot, but is otherwise something of an ergonomic nightmare, with a profusion of small analogue instruments vying for attention.

Above: Seen from head-on, the AH-1F's low-speed sensor probe is clearly visible, projecting from the starboard side of the cockpit. The top-of-the-line AH-1F has been exported to Israel, Japan, Jordan, South Korea, Thailand and Pakistan.

communications, an IFF transponder and a Doppler navigation system. Most importantly, the AH-1F has an entirely new fire control sub-system, with a Hughes laser rangefinder and a ballistics computer, and a Kaiser HUD for the pilot. A bulge on the leading edge of the sail was to have accommodated a Rockwell AN/AAS-32 spot tracker, but this was never fitted. A low-speed sensor probe is fitted to the starboard forward fuselage, and this serves the Marconi Avionics Air Data System.

The AH-1F has been subject to a series of upgrades and modifications. These have included the fitting of a new engine air filter, a redesigned swashplate, AN/ARV-2 laser-warning system and improved stability-control augmentation system. Provision has also been made for aircrew to use the M-43 NBC respirator. C-FLEX (Cobra Fleet Life EXtension), ATAS (Air-To-Air Stinger) and C-Nite (Cobra Night-attack) modification programmes have also been incorporated, although C-Nite has only been applied to 50 US Army aircraft and is available as a retrofit for export customers.

Further updates are possible, and a Cobra Update Package is ready for launch, depending on customer demand. This was developed jointly by Bell and Textron Lycoming, and consists of a conversion kit to uprate the T53-L-703 to -70X standard, with a rating of 2,000 shp, a 46-ft diameter Bell 412 four-bladed main rotor, with a composite yoke replacing the normal titanium hub, a stretched tailboom (by 20 in) and a needle-bearing tail rotor (as used on Israeli Cobras and on the Bell 412). To these are added a digital three-axis stability-augmentation system, reliability and maintainability improvements. These will allow the aircraft to carry 1,000 lb more in payload and to manoeuvre down to below 0.5 *g*. Performance will also be significantly improved.

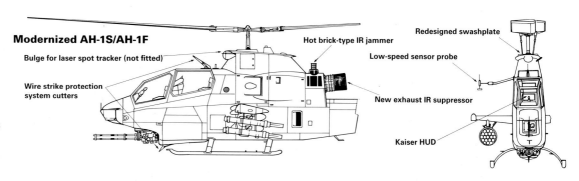

Modernized AH-1S/AH-1F

Bulge for laser spot tracker (not fitted)

Wire strike protection system cutters

Hot brick-type IR jammer

Redesigned swashplate

Low-speed sensor probe

New exhaust IR suppressor

Kaiser HUD

Above: An AH-1F (nearest) and an AH-1W on the production line. Differences are already visible.

*Above: An AH-1F armed with rocket pods and **TOW** missiles, and wearing the desert sand colour scheme adopted during **Operation Desert Shield.***

Above right: A brand new AH-1F (destined for Jordan) is test flown at Fort Worth. The colour scheme of natural metal and zinc chromate primer shows up airframe details to advantage.

Right: All Israeli Cobras wear an inverted yellow 'V' recognition marking.

Bell AH-1F Cobra

The Royal Jordanian Air Force received some 24 AH-1F Cobras, and their associated BGM-71 TOW anti-tank missiles, in a $196-million deal signed in 1981. The Cobras are still operational with Nos 10 and 12 Squadrons, which are variously reported as being located at Amman's King Abdullah air base or at King Faisal air base at Jafr. The AH-1s represented the air arm's first attack helicopter type, and Nos 10 and 12 Squadrons were newly formed to operate the aircraft when they arrived in 1985. Israel's acquisition of the AH-64 Apache has led to Jordanian desires for more anti-tank and anti-helicopter helicopters.

Colour scheme

This AH-1 wears the distinctive desert camouflage colour scheme of the Royal Jordanian Air Force. This consists of the standard tan and brown desert colours used on Iranian and Israeli (tan only) Cobras, in conjunction with forest green and the darker US Army aircraft green (on the nose and wingtips). National insignia (in the form of the air force roundel in Arabic, black, green, white and red) is carried very small on the sides of the nose.

Bell 'Modernized' AH-1F HueyCobra

1 M65 Laser Augmented Airborne TOW (LAAT)
2 Sight visual position indicator
3 Gimballed sight mounting
4 Laser electronics unit
5 Forward AN/APR-39 radar warning receiver, port and starboard
6 Cannon barrels
7 M197 20-mm three-barrelled rotary cannon
8 Cannon elevation control gear
9 Swivelling gun turret mounting
10 Azimuth control gear ring
11 Ammunition feed chute
12 Co-pilot/gunner's instrument panel
13 AN/APX-100 lightweight IFF unit
14 Instrument panel shroud
15 Windscreen rain dispersal air ducts
16 Flat plate windscreen panels
17 Stand-by compass
18 Rear view mirror
19 Sighting system viewfinder
20 Sight control handle and trigger
21 Starboard side cyclic pitch control lever
22 Co-pilot/gunner's seat
23 Seat armour
24 Safety harness
25 Cockpit side window/entry hatch
26 Entry hatch handle
27 Port console mounted collective pitch control lever
28 Energy absorbing seat mountings
29 Boarding step
30 Ammunition magazine, 750 rounds
31 Ammunition bay access door, port and starboard
32 Automatic flight control system equipment (AFCS)
33 Lateral equipment ducting
34 Armoured cockpit sidewalling
35 Control linkages
36 Port side console panel
37 Anti-torque rudder pedals
38 Collective pitch control lever
39 Cyclic pitch control column
40 Pilot's instrument panel shroud
41 Head-up display
42 Co-pilot/gunner's helmet mounted sight attachment
43 Low speed omni-directional air data sensor system probe
44 Cockpit roof glazing
45 Starboard TOW missile
launchers
46 Pilot's starboard side entry hatch
47 Starboard side console panel
48 Seat armour
49 Pilot's seat
50 HF aerial rail
51 DF loop aerial
52 Skin panelling coated with radar absorbent material
53 Upper fuselage equipment bay
54 Generator
55 Hydraulic system reservoir
56 Control linkage mixing unit
57 Position of refuelling connection on starboard side
58 Forward fuselage self-sealing tank, total fuel capacity 980 litres (259 US gal)
59 Fuel tank access panel
60 Crash-resistant bag-type fuel tanks
61 Landing skid front strut
62 Ventral Doppler antenna
63 Fuel system equipment
bay
64 Port inboard stores pylon
65 Port stub wing construction
66 Stub wing attachment joints
67 Gearbox oil sump
68 Wing/fuselage/gearbox main frame
69 Anti-vibration gearbox mounting
70 Alternator
71 Engine air intake
72 Rotor head contol jack (three)
73 Gearbox input shaft
74 Main gearbox
75 Swash plate mechanism
76 Rotor head torque link
77 Pitot head
78 Fresh air intake
79 Starboard wing tip stores pylon
80 Laser spot tracker housing
81 Rotor head fairing
82 Rotor blade root attachment joints
83 Drag links
84 Blade pitch control links
85 Teetering rotor head attachment
86 Blade pitch control rods
87 Main rotor mast
88 Anti-collision light
89 Oil tank vent
90 Main oil tank
91 Oil filler cap
92 Engine intake particle separation plenum
93 Fireproof bulkhead
94 Fuselage upper longeron
95 Rear self-sealing crashproof
fuel tank
96 Fireproof engine mounting deck
97 Engine mounting struts
98 Engine fuel control equipment
99 Avco-Lycoming T53-L-703 turboshaft engine
100 Engine turbine section
101 Rotor head tail fairing
102 Exhaust air mixing intake grille
103 Infra-red jammer unit
104 All-composite main rotor blade
105 Laminated glass-fibre main spar
106 Honeycomb core construction
107 Laminated glass fibre skin panelling
108 Exhaust mixer air plug
109 Infra-red suppression exhaust nozzle

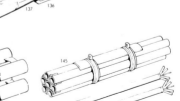

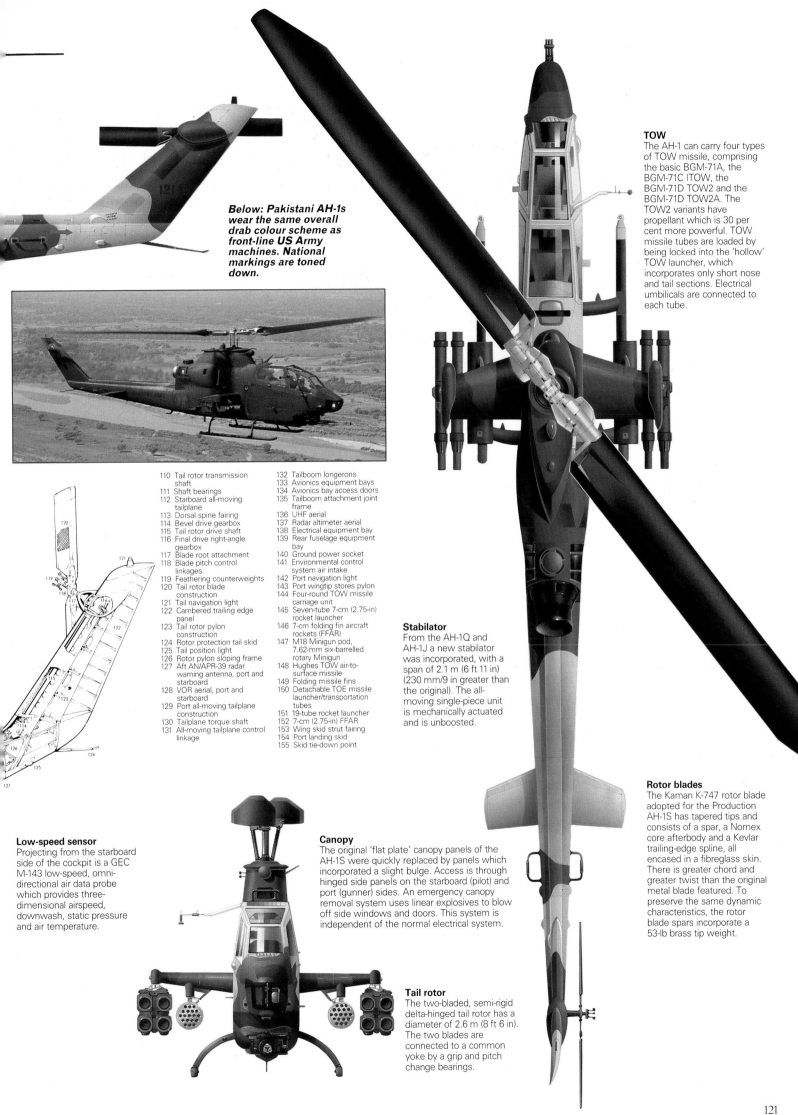

TOW
The AH-1 can carry four types of TOW missile, comprising the basic BGM-71A, the BGM-71C ITOW, the BGM-71D TOW2 and the BGM-71D TOW2A. The TOW2 variants have propellant which is 30 per cent more powerful. TOW missile tubes are loaded by being locked into the 'hollow' TOW launcher, which incorporates only short nose and tail sections. Electrical umbilicals are connected to each tube.

Below: Pakistani AH-1s wear the same overall drab colour scheme as front-line US Army machines. National markings are toned down.

110 Tail rotor transmission shaft
111 Shaft bearings
112 Starboard all-moving tailplane
113 Dorsal spine fairing
114 Bevel drive gearbox
115 Tail rotor drive shaft
116 Final drive right-angle gearbox
117 Blade root attachment
118 Blade pitch control linkages
119 Feathering counterweights
120 Tail rotor blade construction
121 Tail navigation light
122 Cambered trailing edge panel
123 Tail rotor pylon construction
124 Rotor protection tail skid
125 Tail position light
126 Rotor pylon sloping frame
127 Aft AN/APR-39 radar warning antenna, port and starboard
128 VOR aerial, port and starboard
129 Port all-moving tailplane construction
130 Tailplane torque shaft
131 All-moving tailplane control linkage
132 Tailboom longerons
133 Avionics equipment bays
134 Avionics bay access doors
135 Tailboom attachment joint frame
136 UHF aerial
137 Radar altimeter aerial
138 Electrical equipment bay
139 Rear fuselage equipment bay
140 Ground power socket
141 Environmental control system air intake
142 Port navigation light
143 Port wingtip stores pylon
144 Four-round TOW missile carriage unit
145 Seven-tube 7-cm (2.75-in) rocket launcher
146 7-cm folding fin aircraft rockets (FFAR)
147 M18 Minigun pod, 7.62-mm six-barrelled rotary Minigun
148 Hughes TOW air-to-surface missile
149 Folding missile fins
150 Detachable TOE missile launcher/transportation tubes
151 19-tube rocket launcher
152 7-cm (2.75-in) FFAR
153 Wing skid strut fairing
154 Port landing skid
155 Skid tie-down point

Stabilator
From the AH-1Q and AH-1J a new stabilator was incorporated, with a span of 2.1 m (6 ft 11 in) (230 mm/9 in greater than the original). The all-moving single-piece unit is mechanically actuated and is unboosted.

Rotor blades
The Kaman K-747 rotor blade adopted for the Production AH-1S has tapered tips and consists of a spar, a Nomex core afterbody and a Kevlar trailing-edge spline, all encased in a fibreglass skin. There is greater chord and greater twist than the original metal blade featured. To preserve the same dynamic characteristics, the rotor blade spars incorporate a 53-lb brass tip weight.

Low-speed sensor
Projecting from the starboard side of the cockpit is a GEC M-143 low-speed, omni-directional air data probe which provides three-dimensional airspeed, downwash, static pressure and air temperature.

Canopy
The original 'flat plate' canopy panels of the AH-1S were quickly replaced by panels which incorporated a slight bulge. Access is through hinged side panels on the starboard (pilot) and port (gunner) sides. An emergency canopy removal system uses linear explosives to blow off side windows and doors. This system is independent of the normal electrical system.

Tail rotor
The two-bladed, semi-rigid delta-hinged tail rotor has a diameter of 2.6 m (8 ft 6 in). The two blades are connected to a common yoke by a grip and pitch change bearings.

TAH-1S

(redesignated TAH-1F in 1988)

Forty one of the AH-1Gs upgraded to Modernized AH-1S standard were modified as dual-controlled pilot trainers. These are externally indistinguishable from the standard AH-1S, although the IRCM jammer and exhaust suppressor are usually removed. They were redesignated TAH-1F in 1988.

Right: The TAH-1F is externally almost identical to the AH-1F, although many are operated with the M197 cannon, IRCM jammer and exhaust suppressor removed. Most, like the aircraft pictured here, wear large patches of Dayglo.

TH-1S 'Surrogate'

Fifteen old 'round-canopy' AH-1Ss were stripped of armament and fitted with some AH-64 avionics, including the PNVS (Passive Night-Vision System) to act as low-cost trainers for AH-64 pilots learning how to make instrument landings at night. The modifications, collectively known as 'Night Stalker', were incorporated by the Electro-Mechanical Division of Northrop. The aircraft had uprated engines, but retained the original canopy and an inoperative M28 turret. They entered service in 1984/85, and are still in service at Fort Rucker.

TH-1S

IFR blackout curtains over rear cockpit

PNVS sensor

Deactivated undernose weapons turret

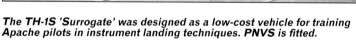
The TH-1S 'Surrogate' was designed as a low-cost vehicle for training Apache pilots in instrument landing techniques. PNVS is fitted.

This AH-1S served as a PNVS trials aircraft and acted as inspiration for the 'Surrogate' conversion programme.

Model 249

Although all production AH-1 variants have so far retained a two-bladed main rotor, Bell have not been blind to the advantages of the four-bladed rotor, which is lighter, capable of absorbing more power, has improved g tolerance, and is quieter and less prone to vibration. It was natural that when a four-bladed rotor was developed for the utility Bell 412, the same rotor would be applied to an AH-1. The union of 412 rotor and AH-1S airframe was a low-risk modification which fitted in well with Bell's philosophy of product improvement by evolution and not revolution, while dramatically improving performance and payload.

The former YAH-1S prototype was modified as the Model 249 prototype, which went on to serve as the 'Cobra II' or 'Improved Attack Cobra' demonstrator,

Right: The Model 249 prototype in flight, laden with dummy Hellfires. The four-bladed rotor, 2,000-shp engine and full IR sighting package were offered as a retrofit package, but the US Army preferred to spend its money on the LHX.

with an increased-chord tailplane incorporating small trailing-edge devices. The four-bladed rotor configuration, a 2,000-shp engine and a full IR-sensor sighting package was offered to the US Army as a retrofit package, which Bell suggested could be incorporated during the remanufacturing cycle of the 290 Modernized AH-1S aircraft. Although the new aircraft would have been a considerably better performer, with AGM-114A Hellfire, the US Army chose to

put its money into the LHX programme.

This setback did not mark the end of the Model 249, which was then proposed as a possible candidate to meet the US Army's Advanced Scout Helicopter requirement to replace the OH-58. Full TADS/PNVS as used by the AH-64 were to have been provided, and the aircraft was to have had a 'mini-wing' with provision for only AAMs and ARMs, and not for air-to-surface missiles. The ASH requirement was eventually dropped in favour of modifying existing OH-58s to OH-58D configuration.

With little prospect of a US military sale, Bell simultaneously promoted the 'Cobra II' as a potential PAH-2 (Panzerabwehr-hubschrauber 2) contender to Germany, with the standard wing, and eight Euromissile HOT missiles, but retaining TADS/PNVS in the nose in place of the standard 20-mm cannon. The prototype undertook a demonstration tour in Europe, with a removeable nose turret, appearing at the 1980 Farnborough air show. Germany eventually chose to develop the PAH-2 as a collaborative venture with France. Since 1983 the Model 249 has been used as the ART (Advanced Rotorcraft Technology Integration) demonstrator, with many of the new navigation, target-acquisition and flight-control systems intended to reduce pilot workload in the new single-pilot LHX. Some of these features, such as the glass cockpit and voice-activated systems, have been suggested as possible retrofits to the Cobra.

The four-bladed rotor of the Model 249

might also still be adopted for retrofit to existing Cobras, since it would solve the 'mast-bumping' problems which have beset the aircraft when limitations are exceeded, as well as providing about 10 per cent more lift even with no engine improvements.

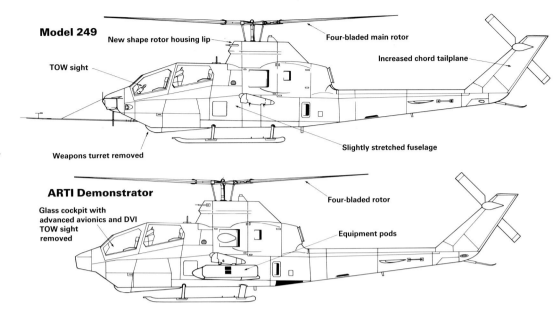

Model 249

New shape rotor housing lip

Four-bladed main rotor

Increased chord tailplane

TOW sight

Weapons turret removed

Slightly stretched fuselage

ARTI Demonstrator

Four-bladed rotor

Glass cockpit with advanced avionics and DVI TOW sight removed

Equipment pods

Left: Having served as the YAH-1S prototype, then the Model 249 prototype, 16019 went on to serve as the PAH-2 and Cobra 2000 demonstrator, before becoming the ARTI technology testbed.

Above: The Model 249 with its optional unarmed nose, containing TADS and PNVS sensors as used by the AH-64. These were necessary for the PAH-2 and US ASH requirements.

Cobra 2000

Bell examined some 60 potential modifications with a view to improving the performance and capability of the Cobra. For the proposed Cobra 2000, only four modifications were eventually put forward. These comprised a four-bladed main rotor, night-attack capability, a new GE T700 engine and improved crashworthiness. The aircraft was never funded, although a FACTS (FLIR Augmented Cobra TOW System) was developed from 1979. This was eventually abandoned in 1983 due to its high cost ($3 million per unit), but some of the technology developed was used in the C-Nite system derived from the FLIR fitted to the M1 tank and installed in some AH-1S Cobras to allow them to fire TOW missiles at night.

Right: Under the Cobra 2000 name, the Model 249 showed what a fully modernised AH-1S could have been. The US Army preferred to spend its money on the AH-64.

Cobra 2000 continued

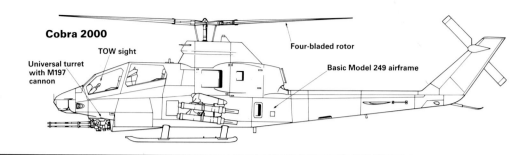

Cobra 2000

TOW sight

Four-bladed rotor

Universal turret with M197 cannon

Basic Model 249 airframe

Bell AH-1 Cobra twin-engined variants

The US Marine Corps preference for a twin-engined helicopter, combined with the existence of twin-engined versions of the transport Huey and Bell's eagerness to gain orders for their product, produced a family of twin-engined Cobra variants. Following the pattern set down by the development of the single-engined Cobras, technological advances, greater engine power and an improving threat led to the development of a succession of twin-engined variants.

Right: The twin-engined AH-1J proved much more suited to the needs of the USMC than the AH-1Gs which they began to receive in 1969. For shipborne, over-water operations, the twin-engined, rotor-brake-equipped AH-1J proved ideal.

AH-1J SeaCobra

As originally envisaged, the AH-1J was to have been a single-engined aircraft, similar to the AH-1G but with a rotor brake (deemed essential for shipborne operations), US Navy standard avionics and heavier armament, as well as better corrosion protection. The AH-1G was already in limited service with the USMC, and the logistic and political advantages of a common American powerplant initially overrode the Marines' traditional desire for a twin-engined machine. The 1968 Tet Offensive generated the need for massive attrition-replacement helicopter orders, and the Marines were given the go-ahead to replace their single-engined Hueys and Cobras with twin-engined machines, albeit that the engine was Canadian.

This allowed the Marines to procure a much more capable aircraft, with a Pratt & Whitney Canada T400-CP-400 (PT6T-4) turboshaft engine and a three-barrelled M197 cannon in a new undernose turret. The new weapon was basically a lightened version of the well-known six-barrelled M61, and came with an internally mounted ammunition box containing 750 rounds. The gun had a nominal rate of fire of 750 rpm, but individual bursts were limited to 16 rounds.

The T400-CP-400, also used by the UH-1N and the Bell 212, consisted of a pair of PT6s driving a single shaft through a common gearbox. The new powerplant was appreciably more powerful than the original Lycoming T53, but its main

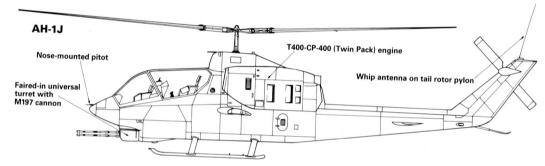

AH-1J

Nose-mounted pitot

Faired-in universal turret with M197 cannon

T400-CP-400 (Twin Pack) engine

Whip antenna on tail rotor pylon

Right: A handful of AH-1Js survived with Marine Reserve squadrons long enough to receive the modern grey and green Marine camouflage and wingtip-mounted chaff/flare dispensers. Some of these elderly aircraft even fought during Operation Desert Storm, although they were outnumbered by more modern AH-1Ws.

advantage lay in the fact that it offered genuine twin-engine reliability. Since the rotor system was unchanged, the AH-1J produced more power than could be used (1,530 shp max continuous), but this gave a useful engine-out hover capability.

The first AH-1J was handed over in October 1969, and four were sent to Patuxent River for evaluation in July 1970. The first AH-1Js were sent to Vietnam in February 1971, where they quickly proved their worth under combat conditions. During their subsequent service, the Marines' AH-1Js have been cleared to carry a wider variety of ordnance than Army Cobra variants, and all now have revised wing pylons and a new canopy-ejection system. Some surviving AH-1Js are to be modified to carry the AIM-9 Sidewinder, and were to have received the AGM-114A Hellfire (the latter having been abandoned), and will continue to serve in Reserve units when AH-1W conversions are complete. Reserve AH-1J units were activated and sent to the Gulf.

Right: This AH-1J was used in support of the AH-1W programme and was fitted with radar jammer and laser scan detector above the rear cockpit, on the rotor pylon. It also carries Sidewinder AAMs.

Model 309 KingCobra

The AH-1 was always regarded as an interim type, and the Army's chosen successor was the Lockheed AH-56 Cheyenne. This advanced and very ambitious helicopter was eventually cancelled due to technical problems, rising costs and the loss of a prototype. In order to fill the gap, Sikorsky promoted its private-venture S-67 BlackHawk, while in January 1971, Bell announced that it would develop the Model 309 KingCobra. Two KingCobras were built, the first a 'Marine' demonstrator powered by the same T400-CP-400 powerplant as the standard AH-1J, but with a strengthened drivetrain allowing the full 1,800 shp to be used, and the second a single-engined 'Army' demonstrator powered by the Lycoming T55-L-7C, flat-rated at 2,000 shp.

The twin-engined aircraft made its maiden flight on 10 September 1971, and was formally unveiled at a presentation on 28 September. At the latter event, the original Model 207 Sioux Scout, which

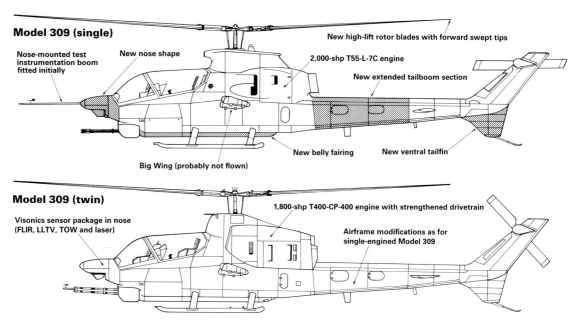

Model 309 (single)

New high-lift rotor blades with forward swept tips
New nose shape
Nose-mounted test instrumentation boom fitted initially
2,000-shp T55-L-7C engine
New extended tailboom section
New belly fairing
New ventral tailfin
Big Wing (probably not flown)

Model 309 (twin)

Visonics sensor package in nose (FLIR, LLTV, TOW and laser)
1,800-shp T400-CP-400 engine with strengthened drivetrain
Airframe modifications as for single-engined Model 309

Left: An unusual view of the single- and twin-engined Model 309 KingCobra prototypes in flight together. The single-engined aircraft is in the foreground.

had been the proof-of-concept aircraft for the AH-1 family, was handed over to the Army Aviation Museum. Although the Model 309 resembled the AH-1J in some ways, it was a very different aircraft. The airframe was strengthened, while the tail boom was lengthened and fitted with a ventral fin to improve directional stability and to allow a larger diameter (48 ft) main rotor to be fitted.

The single-engined 309 was similar, except for its engine pack, and indeed commonality was sufficient for the twin-engined aircraft to be rebuilt with a single engine after the original single-engined 309 was destroyed in an accident. All flight goals for the twin-engined variant had been achieved, but a single-engined prototype was still required for the AAFSS fly-off.

The main rotor featured a distinctively-shaped, new, high-lift blade developed by Professor Franz Wortman. This had a very broad chord and an asymmetric section, and also had unusual-looking forward-swept tips. These delayed the onset of compressibility and reduced the distinctive thudding noise signature associated with twin-rotor Hueys and Cobras.

While the AH-1G and AH-1J were effectively 'day only' helicopters, the Model 309 was intended from the start to be capable of day and night operation, and the aircraft was given a sophisticated package of advanced sensors and avionics equipment. For navigation, a Litton INS was provided, which could be easily updated from the Doppler, and which could provide bearing and range information to 16 pre-set locations as well as providing attitude references to the gunner, fire-control computer and TOW missile system.

The original AH-1G-style nose was soon replaced by a longer unit housing an electro-optical or 'Visonics' sensor package, including a FLIR, a low-light TV, the TOW missile tracker and a laser rangefinder. This Stabilised Multi-sensor Sight (SMS) unit was adapted from the turret designed for the AH-56, and could display information on the gunner's TSU and the pilot's HUD. Both crewmen wore Sperry Univac helmet-mounted sights to allow rapid target acquisition. The pilot had his own independent LLTV system mounted at the front of the rotor fairing, and this allowed him to fly in total darkness even when the FLIR was being used by the gunner.

Avionics equipment was comprehensive. A VHF/FM homer was fitted, together with ADF, IFF and even a radar altimeter with a ground-proximity warning. The communications system covered UHF/AM and VHF/AM and FM,

and there was provision for HF and secure voice communications. A bulge added below the fuselage covered a huge ammunition tank adapted from the unit fitted to the F-111! Although the Model 309 retained the M197 cannon of the AH-1J, the main weapon of any production version would have been the Hughes TOW missile.

A 13-ft span 'Big Wing' developed for the Model 309 was probably never flown, though a mock-up was fitted to at least one of the KingCobras. It would have contained extra fuel and would have allowed the innermost weapons pylons to be mounted further out from the fuselage, perhaps allowing an ECM pod to be carried on the fuselage 'shoulder'. Hardpoints on the tips would have allowed the carriage of AIM-9 Sidewinder, Redeye or Stinger missiles.

After a fly-off against the S-67, the Army decided that neither contender met its requirement, and drew up a fresh requirement for an Advanced Attack Helicopter (AAH) better suited to low-level nap-of-the-earth operation. This eventually led to the Bell YAH-63 and the Hughes (now McDonnell Douglas) YAH-64 Apache. The huge amount of effort expended on the Model 309 was not wasted, however, since much of the technology developed was injected back into the UH-1 family, and into later AH-1s.

Right: The original single-engined Model 309 was lost in an accident and the twin-engined aircraft was rebuilt with a single engine after its own trials were complete. The twin-engined aircraft is seen here in its original configuration.

AH-1J International

The Model 309 KingCobra had marked a dramatic improvement over previous Cobra variants, and when the Shah of Iran decided to order AH-1s for his army, he specified a TOW-compatible AH-1J derivative which incorporated many features previously tried and tested by the Model 309. The $704-million contract, for what was to be the biggest single export programme ever undertaken by Bell, was signed on 21 December 1971, and covered the sale of 287 Model 214 utility helicopters and 202 AH-1Js.

The 'Iranian J', as it was sometimes dubbed, was powered by an uprated T400-WV-402, with a new transmission system derived from that of the Model 211 HueyTug flying crane. This gave the J International much improved hot-and-high performance, with a rating of 1,673 shp (maximum continuous).

The AH-1J International incorporated a number of other improvements, including an improved turret with a recoil

Right and below right: Two different standards of AH-1J were delivered to Iran, some equivalent to the USMC AH-1J but with the T400-WV-402 engine, and some with TOW sight and missiles. Both AH-1J International sub-variants are pictured here.

compensator, a stabilised pantograph sight and even a vibration damped gunner's seat. Some Iranian AH-1J Internationals were not TOW compatible. South Korea was the only other user of the AH-1J International, taking delivery of eight TOW aircraft in 1978.

Perhaps the greatest significance of the AH-1J was that it led directly to the development of the AH-1T and indirectly to the AH-1W, the most capable members of the Cobra family to enter front-line service.

Below: South Korea was the only other customer for the TOW-armed AH-1J.

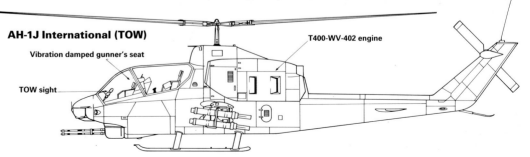

AH-1J International (TOW)

Vibration damped gunner's seat

TOW sight

T400-WV-402 engine

AH-1T Improved SeaCobra

The AH-1T was the first production Cobra variant with a new fuselage, necessitated by the upgraded powerplant and transmission system of the new variant. The US Marine Corps had been relatively pleased with their AH-1Js, but wanted the TOW missile, and wanted a more capable Cobra from which to launch it. It was decided to provide more power, which in turn meant switching to a new engine (the 1,970-shp Pratt & Whitney Canada T400-WV-402 twin-pac) and a new transmission system. In fact, the transmission system of the Bell 214 was used virtually unmodified.

To absorb the extra power, the AH-1T was also given a new, larger, 48-ft diameter rotor, similar to that used by the Bell 214, with blades whose chord had been increased from 27 to 33 in. The hub was strengthened, and given Lord Kinematics Lastoflex Elastomeric and Teflon-faced bearings. Swept tips were incorporated for reduced noise and to improve high-speed performance. The increased diameter of the main rotor made it necessary to lengthen the tailboom, and to provide a more powerful tail rotor with increased diameter and larger tail surfaces. This gives the AH-1T an unmistakable appearance, with its characteristic ventral fin and double kink on the lower fuselage. To maintain the centre of gravity the forward fuselage was also stretched, making room for an additional avionics bay and 400 lb more fuel. Longer undercarriage skids are also used.

Even the last single-engined Cobra, the AH-1S, was hardly over-powered, but the adoption of the T400-WV-402 engine gave the AH-1T a dramatic increase in available power, allowing heavy payloads to be carried even with full internal fuel and giving the new variant, despite its much greater empty weight, a really impressive performance. The promise shown by the AH-1T was such that only 67 of the planned 124 AH-1Js were delivered, production immediately switching to the new variant.

The last two AH-1Js built served as AH-1T prototypes, the first flying in its new guise on 20 May 1976. They were followed by 57 production aircraft. TOW compatibility was not provided from the start on the first 33 aircraft, due to budgetary constraints, but the survivors were given a retrofit programme including a nose sight, Sperry Univac helmet sights for both crew, and a recoil compensator to allow the TSU to be used with the M197 gun. This programme has given them compatibility with the TOW missile, and other modifications were to have allowed them to use the newer Hellfire. The second batch of 24 AH-1Ts was built with full TOW compatibility. Thirty-nine of the surviving AH-1Ts are to be brought up virtually to AH-1W standard in an ambitious upgrade programme, with General Electric T700-GE-401 engines and a more crashworthy fuel system.

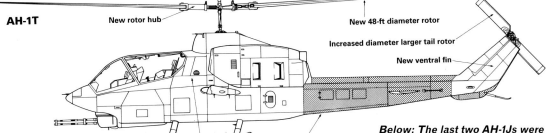

AH-1T — New rotor hub · New 48-ft diameter rotor · Increased diameter larger tail rotor · New ventral fin · Lengthened tailboom · Swept main rotor tips · Slightly stretched forward fuselage

AH-1T (TOW) — TOW sight fitted from 33rd AH-1T

Below: The last two AH-1Js were taken off the assembly line before completion, and modified to serve as the AH-1T prototypes. This, the first, lacked a TOW sight.

Left: Another view of the first AH-1T, seen here armed with Sidewinders.

Inset and below: The AH-1T prototype was eventually fitted with a stabilised FLIR/laser-designator turret during trials to find a replacement for the M65 TSU.

Below left: This AH-1T, named 'Le Tigre', is seen over Grenada during the US invasion. This particular machine accounted for two enemy ZSUs.

AH-1T+

The AH-1T+ began its life as a paper proposal to Iran for a further enhanced SeaCobra incorporating the General Electric T700-GE-700 engines and transmission system of the Bell Model 214ST, which was to have been produced under licence in Iran. The new aircraft offered 75 per cent more power than the AH-1J then in Iranian service, with 25 per cent better fuel burn. It was to have had sand filters, better recoil compensation for the gun and enhanced avionics. It was also intended to demonstrate a top speed of 173 kt. The overthrow of the Shah deprived Bell of their intended customer, and the Marines made no secret of the fact that they wanted some AH-64s and did not want another 'warmed over' Cobra. Work on the new aircraft continued, however, and an AH-1T was flown with the 1,258-shp (max continuous) General Electric T700-GE-700 in April 1980.

Right: The AH-1T+ prototype in flight. Designed for the Shah of Iran, the aircraft eventually resulted in the definitive Marine AH-1W. It lacked the prominent cheeks of the later AH-1W and had more crudely shaped engine nacelles.

AH-1W SuperCobra

In 1981, Congress refused to grant any funds for a Marine procurement of the AH-64; instead, Bell were given a $4.1-million contract to qualify the T700-GE-401 (used by the Sikorsky SH-60 Seahawk, and to re-engine the Kaman SH-2F) in the AH-1T. Bell then proceeded to add a host of new improvements and updates to the AH-1T+ prototype (161022), which was given prominent exhaust suppressors and bulged 'cheek' fairings which marked the relocation of TOW electronics previously carried in the tailboom. Sidewinders, Hellfire and TOW were all carried by the prototype, which was also given an AN/ALQ-144 IRCM set and AN/ALE-139 chaff/flare dispensers.

When funds were granted to develop the AH-1T+ as a production aircraft, Bell repainted it from dark green to glossy black, with a gold snake slithering down the fuselage sides. The first production aircraft was redesignated AH-1W. An initial order for 44, plus a single TAH-1W trainer, was followed by orders for 34 for delivery between June 1990 and June 1991, and six more were funded in FY 1990. The 39 remaining AH-1Ts are to be modified to AH-1W configuration, and 17 had been completed by February 1990.

In service, the US Marine Corps has made the most of its AH-1Ws, vastly increasing the Cobra's already formidable firepower. The M197 three-barrel Vulcan cannon has been qualified to fire an improved armour-piercing round consisting of a discarding sabot and a high density sub-calibre projectile. This leaves the barrel at about twice the normal velocity because of the increased size and mass of the sabot, which falls away. This lets the dense projectile fly on unimpeded, and it has roughly three times the armour-penetration capability of a standard round.

Extra gun capability can be added by fitting a pair of General Electric GPU-2/A 20-mm cannon pods, each containing an M197 gun and 300 rounds of ammunition, while a variety of free-fall bombs, fuel/air explosive weapons and cluster munitions have also been cleared for use with the

AH-1W. A new outboard stores station may be fitted above the tip of each stub wing, and these can each mount an AIM-9L Sidewinder IR-homing air-to-air missile, or the similar AGM-122 Sidearm, which is essentially a rebuilt AIM-9C modified to serve as a lightweight anti-radar missile. A night-capability package, consisting of a FLIR and a laser ranger/designator, is being developed jointly with Israel, while an enhanced EW system has been tested and the AN/APN-217 navigation system is being considered as a retrofit item. Turkey reportedly has plans to acquire at least five AH-1Ws.

Above: The AH-1T+ prototype after conversion to 'SuperCobra' standards, and wearing the gaudy SuperCobra colour scheme. Above right: The same aircraft in overall green (with Dayglo panels) firing chaff/flare cartridges.

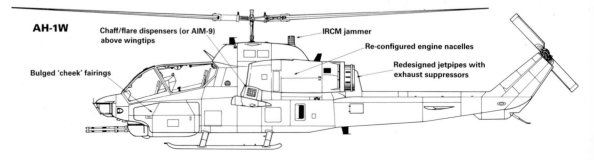

4BW

The last production AH-1T (161022), previously the AH-1T+ and AH-1W prototype, was converted by Bell with the all-composite, bearing-free, Model 680 four-bladed rotor, first test-flown on a Bell 222. The new rotor is much simpler to make and maintain, and has a much longer life, as well as giving the SuperCobra improved manoeuvrability, increased top speed (by 20 kt) and less vibration. It is much stealthier than existing rotors, and Bell hope to demonstrate an ability to withstand direct hits by AAA of up to 23-mm calibre. The Model 680 rotor has been chosen for the McDonnell Douglas/ Bell LHX submission.

Known only as the 4BW (Four-Bladed Whiskey), the former AH-1T+ demonstrator aircraft was also fitted with new tail surfaces, positioned further aft by some 60 in, and with end-plate fins. The aircraft also incorporated a digital flight-control system and the night-targetting sights and Doppler-based navigation system under consideration for the AH-1W. Various new names have been suggested for the aircraft, including CobraShark. The possibility of USMC AH-1Ws receiving the Model 680 rotor as a retrofit cannot be ruled out, and a proposal to this effect has been submitted by Bell. With USMC evaluations complete, the 4BW prototype

aircraft has reportedly been returned to stock AH-1W configuration and will be returned to the USMC.

Various 4BW derivatives have been sketched, including one with retractable wheeled landing gear and gull wings. Another derivative is being offered by Bell to meet the UK's requirement for an attack helicopter, in competition with the AH-64 Longbow Apache and the Franco-German Tiger. The Bell aircraft is reportedly back in the running after two years during which Britain became 'focused on the AH-64 Apache'. GEC (already helping Bell to redesign the AH-1W cockpit) would be a likely partner.

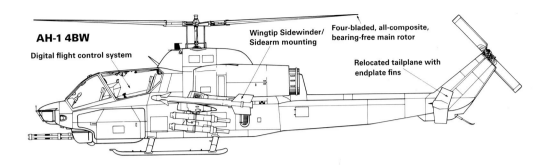

AH-1 4BW

Digital flight control system

Wingtip Sidewinder/ Sidearm mounting

Four-bladed, all-composite, bearing-free main rotor

Relocated tailplane with endplate fins

Left: *The AH-1W prototype (previously the AH-1T+) went on to serve as the 4BW demonstrator, as seen here. The Model 680 four-bladed rotor was tested first on a Bell 222.*

Above: *Yellow primer picks out some of the changes made to 161022 as the 4BW demonstrator. A rear-located tailplane with endplate fins was fitted, along with a bulged fairing along the belly.*

Above: *Close-up of the nose-mounted sensor turret fitted to the 4BW demonstrator by the time it participated in the 1990 Farnborough SBAC show. The many advances pioneered by this aircraft now seem unlikely to be retrofitted to production Cobras.*

Left: *An unconventional-looking 'Future SuperCobra' drawn up by the Bell marketing department. Based on the 4BW the aircraft has distinctive gull wings and retractable undercarriage. In the present climate this configuration is unlikely to even reach mock-up or prototype form, and it seems likely that the AH-1W will be the last production Cobra variant.*

The Soviet Withdrawal from Europe

Part Two: POLAND

In the second of a series of articles documenting the Soviet withdrawal from Eastern Europe, *World Air Power Journal* details the composition of the air forces of the Northern Group of Forces (once known as the 37th Air Army) and their bases in Poland. With the withdrawals from Hungary and Czechoslovakia completed by mid-1991, only Poland and the former East Germany were left with Soviet military forces on their territory. The withdrawal from East Germany has been carefully phased to gain the maximum financial compensation from the German government for the disruption caused by re-location, and will thus last until 1994. In Poland, where there is unlikely to be any financial compensation, withdrawal of forces is likely to be considerably more rapid.

Below: Armed with only a single rocket pod underwing, one of Szprotawa's Su-24 'Fencer-Ds' screeches past the flight line as it takes off on a training mission. The Soviet air forces in Poland retain a substantial strike element, with full regiments of 'Fencer-Ds' at Zagan and Szprotawa. The Su-24 is the Soviet equivalent of the F-111 and Tornado, and carries a wide range of weapons, including guided missiles of various kinds.

Since Poland shared no borders with NATO, the need for large Frontal Aviation air assets was less than it was in East Germany. Nevertheless, the Northern Group of Forces was a powerful military force, which would have played a crucial role in any war, and its Air Army was of corresponding size, representing some 15 per cent of Soviet air power strength in Central Europe. This made the 37th Air Army second in size only to the 16th Air Army in former East Germany. The Soviet air forces in Poland were largely located in the west of the country, close to the border with the DDR, where they could best support both the Northern Group of Forces and the Western Group of Forces in former East Germany. Before the beginning of the withdrawals from Europe, the Soviet Army controlled 70,000 acres in Poland, including eight active and five reserve airfields and four huge exercise areas.

Soviet Army ground forces in Poland consist

Above: A 'Fencer-D' takes off from Szprotawa, its landing gear already tucking away. The way in which the main gear doors can also act as airbrakes can clearly be seen.

Left: The Soviet air forces in Poland include three regiments of Su-24 'Fencers' at Zagan, Szprotawa and Osla, operating in the nuclear strike, conventional interdiction and possibly reconnaissance roles. The Su-24s at Osla, usually described as being recce assigned, are actually 'Fencer-Cs', and not dedicated 'Fencer-E' or 'Fencer-F' reconnaissance variants.

of only two tank divisions, both of which are classified as being at Category I Readiness state. The Soviet Northern Group of Forces is thus smaller than the Southern Group of Forces in Hungary (which had two tank divisions and two Guards motor rifle divisions), and the Central Group of Forces in Czechoslovakia (which had two tank divisions and three Guards Motor Rifle Divisions), although its small size belied its importance. (The Western Group of Forces in Germany was of an entirely different order of magnitude, with five armies, each with about four divisions.)

Soviet airfields in the north and east of Poland did exist, but these were normally kept under 'Care and Maintenance' status, and would have been activated only to act as Forward Operating Bases for the strategic and tactical bombers of the 46th Strategic Air Army (headquartered at Smolensk) normally based in the USSR. The Strategic Air Armies are directly subordinated to the

High Command Reserve. The 46th Strategic Air Army was a massive and powerful force and consisted of some four divisions, with seven Tu-16 'Badger' regiments, three Tu-22 'Blinder' regiments and two Tu-26 'Backfire' regiments. These are supported by three independent recce /EW regiments operating a mix of Su-24s, MiG-25s and Yak-28s. Tanker support is probably provided by independent tanker units, perhaps operating the new Ilyushin Il-78 'Midas'. This huge nuclear strike force was broadly equivalent to one of Strategic Air Command's two numbered air forces, albeit with slightly smaller, shorter-range aircraft than SAC's B-52 and B-1Bs, and without its own strategic missile forces. Some of the 46th Strategic Air Army would have deployed to under-used airfields in western Poland in time of war.

Strategic strike

Some of the units permanently based in Poland (like those which would have used the FOBs mentioned above) do not come under the direct control of the Northern Group of Forces, these being the Su-24 'Fencer' strike units, which (together with those now withdrawn from former East Germany) belong to the 24th Strategic Air Army headquartered at Legnica. Su-24 regiments in the western USSR (and those formerly based in Hungary) belong to the 4th Strategic Air Army, headquartered at Vinnitsa in the Ukraine.

The exact organisation of the Soviet air forces in Poland remains uncertain, some of the air

superiority units perhaps being assigned to the 24th Strategic Air Army for escort duties rather than to the Northern Group of Forces as has traditionally been supposed. The two Su-27 regiments at Kluczewo/Stargard and Chojna, for example, may have transferred to the 24th Strategic Air Army on conversion to the new type, whose long range does make it a useful escort aircraft. At least one of these units transferred from the MiG-23 to the MiG-29 'Fulcrum-C' (which had a range broadly equivalent to the short-legged 'Flogger') before transitioning to the Su-27.

The tabular order of battle given below must therefore be regarded as being at least partially speculative insofar as organisation goes, and it may be that virtually all of the fixed-wing aircraft now based in Poland are actually assigned to the 24th Strategic Air Army and not to the Northern Group of Forces. The opening-up of Poland means that the actual locations and strengths of Soviet units in Poland are known, but security remains tight, and unit designations remain largely unknown. There is not the same degree of tolerance to Western photographers and aircraft spotters as there has been recently in eastern Germany (and even there you can be arrested!) so there has not been as much information flowing back. The Soviets in Poland reportedly still retain a degree of jurisdiction in the environs of any base, and can carry and use weapons up to 1 km from any Soviet facility. While we would strongly discourage readers from attempting

An underside view of an Osla-based 'Fencer-C' shows no provision for built-in cameras or other optical or electro-optical sensors. There may, of course, be a SLAR in the forward fuselage, with an over-painted flush radome, or podded recce equipment may be carried. Alternatively, these aircraft may serve as the attack half of a 'Foxbat-F'/'Fencer' hunter/killer 'Wild Weasel' team.

Above: Another Osla-based 'Fencer-C'. This aircraft appears to have a non-standard nose sensor, with side-by-side pitots below the curved 'hockey stick'. It also seems to have an extra projection on the undernose sensor. This may merely represent a later production batch airframe, or may indicate compatibility with a particular weapons system.

photographic or spotting trips in countries like Poland, we would obviously be interested to see any photos or reports from those lucky enough to return from such foolish trips!

Throughout Central Europe, the deployment, composition and structure of Soviet forces underwent major changes during the 1970s and 1980s. During the late 1970s and early 1980s, the air forces of the Groups of Forces began to become more offensive, with MiG-27 and Su-17 fighter-bomber regiments replacing MiG-21 and MiG-23 fighter regiments. At the same time, there were an increasing number of Su-24 strike regiments deployed outside Soviet territory. Later in the decade, in response to the changing international situation, the accent switched again to a more defensive posture, and in former East Germany in particular there was a widespread

Below: Although all of Osla's 'Fencers' carry two-digit white tactical codes, a handful have these outlined very thinly in red. This may indicate assignment to a different squadron within the regiment.

exchange of overtly offensive aircraft for MiG-29s. The latter process was not experienced to the same degree in Poland, where there was a small reduction in the total numbers of aircraft deployed through the withdrawal of a MiG-23 'Flogger' regiment from Brzeg to a base near Smolensk in May 1991, the withdrawal of a MiG-25R/Yak-28-equipped recce/EW unit from Brzeg in 1990 and the withdrawal of the MiG-25BM 'Foxbat-F' defence suppression aircraft, which were probably based at Chojna, on an unknown date.

MiG-23 withdrawal

The MiG-23MLDs from Brzeg had previously been based at Bagicz/Kolobrzeg on the Baltic coast, and moved to Brzeg due to noise complaints, their place at Bagicz/Kolobrzeg being taken by the sole army Mil Mi-24/-17 combat helicopter regiment in Poland. The removal of the MiG-23 regiment (which had operated the top-of-the-line 'Flogger-K') completed the transformation of the old three-regiment short-range tactical fighter division into a two-regiment long-range fighter-interceptor division, since Su-27s replaced MiG-23s and MiG-29s in the surviving regiments.

The MiG-29, which has formed the backbone of Soviet air forces elsewhere in Europe, is thus absent from the present Northern Group of Forces order of battle, and served only briefly in Poland, never totally replacing the MiG-23

before the Su-27 made its debut as a Frontal Aviation interceptor.

Why a single MiG-23 unit was retained alongside the new 'Flankers' (instead of a MiG-29 regiment) is unknown, unless it had been planned to convert the Brzeg-based unit to the Su-27. Although the lightened and aerodynamically refined MiG-23MLD represented a considerable improvement over earlier members of the 'Flogger' family, it has no modern pulse-Doppler radar (thus lacking any real lookdown/shootdown and multiple target-tracking capability), and lacks agility.

It is also hampered by being armed with the ageing R-27 (NATO AA-7 'Apex') semi-active

Above: Long-range transport is usually provided by Aeroflot aircraft, which are often crewed by VTA crews, and which would pass to the VTA in time of war anyway. Here an Aeroflot Tupolev Tu-154 is seen visiting Osla. When the Soviet withdrawal from Poland really gets underway, Aeroflot visitors will become increasingly common, with Tu-154s performing trooping while An-22s and An-124s carry heavy freight.

Right: Transport requirements within the Northern Group of Forces area are assigned to a Theatre Transport Regiment at Legnica, which operates blue-coded Antonov An-26s and Mil Mi-8s, with a handful of An-12s and An-74s.

Below: Army aviation assets in Poland consist of a single large regiment of Mil Mi-8 and Mi-17 'Hips' and Mi-24 'Hinds'. These are now based at Kolobrzeg on the Baltic Coast, following the withdrawal of MiG-23s from that base. Here an Mi-8 lifts off into the hover.

Above: Continuation training is provided by the MiG-23UB. These aircraft lack a fire control radar, so are fitted with a missile guidance/ illuminator pod under the starboard wing when live firing needs to be undertaken.

Right: Colonel Nikolai Zemstov, commander of the Brzeg-based regiment, wears a thick leather flying coat over his two-piece 'dungaree-and-jacket' flying suit. The aircraft behind him shows clear evidence of the regiment's previously-used blue codes, changed to yellow after the move from Kolobrzeg.

Above: Proud of its Great Patriotic War traditions, the Brzeg-based 'Flogger' regiment displayed its 1941-45 'Guards' battle honours prominently inside the base.

Below: This Brzeg-based MiG-23MLD 'Flogger-K' is unusual in that it lacks the top-surface chaff/flare dispensers usually associated with this advanced MiG-23 variant. Notches in the leading edge of the wing glove are clearly visible, however.

radar-homing missile, and not the more modern and more effective AA-10 'Alamo' carried by both the MiG-29 and the Su-27. It is not known whether the MiG-23MLD can carry the modern AA-11 'Archer' IR-homing dogfight missile, or whether it relies solely on the older and less effective R-60 (NATO AA-8 'Aphid').

Before leaving Poland on 10 June 1991, the unit commander, Colonel Nikolai Andreyevich Zemstov, spoke to one of our correspondents. Regimental commander for some two years, the 40-year-old Zemstov (a first class pilot) had amassed some 2,500 jet fighter hours on aircraft as diverse as the MiG-17, Su-9 and MiG-23. He revealed that the regiment had been formed at Pushkin on 2 February 1940, flying the Polikarpov I-16. The unit moved to Kolobrzeg in 1953, by which time it was flying the MiG-17. Since then the regiment has flown various types of MiG-21s and MiG-23s, moving to Brzeg (then a busy recce base with Su-24s and MiG-25s) in August 1989.

Flying had been unrestricted at Brzeg, but 0300 take-offs proved unpopular with the locals, and by the time the regiment moved back to the USSR it was flying on only two of three nominated days per week, and only between 0600 and 2200 (only until 1500 on Saturdays, and not at all on Sundays). The base, with its huge apartment blocks, was handed over to the Polish government in July 1991, the majority of its personnel (and their families) travelling back to the USSR by train. The Brzeg regiment adopted yellow regimental codes when it moved from Kolobrzeg, where blue codes had been in use.

The withdrawal of the 'Floggers' from Brzeg left the air defence of Soviet Forces in Poland as the responsibility of two regiments of Sukhoi Su-27 'Flankers', the only examples of this powerful and extremely agile long-range interceptors based outside the Soviet Union, and two of the handful of Su-27 regiments controlled by the air forces and not by the IA-PVO home defence interceptor force.

Sukhoi 'Flankers'

Each regiment operates some 30 Su-27s, with three two-seaters. The unit based at Kluczewo (variously known as Stargard) is the only Soviet air force unit in Poland whose designation is known, this being the 159th Fighter Interceptor Regiment. Its aircraft carry red regimental codes. The Su-27s at nearby Chojna carry black or very dark blue code letters.

*Above: Laden with three fuel tanks, 'Yellow 08' taxis out prior to its ferry flight back to the **USSR**. Chaff/flare dispensers are mounted on the upper decking of the fuselage, immediately adjacent to the wingroot. Each contains two dispensers, mounted in tandem. They are similar to the units housed in the fin leading edge extensions of the **MiG-29 'Fulcrum'**.*

The exchange of overtly offensive MiG-27 fighter-bombers for 'reconnaissance' Su-24 'Fencers' at Osla, once thought to be an example of down-scaling offensive forces, may not be all it seems, however. It now appears that the Su-24s based at Osla are actually 'Fencer-Cs' (traditionally regarded as bombers) and not the 'Fencer-E' or 'Fencer-F' variants normally associated with recce and EW tasks. On the other hand, the Su-24s seen at Pushkin were 'Fencer-Cs' (*World Air Power Journal*, Volume 6), and these were believed to be operating in, or undergoing conversion to, the EW/recce role. All other aircraft at Osla, which include MiG-25s (possibly those supposedly withdrawn to the USSR from Brzeg) and three Il-20/Il-22 'Coot-A/Bs' seem to have a reconnaissance/EW role. The single Il-22 'Coot-B' may be an airborne command post aircraft. Osla is the most likely base for any MiG-25BM 'Foxbat-Fs' which remain in Poland, though their presence cannot be confirmed. Osla's Su-24s wear white codes (some of them outlined thinly in red), while the MiG-25s and Il-20s have red codes.

'Fencer' roles

Whatever the role of the 'Fencer-Cs' at Osla, it is unlikely to be purely nuclear strike, since even the advanced 'Fencer-Ds' at Szprotawa and Zagan/Stara Kopernia now seem to have embraced a conventional interdiction/air support role. They are now most commonly seen armed with rocket pods, although nuclear capability is presumably still retained. The full range of conventional Soviet air-to-ground ordnance is also available to Polish-based 'Fencers'. This includes the Kh-58 (NATO AS-11 'Kilter') anti-radiation missile, the Kh-23 (NATO AS-7 'Kerry'), Kh-25 (NATO AS-10 'Karen'), Kh-29 (NATO AS-14 'Kedge') ASMs and the new Kh-31, which has no NATO codename, but is described as a medium-range anti-radar missile with four rocket boosters. The Kh-25 is available in three

Above: The Brzeg-based 'Flogger-Ks' wore a fairly dark colour scheme of brown, green and olive drab, with light grey undersides. This proved particularly effective at low level.

Below: The flight line at Brzeg was typical of front-line WarPac fighter bases, with its sloping blast deflector, fixed ground power units and huge lighting stands. Several of the MiG-23s have their avionics bay hatches open.

Above: The Sukhoi Su-27 'Flanker-Bs' based at Chojna wear black or dark blue regimental codes. Many aircraft have dark green radomes and dielectric panels (newer aircraft have white). 'Black 24' seen here has an unusual two-tone radome, and wears an excellence award and several tiny red stars (kill markings?) below the cockpit.

versions: radio command-guided, passive radar-guided, and semi-active laser-guided. The newer Kh-29 is also available in two variants: TV and semi-active laser-guided.

A huge range of bombs (guided and unguided, slick and retarded), cluster bomb and other dispenser weapons, unguided rockets (podded and unpodded) and gun pods are also standard equipment on the Su-24. All known 'Fencer' variants are equipped with an internal GSh6-23M 23-mm cannon. Some Su-24 'Fencer-Ds' have been photographed carrying a buddy-buddy refuelling store under the centreline, and some of these may be available to the Su-24s based in Poland. The Su-24s at Zagan/Stara Kopernia and Szprotawa carry white regimental codes. The three Su-24 bases form a 'clutch' of airfields close to the German and Czech borders.

Supporting the front-line fighters, bombers and reconnaissance aircraft is a single Theatre Transport Division, which operates both fixed-wing types and helicopters. The fixed-wing types consist largely of Antonov An-26s and An-72/-74s, augmented by a handful of VIP-configured An-24s, and by An-12s for heavylift duties. These transport aircraft all carry blue codes, although at least some of the An-72/-74s may operated in Aeroflot colours. A separate transport helicopter squadron operates Mil Mi-8 and Mi-17 'Hips', and may have one or two Mi-6 'Hooks' on charge. These also wear blue regimental codes.

Transports and helicopters

The transport aircraft and helicopters, all of which are based at Legnica, can be augmented by Aeroflot or air force transport aircraft normally based in the Western USSR. Such aircraft types are regular visitors to all the Soviet airfields in Poland, and the flightline at Legnica normally includes examples of Aeroflot Il-76s, Tu-154s and the like. Legnica also houses a major maintenance and overhaul facility, reportedly with a fasci-

nating 'graveyard' of crashed and withdrawn aircraft gathered up from the other bases in Poland.

The distance from the NATO front line meant that the Northern Group of Forces was never over-generously endowed with combat helicopters and close support aircraft. At one time Su-25s were reported as operating from Chojna, but they were either on a short detachment or were quickly withdrawn. Similarly, while there were at least 10 Combat Helicopter Regiments in former East Germany, there is only one in Poland, based at Bagicz/Kolobrzeg on the Baltic Coast. The 'Sevastapolski' combat helicopter regiment consists of three squadrons, one equipped with Mi-8s and Mi-17s (known in Soviet military service as Mi-8TVs), one with Mi-24Vs ('Hind-Es') and Mi-24Ds ('Hind-Ds') and one with Mi-24Vs and Mi-24Ps ('Hind-Fs'). The 'Hips' are, or can be, armed with a variety of bombs and rockets, as can the 'Hinds' which also carry AT-6 'Spiral' tube-launched ATMs and which are armed with 12.7-mm machine-guns or 30-mm cannon.

Special variants?

Kolobrzeg's helicopters mostly wear black or yellow codes (Mi-24s) or white codes (Mi-8/-17s). Unusually, no ECM jamming, Elint or airborne command post 'Hip' variants have been noted at Kolobrzeg, yet the Soviet army seldom operates without these 'special purpose' Mi-8/17 variants. Similarly the NBC monitoring Mi-24 RCh ('Hind-G') and the Mi-24K ('Hind-G2') have not yet been noted in Poland. In time of war, armies moving forward into Poland from the USSR would almost certainly have been accompanied by their own assault and transport helicopter regiments, and perhaps by Su-25 'Frogfoot' and even Su-17 'Fitter' units.

While seven airfields in Poland remain active, severe restrictions on flying activities are in force, imposed by financial considerations, and the need to avoid annoying the local population (the latter being an entirely new consideration for

Left: This Chojna-based Su-27 carries a single acquisition round for an AA-11 'Archer' IR-homing AAM under the port outboard underwing pylon. When fully armed the 'Flanker-B' would carry four of these advanced dogfight missiles and up to six AA-10 'Alamo' medium-range AAMs in a mix of IR- and semi-active radar-homing versions.

Above: Red regimental codes on the intakes (and repeated on the tailfins) identify this Sukhoi Su-27 as an aircraft from the Kluczewo-Stargard-based 159th Fighter Interceptor Regiment. The landing gear has to be retracted quickly, to avoid exceeding its limiting speed, since even at this steep angle of climb, the 'Flanker' accelerates very rapidly.

Right: Three of the 159th Fighter Interceptor Regiment's 'Flankers' made history during 1991 by visiting first the Poznan international air show, and then an air show at Kbely in Czechoslovakia. At each of these events the 'Flankers' appeared beside contemporary Western fighters. Here 'Red 51', flown by Captain Alexander Michaelyov, taxis in at Poznan.

Below: The sheer size of the Su-27 is clearly evident in this view of one of the aircraft at Kbely. The Su-27s based in Poland operate primarily as long-range interceptors.

Right: 'Red 48' was flown at Kbely by Captain Alexander Dudarenko of the 159th Fighter Interceptor Regiment at Kluczewo-Stargard. The aircraft is seen here with its spine-mounted airbrake deployed, and using its twin white and Dayglo braking parachutes. The latter are seldom seen, since aerodynamic and wheel braking is usually enough to give the 'Flanker' a very short landing run.

Above: The Poland-based Su-27s have an important secondary role as long-range escort fighters. With full fuel they could accompany Su-24s to their targets, and could even reach eastern England. These large and heavy fighters, however, are astonishingly agile.

Soviet commanders!). Only at Legnica, home to the Theatre Transport Division's transport aircraft (and a major maintenance/overhaul facility), Osla and Kolobrzeg does flying take place every day. At Chojna the Su-27s fly only on Tuesdays, Thursdays and Saturdays, while the Su-27s at Kluczewo/Stargard fly only on Tuesdays and Thursdays. The Su-24 bomber bases at Szprotawa and Zagan/Stara Kopernia take it in turns to have a flying week from Monday to Saturday. Where Soviet airfields are restricted to flying only on certain days of the week, they usually alternate with a local Polish air force unit, most of which fly very little due to financial constraints. The constraints on flying have reduced still further the amount of flying time logged by front-line Soviet pilots, widening the gulf between them and their NATO counterparts.

Although Soviet training philosophy maximises the value of time spent in the air by extensive use of simulators and exhaustively going through every exercise on the ground, the effectiveness of pilots handling the more-sophisticated weapons systems must now be open to doubt.

Although the Soviets have not published a formal withdrawal timetable (as they have for their forces based in former East Germany) the process is likely to be rapid. There is no Polish support for the continued presence of Soviet troops, whose role has almost completely

vanished. Their continued presence cannot be used to wring financial concessions from the Polish government, which is virtually bankrupt, and it is only a matter of finding places in the reliable Slavic republics to which the units can return. The final dissolution of the USSR has meant that homes will be found, wherever possible, in Russia itself, especially for the higher-value assets. The Russian government is keen to concentrate control of the armed forces in its own hands, and this will be easier to justify when it applies to units based on Russian territory.

Treaty obligations

The Soviets are treaty bound to quit Poland by the end of 1993, and have undertaken to leave all bases within 50 km of the German border by the end of 1992. Chojna, Osla, Kluczewo/Stargard and Zagan/Stara Kopernia all fall into the latter category. It is thus widely expected that all Polish-based units will have gone home by the end of 1992, and Chojna was expected to close before the end of 1991. During 1991, Soviet Su-27s based at Kluczewo/Stargard participated in air shows at Poznan, Poland, and at Kbely, Czechoslovakia, and it is expected (and hoped) that other Poland-based Soviet aircraft may participate in these and other air shows in Central Europe before the final pull-out. If they do, it will be a remarkable curtain call for what has always been a very shadowy and little-known organisation.

With the Soviets already having pulled out of Czechoslovakia and Hungary, the final withdrawal from Poland will leave the enormous Western Group of Forces in the former East Germany as an island, completely cut off from the territories of the former USSR. The lack of access to airfields in Poland, and to the military railway system in that country, is sure to complicate the final Soviet withdrawal from the territories of its former Warsaw Pact allies.

Left: A Kluczewo-based Su-27 demonstrates its agility at low level, and incidentally shows off its attractive blue-grey air defence colour scheme. The Su-27 uses inboard flaperons and differential tailplanes for roll control. The extended tailcone houses a pair of brake chutes, ECM equipment and chaff/flare dispensers.

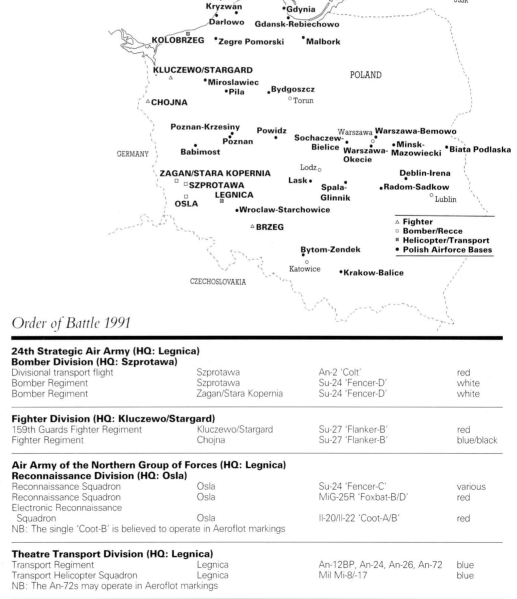

Order of Battle 1991

24th Strategic Air Army (HQ: Legnica)
Bomber Division (HQ: Szprotawa)

Divisional transport flight	Szprotawa	An-2 'Colt'	red
Bomber Regiment	Szprotawa	Su-24 'Fencer-D'	white
Bomber Regiment	Zagan/Stara Kopernia	Su-24 'Fencer-D'	white

Fighter Division (HQ: Kluczewo/Stargard)

159th Guards Fighter Regiment	Kluczewo/Stargard	Su-27 'Flanker-B'	red
Fighter Regiment	Chojna	Su-27 'Flanker-B'	blue/black

Air Army of the Northern Group of Forces (HQ: Legnica)
Reconnaissance Division (HQ: Osla)

Reconnaissance Squadron	Osla	Su-24 'Fencer-C'	various
Reconnaissance Squadron	Osla	MiG-25R 'Foxbat-B/D'	red
Electronic Reconnaissance Squadron	Osla	Il-20/Il-22 'Coot-A/B'	red

NB: The single 'Coot-B' is believed to operate in Aeroflot markings

Theatre Transport Division (HQ: Legnica)

Transport Regiment	Legnica	An-12BP, An-24, An-26, An-72	blue
Transport Helicopter Squadron	Legnica	Mil Mi-8/-17	blue

NB: The An-72s may operate in Aeroflot markings

Combat Helicopter Division (HQ: Bagicz/Kolobrzeg)

Combat Helicopter Regiment	Bagicz/Kolobrzeg	Mil Mi-24V, P, Mil Mi-17	various

US Navy

The US Navy is one of the most powerful fighting forces the world has ever seen. Its organic aviation alone represents the world's third-largest air arm, with some 250 squadrons. The backbone of US Naval Aviation is a force of powerful aircraft-carriers, each of which can project an almost unbelievable degree of power, with its own nuclear-capable bombers, fighters, electronic warfare aircraft, AEW platforms and ASW assets. To support these front-line carrier air wings the US Navy has significant numbers of shore-based training and support aircraft, and also deploys ASW helicopters on a huge fleet of cruisers, destroyers and frigates. Today Naval Aviation faces its toughest battle, which is for funding.

USS Abraham Lincoln, *one of 15 front-line US Navy carriers is seen conducting operations in the Indian Ocean, with the two waist cats almost clear of parked aircraft.*

From its humble beginnings in 1910, when civilian Eugene Ely made the first take-off in a fixed-wing aircraft from a ship (from the battleship USS *Birmingham*), US Naval Aviation has come a long way. Restricted largely to land-based coastal patrolling during World War I, the US Navy followed European developments during the 1920s and 1930s with great interest, embarking on a massive aircraft-carrier construction programme and the development of dedicated aircraft and flying techniques. By the end of World War II, the US Navy had 41,000 aircraft and nearly 140 aircraft-carriers. In the Atlantic its escort carriers had made a crucial contribution to keeping the sea lanes open, while US victory against Japan would have been impossible without the aircraft-carriers.

Throughout the post-war period, the US Navy's aircraft-carriers and land-based aircraft have provided the 'tip of the spear' for US foreign policy makers, making an incalculable contribution during the Cold War and a more concrete one in Korea, Vietnam and, most recently, the Persian Gulf. In the 1950s, the US Navy was enthusiastic in embracing British developments like the angled deck, the steam catapult and the mirror landing sight. Many US Navy admirals are proud to point out that the usual Presidential reaction to crisis has always been to ask, "Where are the carriers?"

Such a question is a natural one to ask, since the carrier force represents one of the most powerful military weapons ever seen. With some 250 squadrons and more than 1,500 front-line aircraft and helicopters, the US Navy has the world's third-largest air arm, whose tremendous capability includes the capacity for launching strategic nuclear strikes.

However, the US Navy is now entering a difficult period, which may turn out to be its toughest battle. With an ever-tightening budget, the US Navy's ineptitude in publicising itself may well prove damaging. During Operation Desert Storm, for example, while the USAF tasked, controlled and co-ordinated coalition air power assets, simultaneously releasing spectacular film of its successes, the US Navy made few efforts to ensure that it received any media exposure at all. The question "Where are the carriers?" took on a new meaning, almost gaining the suffix "and what are they doing in the Gulf?" These mistakes may well bring severe repercussions when the funding battle gets fiercest. Already the US Navy has lost its A-12 Avenger (designed as an A-6 replacement), the P-7 patrol aircraft (destined to replace the Orion), and cancellation of both the V-22 and the F-14 have been recommended. Since FY 1985, the percentage of Pentagon funding allocated to naval aviation has shrunk more than twice as quickly as the overall defence budget, giving the US Navy's aviators an ever-shrinking slice of a diminishing pie.

The E-2C Hawkeye and F-14 Tomcat team provides outer zone air defence for the carrier battle group. These are from VF-142, VF-143 and VAW-121.

Deployed Operations – The Carriers

The US Navy has two separate chains of command, operational and administrative. Thus an individual squadron will be assigned to a 'type commander' for administrative control during training and other periods spent ashore. The same squadron may also be assigned to a Carrier Air Wing (CVW) for advanced training and operations prior to deployment. Thirdly, the CVW itself may be assigned to an individual aircraft-carrier (CV or CVN) for operations.

Operationally, like Air Force, Army and Marine assets in a given area, all US Navy assets come under one of two unified commands: CINCLANT in the Atlantic and CINCPAC in the Pacific, or directly under the Deputy CNO Air Warfare for shore-based units. All carrier- and land-based US Navy aircraft are controlled through the numbered operational fleets, the Second (headquartered at Norfolk, VA) in the Atlantic, the Third (headquartered at Pearl Harbor) in the Eastern Pacific, the Sixth (headquartered at Gaeta, Italy) in the Mediterranean, and the Seventh (headquartered at Yokosuka) in the Western Pacific and Indian Ocean. Each is commanded by a four-star admiral.

While aircraft-carriers tend to remain allo-

VF-1 'Wolfpack' was the first F-14 Tomcat squadron. The 'NE' tailcode indicates allocation to USS Ranger, *presently assigned to the Pacific Fleet.*

cated either to the Atlantic or Pacific, they do often move between the numbered fleets on an as-required basis. The maintenance of a huge fleet of expensive, nuclear-powered supercarriers is becoming increasingly hard to justify. The dramatic reduction in tension with the former USSR has largely removed any challenge to US maritime superiority, lending weight to the arguments of those who believe that smaller, cheaper ships should be built which are less expensive to maintain and to run. Others believe that large aircraft-carriers are simply too vulnerable to contemporary anti-ship missiles. US Navy plans to have a

'F-31 'Tomcatters' are the oldest squadron in the US Navy. They flew their Tomcats from the USS Forrestal until that carrier was withdrawn for conversion to training duties.

The 'Knighthawks' of VFA-136 fly F/A-18 Hornets from the USS Dwight D. Eisenhower as part of Air Wing Seven.

Air Wing One's CAG (Commander Air Group) nominally 'owns' this Hornet from VFA-82 'Marauders', which has a CVW-1 fin badge in place of the normal unit marking.

A handful of S-3 Vikings still wear the old-style grey and white colour scheme. This aircraft serves with VS-29.

VFA-82's shipmates aboard the USS America are VFA-86 Sidewinders', the second light attack unit with CVW-1.

A VS-28 S-3B Viking takes a wire aboard the USS Forrestal, withdrawn in late 1991 to become the USN training carrier.

VFA-113's 'CAG Bird' wears a black fin, with rainbow stripes indicating the Air Wing's other squadrons. It is seen as it appeared when operating from Constellation.

The E-2C Hawkeye serves aboard every US Navy carrier in the airborne early warning role. This one wears the markings of VAW-114.

The remaining three 'Forrestal'-class carriers, USS Saratoga, USS Ranger and USS Independence, along with the USS America (essentially an improved Forrestal), are now scheduled to decommission during the remainder of the decade, Ranger in FY 1993, Saratoga in FY 1995, America in FY 1996 and Independence in FY 1998. The USS America is being retired ahead of the other three 'Kitty Hawk'/'John F. Kennedy'-class ships because it has not undergone the SLEP (Service Life Extension Program) which can extend a carrier's normal 30-year life by some 15 years.

Plans for USS John F. Kennedy to undergo a SLEP are presently under (vigorous) discussion. Sister-ship USS Kitty Hawk received her SLEP at Philadelphia between July 1987 and November 1989, while Constellation is currently in SLEP, and due to rejoin the fleet in 1993.

Most of the newer nuclear-powered carriers seem to have a long life stretching ahead of them, although a cloud hangs over Enterprise, presently laid up for the nuclear refuelling which would provide power for another 13 years of operation. This simple-sounding operation is in fact very costly and complex. When she was last refuelled, in 1971, the eight new nuclear cores cost $80 million, and installation came to $17 million. Enterprise is a one-off, built to a modified Forrestal design, and has two reactors for each of the ship's four shafts. The newer 'Nimitz'-class ships have only two reactors. Three nuclear-powered carriers have yet to commission. These are CVN-73 George Washington (due to commission in 1993), CVN-74 John Stennis (in 1994) and CVN-75 USS United States (in 1998).

Front-line carriers America, Kennedy, Saratoga, Roosevelt and Eisenhower (to be joined by Washington in 1993) are presently in service in the Atlantic Fleet, with Ranger, Independence, Kitty Hawk, Nimitz, Vinson and Lincoln in the Pacific. Enterprise and Constellation are refuelling, or in SLEP, while Forrestal has been relegated to training.

Carriers

Atlantic Fleet	
CV-60: USS Saratoga	Air Wing Seventeen (CVW-17/AA)
CV-66: USS America	Air Wing One (CVW-1/AB)
CV-67: USS John F. Kennedy	Air Wing Three (CVW-3/AC)
CVN-69: USS Dwight D. Eisenhower	Air Wing Seven (CVW-7/AG)
CVN-71: USS Theodore Roosevelt	Air Wing Eight (CVW-8/AJ)
CV-59: USS Forrestal	ex-Air Wing Six (CVW-6/AE), became AVT-59 training carrier on 1 January 1992
CVN-73: USS George Washington	to be commissioned July 1993
AVT-16: USS Lexington	retired November 1991

Pacific Fleet	
CV-61: USS Ranger	Air Wing Two (CVW-2/NE)
CV-62: USS Independence	Air Wing Five (CVW-5/NF)
CVN-68: USS Nimitz	Air Wing Nine (CVW-9/NG)
CVN-70: USS Carl Vinson	Air Wing Fifteen (CVW-15/NL)
CVN-72: USS Abraham Lincoln	Air Wing Eleven (CVW-11/NH)
CV-41: USS Midway	decommissioned April 1992, Air Wing to CV-62
CV-63: USS Kitty Hawk	temporarily assigned to AIRLANT while undergoing SLEP, rejoined AIRPAC December 1991
CV-64: USS Constellation	temporarily assigned to AIRLANT while undergoing SLEP, will return to AIRPAC by December 1993
CVN-65: USS Enterprise	temporarily assigned to AIRLANT while undergoing nuclear refuelling and modernisation; area of service to be decided in 1994

15-carrier navy in the 1990s have thus been dramatically down-graded, and even a 12-carrier force is beginning to look optimistic.

Unfortunately for the supporters of the aircraft-carrier, these arguments have coincided at a time that more than half the present fleet has reached the midway point in their nominal 45-year lifespan, the very point at which replacements should be being planned. Although there are now three CVNs under construction, further vessels will find it very hard to attract funding.

The last of the wartime carriers (Lexington fought in the Pacific, including the ferocious Marianas Turkey Shoot, while Midway was

launched in March 1945) have now finally been retired. Lexington, the training carrier since 1962, has been replaced by USS Forrestal which has been re-designated from CV-59 to AVT-59, retaining a measure of operational capability for contingencies. USS Midway became the first carrier home-ported outside the USA by being based at Yokosuka, Japan. This allowed the ship to be readily available for rapid deployments in the Pacific. USS Independence has now taken over both Midway's role and its Air Wing Five, leaving its own CVW-14 (which played a major part in Operation Desert Storm) ashore for possible re-assignment.

Deployed Operations – Carrier Air Wings

The US Navy's remaining carriers share 12 Carrier Air Wings (CVWs), six per fleet. These air wings are not all of the same composition, since different types of ships can accommodate different numbers of aircraft, and since not all carriers can accommodate all aircraft types in use. In addition, there have been experiments in air wing composition in order to try to find the most efficient type, and some non-standard air wings are still deployed. The eventual aim, however, is to end up with a standard air wing, with the same number of aircraft of the various different types. This will bring great benefits in training and operability.

Nine of the existing air wings are similar in composition (known as 'Conventional CVWs'), with a total of 86 aircraft. This total includes two long-range all-weather fighter/intercept squadrons equipped with 24 F-14 Tomcats, two fighter/light-attack squadrons equipped with 24 F/A-18 Hornets, a single medium-attack squadron equipped with 10 A-6E and four KA-6D Intruders, and single ECM/EW, ASW, AEW and SAR/ASW squadrons equipped respectively with four EA-6B Prowlers, 10 S-3 Vikings, four E-2C Hawkeyes and six SH-3H Sea King or SH-60F Sea Hawk helicopters.

The 'attack heavy' CVW-8 on board the USS *Roosevelt* represents the future composition of the air wing, which again has a total of 86 aircraft. It differs in having a second A-6E Intruder squadron, with a total of 20 of these powerful aircraft on charge, some equipped with buddy refuelling pods. Hornet and Tomcat numbers are reduced by four aircraft of each type, and no dedicated KA-6Ds are carried. An extra EA-6B and an extra E-2C make up the total.

The 66-aircraft CVW-5 previously on USS *Midway* also had a second Intruder unit (with a total of 16 of these aircraft, and no KA-6Ds) and also an extra Hornet unit (bringing the total to 36 F/A-18s), but lacked any F-14s or S-3s. The air wing was otherwise identical to the 'Conventional' type. Moving to the *Independence*, CVW-5 initially retained its present structure, although the individual squadrons could theoretically have been expanded to take advantage of the extra space afforded by the larger 'Forrestal'-class carrier. Expansion and conversion to the normal 'conventional' or 'Roosevelt'-type wing may be more difficult, since there are barely sufficient F-14s to form two additional units, and since there is also a shortage of S-3 Vikings. Possibly as a temporary measure, the two CVW-14 Tomcat units have deployed to Atsugi, Japan, where they have been seen flying with CVW-5's 'NF' tailcodes, and VS-21 has been allocated to CVW-5. The wing now has only two F/A-18 units. In any case, since CVW-5 is shore-based at Atsugi, the use of large numbers of F/A-18s fits in well with the forward basing of USMC F/A-18s at Iwakuni, Japan.

CVW-2 on *Ranger* has two Intruder units (24 A-6Es, four KA-6Ds) and no Hornets, but is otherwise similar to the 'conventional' wing, albeit with a total of only 76 aircraft. The impending early retirement of *Ranger* makes its conversion to a more standard CVW (incorporating Hornets) unlikely.

Perhaps the biggest change on US Navy carrier decks in recent years has been the substitution of the ageing A-7 Corsair II by the multi-role F/A-18 Hornet. The last A-7 units remained in service just long enough to participate in Desert Storm, but all have now been replaced. Although it lacks range (a fault admitted by even its most devoted admirers), the F/A-18 has revolutionised the light-strike community, bringing an undreamed-of measure of versatility and survivability. Every Hornet on a carrier deck represents both a modern ground-attack aircraft, capable of delivering the most modern types of ordnance with pinpoint accuracy, and also a highly effective air combat aircraft.

The original F/A-18A and its two-seat equivalent, the F/A-18B, have now been replaced on the production line by the F/A-18C and F/A-18D, respectively. The first 137 F/A-18Cs and 31 F/A-18Ds incorporated improved avionics and featured AMRAAM and IR-Maverick compatibility, while the latest aircraft have been equipped to full night-attack standard, with a Kaiser AV/AVQ-28 raster HUD, AN/AAS-38 thermal imaging and colour MFDs.

The proposed F/A-18E and F/A-18F offer increased range, two extra stores stations and enhanced performance with uprated engines and a bigger wing. The two-seat F/A-18D has already started to replace the A-6E Intruder in US Marine Corps all-weather attack units, trading survivability and accuracy for a slight reduction in range and endurance.

The importance of the F/A-18 Hornet to the US Navy of the 1990s cannot be understated. Although the engine problems which crippled the F-14 Tomcat were finally solved in the F-14A(Plus), since re-designated F-14B, the aircraft is increasingly being seen as an expensive luxury which is no longer needed with the demise of the Soviet Union and the Warsaw Pact, and whose fleet defence role can be as effectively fulfilled by AMRAAM-equipped Hornets operating in conjunction with ship- and land-based AEW platforms. One-time plans to build 127 advanced F-14Ds, and produce 400 more by conversion, were dramatically cut back, and now only 37 of these aircraft will be built, with 18 more produced by conversion of F-14As. The F-14D introduces new avionics, including APG-71 radar and a new IRST set. Even the interim re-engined F-14B (which retains F-14A avionics) will now only equip six front-line squadrons, with 38 being built new, and 32 more being produced through conversion of F-14A airframes. The F-14 will remain in service for many years to come, but procurement has already been virtually halted, and the size of some F-14 squadrons has been reduced, making room for more multi-role Hornets and A-6E Intruders.

The A-6E Intruder, despite its age, remains crucially important. All operational aircraft are now to A-6E TRAM (Target Recognition and Attack Multi-sensor) standard, although most A-6 units also include a handful of dedicated KA-6D tankers. Some 80 of the remaining 300

VA-36, known as the 'Roadrunners', is one of two A-6 units with CVW-8 aboard Roosevelt. The other unit is VA-65, known as the 'Tigers'.

Grumman's ageing A-6E continues to perform the vital long range, all-weather attack role on board US Navy carriers. This one serves with VA-95 'Green Lizards' aboard Lincoln.

USS Ranger's Air Wing Two wear 'NE' tailcodes. EW support is provided by the EA-6B Prowlers of VAQ-131 'Lancers'. Ranger does not embark any F/A-18 Hornets.

Before structural problems intervened, grounding most of the F-16Ns, VF-43 'Challengers' at Oceana operated these aircraft on adversary missions.

Led by an F-16N are two of VF-45's elderly McDonnell Douglas A-4 Skyhawks. They are based at NAS Key West. Both wear gaudy 'adversary' colour schemes.

Atlantic Fleet **COD** duties are performed by **VRC-40** 'Codfish Airlines', based at **NAS** Norfolk as part of **Carrier Airborne Early Warning Wing 12.**

VF-101 'Grim Reapers' are the East Coast Tomcat **FRS** (Fleet Readiness Squadron), responsible for aircrew training and conversion.

VF-43's F-16Ns are augmented by a substantial number of similarly painted, stripped and lightened A-4 Skyhawks. These simulate older threat aircraft very well.

Lightweight supersonic enemy aircraft like the MiG-21 can be simulated by the F-5E. This one wears the distinctive markings of VF-43.

The EA-6A Intruder remains in service only with **VAQ-33** 'Firebirds' as electronic adversaries, simulating **Soviet** electronic warfare aircraft in exercises.

This 'Grim Reaper' tail marking is applied to the Tomcats of the East Coast **FRS**, **VF-101**. The unit also uses the tailcode '**AD**'.

VAW-120, known as the 'Cyclones', is the Atlantic Fleet E-2C Hawkeye **FRS**. This is their unit insignia.

The 'Lamplighters' of HSL-36 apply this winged torch badge to their '**HY**'-coded Kaman SH-2F Seasprites.

This is the tailfin marking of **VP-23**, the 'Sea Hawks', a P-3 Orion squadron which serves with **Brunswick's Patrol Wing Five.**

The 'Pelicans' of **VP-45** are co-located with **VP-23**. Orions rarely wear even these toned-down markings, appearing anonymous.

A-6E airframes are now severely g-limited because of fatigue problems, and during Desert Storm many had to be relegated to performing tanker duties only. Cancellation of the A-12 leaves re-winging these aircraft as the only realistic option apart from replacing them with the two-seat all-weather F/A-18D (or a more advanced Hornet derivative) or one of the proposed strike versions of the Tomcat, for which Grumman are lobbying hard but which would offer little more than an F/A-18 apart from (irrelevant) supersonic performance. One hundred and seventy eight sets of new composite wings have been contracted for, and options on 72 or 144 more may be exercised. Ninety four wing sets had been delivered by the beginning of 1990, and 22 sets had been fitted by Grumman and the two NADEPS at Norfolk and Alameda. Current plans call for Grumman to install three sets per month, and for each of the NADEPS to install one set.

Mainstream US Navy Carrier Air Wings adopted the ASW role (previously assigned mainly to shore-based aircraft, ship-based helicopters and a handful of specialist carriers) during the mid-1970s, and what had been attack carriers (CVAs) became general-purpose carriers (CVs). ASW aircraft are used with a core of fighter and strike aircraft, alongside the various support types. Thus all current types of CVW include six helicopters (with a dual SAR and ASW role) and all except CVW-5 also include between eight and 10 S-3 Vikings.

The remarkable Viking (affectionately dubbed the 'Hoover' because of the peculiar hoot of its turbofan engines) has proved extraordinarily successful in service, and has even been pressed into service as a bomber (this latter role being demonstrated during the Gulf War). The Viking is unique among US Navy carrierborne aircraft in that its crew includes an enlisted man – the only 'White Hat' to fly in an ejection seat! In 1981, Lockheed received a contract to upgrade 160 of the 187 S-3As built to S-3B standards, with increased acoustic processing capacity, expanded ESM, better radar processing, provision for the Harpoon missile and a new sonobuoy telemetry receiver. These modifications are being incorporated at NAS Cecil Field, and at the time of writing all Atlantic Fleet units have S-3Bs, while Pacific Fleet units largely retain the older S-3A.

The basic S-3 airframe has been used to provide a COD platform (the US-3A) and was used when the USN needed a replacement for the ageing Skywarrior in the carrierborne Elint role, producing the ES-3A, which has recently flown in prototype form. This will allow new squadrons VQ-5 and VQ-6 to form at Agana and Cecil Field, and these will operate Elint aircraft from carriers for the first time since 1987, when a Skywarrior crash (on 21 November) on the USS *Nimitz* led to the type being restricted to shore bases. VQ-1 discarded its Skywarriors in December 1988, followed by VQ-2 in October 1991, leaving these units operating only the EP-3 Orion. VQ-2 used the EA-3B operationally in the Gulf, but only VAQ-33 at Key West retains the type today.

The carrierborne 'Inner Zone' ASW role is handled by helicopters. The trusty Sikorsky SH-3H Sea King is only now being replaced by the SH-60F version of the Sea Hawk. The newer helicopter has made one deployment with HS-2 aboard the USS *Nimitz*, and is entering service with HS-3, HS-4 and HS-6. By comparison with the SH-60B used for outer-zone ASW work and deployed on smaller ships, the SH-60F lacks MAD gear, ESM and data-link, and carries only eight sonobuoys. The aircraft lacks the SH-60B's underfuselage radar scanner, and instead has a dunking sonar. The SH-60F can carry the Mk 46 or Mk 50 homing torpedo. When they deploy, SH-60F units will eventually have six Ocean Hawks and two HH-60Hs for combat SAR.

Another vitally important support type is the Grumman E-2C Hawkeye. Deployed aboard every carrier in fours (or fives), the turboprop-powered 'hummer' serves as an airborne early warning and radar command post, and is chiefly used for the control of F-14 interceptors. The aircraft is reputed to be one of the most difficult types to bring aboard a carrier. Early E-2Cs were equipped with the AN/APS-139 radar, but all will be retrofitted with the newer AN/APS-145.

To support and protect packages of strike aircraft, every carrier has a detachment of EA-6B Prowler ECM/EW aircraft. Developed from the A-6 Intruder, the Prowler is a dedicated electronic warfare platform, with four crew sitting in tandem pairs of side-by-side ejection seats. First deployed in Vietnam, the aircraft has been continuously updated and upgraded, so that several standards of Prowler are now in use. Representing today's baseline is the EA-6B ICAP-1, which introduced increased jamming capability with an eight-band expanded jamming system, reduced response time, and a multi-format display, along with an automatic all-weather carrier landing system, and new navigation and communications systems. Twenty three basic aircraft were followed by 25 EXCAP EA-6Bs, all of which have now been retired or upgraded. Twenty one surviving basic production aircraft were modified to ICAP-1 standard, followed by 45 new-build aircraft. The ICAP-2 modification further enhanced jamming capability with a new AYK-14 computer with four times the memory and three times the processing speed. This enables the system to operate effectively across nine frequency bands. Each of the five external jammer pods can generate signals in one of seven frequency bands (instead of one!) and can jam in two frequency bands simultaneously. New-build ICAP-2 aircraft began rolling off the line during 1984.

The latest EA-6B equipment standard is known as ADVCAP. ADVCAP aircraft are compatible with the HARM missile and incorporate the new Lockheed-Sanders AN/ALQ-149 communications jammer. Various other new jammers are incorporated, along with extra chaff/flare dispensers, Navstar GPS and JTIDS. The increased weight is compensated by uprated engines and a host of aerodynamic improvements, including an increased-height tailfin, recontoured slats and flaps, drooped wing leading edges and new strakes on the forward fuselage. Some 100 ADVCAPs are to be converted from ICAP-2 standard aircraft.

AIRLANT

Air Wing One (USS America)

VF-102 'Diamondbacks'	F-14A TARPS	Codes commence AB/100
VF-33 'Starfighters'	F-14A	Codes commence AB/200
VFA-82 'Marauders'	F/A-18C	Codes commence AB/300
VFA-86 'Sidewinders'	F/A-18C	Codes commence AB/400
VA-85 'Buckeyes'	A-6E/KA-6D	Codes commence AB/500
VAW-123 'Screwtops'	E-2C	Codes commence AB/600
VAQ-137 'Rooks'	EA-6B	Codes commence AB/604
HS-11 'Dragon Slayers'	SH-3H	Codes commence AB/610
VS-32 'Maulers/ Norsemen'	S-3B	Codes commence AB/700

(VF-33 were previously known as the 'Fighting Tarsiers')
(VA-85 have been known as the 'Black Falcons')

Air Wing Three (USS John F. Kennedy)

VF-14 'Tophatters'	F-14A	Codes commence AC/100
VF-32 'Swordsmen'	F-14A TARPS	Codes commence AC/200
VFA-37 'Bulls'	F/A-18C	Codes commence AC/300
VFA-105 'Gunslingers'	F/A-18C	Codes commence AC/400
VA-75 'Sunday Punchers'	A-6E/KA-6D	Codes commence AC/500
VAW-126 'Seahawks'	E-2C	Codes commence AC/600
VAQ-130 'Zappers'	EA-6B	Codes commence AC/604
HS-7 'Big Dippers'	SH-3H	Codes commence AC/610
VS-22 'Vidars'	S-3B	Codes commence AC/700

Air Wing Six
(Presently unassigned)

VF-11 'Red Rippers'	F-14A	Codes commence AE/100
VF-31 'Tomcatters'	F-14A TARPS	Codes commence AE/200
VFA-132 'Privateers'	F/A-18C	Codes commence AE/300
VFA-137 'Kestrels'	F/A-18C	Codes commence AE/400
VA-176 'Thunderbolts'	A-6E/KA-6D	Codes commence AE/500
VAW-122 'Steeljaws'	E-2C	Codes commence AE/600
VAQ-133 'Wizards'	EA-6B	Codes commence AE/604
HS-15 'Red Lions'	SH-3H	Codes commence AE/610
VS-28 'Gamblers'	S-3B	Codes commence AE/700

Air Wing Seven (USS Dwight D. Eisenhower)

VF-143 'Pukin' Dogs'	F-14B TARPS	Codes commence AG/100
VF-142 'Ghostriders'	F-14B	Codes commence AG/200
VFA-136 'Knighthawks'	F/A-18C	Codes commence AG/300
VFA-131 'Wildcats'	F/A-18C	Codes commence AG/400
VA-34 'Blue Blasters'	A-6E/KA-6D	Codes commence AG/500
VAW-121 'Bluetails'	E-2C	Codes commence AG/600
VAQ-140 'Patriots'	EA-6B	Codes commence AG/604
HS-5 'Night Dippers'	SH-3H	Codes commence AG/610
VS-31 'Top Cats'	S-3B	Codes commence AG/700

Air Wing Eight (USS Theodore Roosevelt)

VF-41 'Black Aces'	F-14A	Codes commence AJ/100
VF-84 'Jolly Rogers'	F-14A TARPS	Codes commence AJ/200
VFA-15 'Valions'	F/A-18A	Codes commence AJ/300
VFA-87 'Golden Warriors'	F/A-18A	Codes commence AJ/400
VA-65 'Tigers'	A-6E	Codes commence AJ/500
VA-36 'Roadrunners'	A-6E	Codes commence AJ/530
VAW-124 'Bear Aces'	E-2C	Codes commence AJ/600
HS-9 'Sea Griffins'	SH-3H	Codes commence AJ/610
VAQ-141 'Shadowhawks'	EA-6B	Codes commence AJ/620
VS-24 'Scouts'	S-3B	Codes commence AJ/700

Air Wing Seventeen (USS Saratoga)

VF-74 'Bedevillers'	F-14B	Codes commence AA/100
VF-103 'Sluggers'	F-14B TARPS	Codes commence AA/200
VFA-83 'Rampagers'	F/A-18C	Codes commence AA/300
VFA-81 'Sunliners'	F/A-18C	Codes commence AA/400
VA-35 'Black Panthers'	A-6E/KA-6D	Codes commence AA/500
VAW-125 'Tigertails'	E-2C	Codes commence AA/600
VAQ-132 'Scorpions'	EA-6B	Codes commence AA/604
HS-3 'Tridents'	SH-60F	Codes commence AA/610
VS-30 'Diamondcutters'	S-3B	Codes commence AA/700

The Fleet Electronic Warfare Support Group operates two NKC-135s and a single converted DC-8 from Chrysler's Wac Field facility.

The East Coast Hornet FRS is VFA-106, the 'Gladiators', based at Cecil Field. The Navy and Marines share three F/A-18 FRSs.

All Atlantic Fleet Viking units, including the FRS, VS-27 'Seawolves', use the S-3B, while some West Coast units retain the S-3A.

VAW-115 'Sun Kings'	E-2C	Codes commence NF/600
VAQ-136 'Gauntlets'	EA-6B	Codes commence NF/604
HS-12 'Wyverns'	SH-3H	Codes commence NF/610
VS-21 'Fighting Redtails'	S-3B	Codes commence NF/700
VFA-151 'Vigilantes'	F/A-18A	Transferred to Lemoore 1991
VA-185 'Knighthawks'	A-6E/KA-6D	Decommissioned 1991 NF/400

(VAW-115 were previously known as the 'Liberty Belles')

Air Wing Nine (USS Nimitz)

VF-24 'Fighting Renegades'	F-14B	Codes commence NG/100
VF-211 'Fighting Checkmates'	F-14B TARPS	Codes commence NG/200
VFA-146 'Blue Diamonds'	F/A-18C	Codes commence NG/300
VFA-147 'Argonauts'	F/A-18C	Codes commence NG/400
VA-165 'Boomers'	A-6E/KA-6D	Codes commence NG/500
VAW-112 'Golden Hawks'	E-2C	Codes commence NG/600
VAQ-138 'Yellow Jackets'	EA-6B	Codes commence NG/605
HS-2 'Golden Falcons'	SH-60F/ HH-60F	Codes commence NG/610
VS-33 'Screwbirds'	S-3A	Codes commence NG/700

Air Wing Eleven (USS Abraham Lincoln)

VF-114 'Aardvarks'	F-14A	Codes commence NH/100
VF-213 'Black Lions'	F-14A TARPS	Codes commence NH/200
VFA-22 'Fighting Redcocks'	F/A-18C	Codes commence NH/300
VFA-94 'Shrikes'	F/A-18C	Codes commence NH/400
VA-95 'Green Lizards'	A-6E/KA-6D	Codes commence NH/500
VAW-117 'Wallbangers'	E-2C	Codes commence NH/600
VAQ-135 'Black Ravens'	EA-6B	Codes commence NH/604
HS-6 'Indians'	SH-60F	Codes commence NH/610
VS-29 'Screaming Dragonfires'	S-3A	Codes commence NH/700
VS-21 'Fighting Redtails'	S-3A	Reassigned to CVW-5

Air Wing Fourteen

(No current assignment, previously USS Independence)

VFA-113 'Stingers'	F/A-18C	Codes commence NK/300
VFA-25 'Fist of the Fleet'	F/A-18C	Codes commence NK/400
VA-196 'Main Battery'	A-6E/KA-6D	Codes commence NK/500
VAW-113 'Black Hawks'	E-2C	Codes commence NK/600
VAQ-139 'Cougars'	EA-6B	Codes commence NK/604
HS-8 'Eight Ballers'	SH-3H	Codes commence NK/610
VF-154 'Black Knights'	F-14A TARPS	Transferred to CVW-5
VF-21 'Freelancers'	F-14A	Transferred to CVW-5
VS-37 'Sawbucks'	S-3A	Transferred to CVW-15

Air Wing Fifteen (USS Carl Vinson)

VF-51 'Screaming Eagles'	F-14D	Codes commence NL/100
VF-111 'Sundowners'	F-14D TARPS	Codes commence NL/200
VFA-27 'Chargers'	F/A-18A	Codes commence NL/300
VFA-97 'Warhawks'	F/A-18A	Codes commence NL/400
VA-52 'Knight Riders'	A-6E/KA-6D	Codes commence NL/500
VAW-114 'Hormel Hawks'	E-2C	Codes commence NL/600
VAQ-134 'Garudas'	EA-6B	Codes commence NL/605
HS-4 'Black Knights'	SH-60F	Codes commence NL/610
VS-37 'Sawbucks'	S-3A	Codes commence NL/700

The 'Sea Stallions' HM-14 fly mine-sweeping MH-53Es and may still have a handful of RH-53Ds. One of the latter is seen here.

This CH-46 serves with Helicopter Combat Support Squadron 16, 'Bullfrogs', based at NAS Pensacola.

VX-1 (known as 'The Pioneers') are a helicopter test and trials unit based at Patuxent River. Their fleet includes this SH-60B.

The 'Tridents' of HS-3 were the first COMNAVAIRLANT SH-60F Ocean Hawk squadron, transitioning from the SH-3.

Toned-down tactical markings have spread to every community, this drab CH-46 belonging to Norfolk-based HC-8 'Dragon Whales'.

HS-5 'Night Dippers' are the ASW/SAR helicopter squadron of CVW-7, deployed aboard the USS Dwight D. Eisenhower.

A CH-46 from the same unit, HC-8, displays the full colour scheme which is now a rarity, even among second-line units.

AIRPAC

Air Wing Two (USS Ranger)

VF-1 'Wolfpack'	F-14A	Codes commence NE/100
VF-2 'Bounty Hunters'	F-14A TARPS	Codes commence NE/200
VA-155 'Silver Foxes'	A-6E/KA-6D	Codes commence NE/400
VA-145 'Swordsmen'	A-6E	Codes commence NE/500
VAW-116 'Sun Kings'	E-2C	Codes commence NE/600
VAQ-131 'Lancers'	EA-6B	Codes commence NE/604
HS-14 'Chargers'	SH-3H	Codes commence NE/610
VS-38 'Red Griffins'	S-3A	Codes commence NE/700

Air Wing Five (USS Independence)

(Shore-based at NAF Atsugi when not deployed.)

VF-154 'Black Knights'	F-14A TARPS	Codes commence NF/100
VF-21 'Freelancers'	F-14A	Codes commence NF/200
VFA-192 'World Famous Golden Dragons'	F/A-18A	Codes commence NF/300
VFA-195 'Dambusters'	F/A-18A	Codes commence NF/400
VA-115 'Eagles'	A-6E	Codes commence NF/500

Operating from Sigonella, Sicily, the 'Black Stallions' of HC-4 provide support for the Sixth Fleet with their CH-53E Sea Stallions.

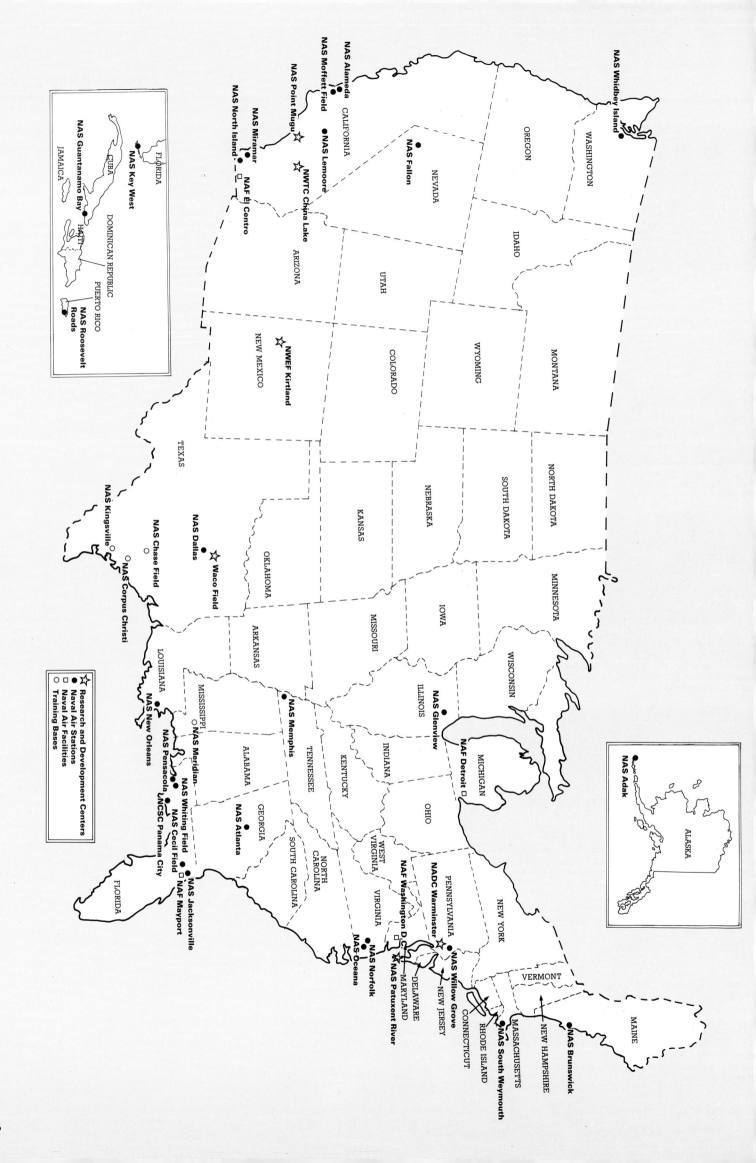

NAS Whidbey Island

OREGON

WASHINGTON

NAS Alameda

NAS Moffett Field

NAS Point Mugu

NAS Miramar

NAS North Island

NAS Lemoore

CALIFORNIA

NAF El Centro

NWTC China Lake

NAS Fallon

NEVADA

IDAHO

ARIZONA

UTAH

WYOMING

MONTANA

NWEF Kirtland

NEW MEXICO

COLORADO

SOUTH DAKOTA

NORTH DAKOTA

TEXAS

OKLAHOMA

KANSAS

NEBRASKA

MINNESOTA

NAS Kingsville

NAS Chase Field

NAS Dallas

Waco Field

NAS Corpus Christi

ARKANSAS

MISSOURI

IOWA

WISCONSIN

LOUISIANA

NAS New Orleans

NAS Pensacola

NCSC Panama City

NAS Memphis

NAS Meridian

MISSISSIPPI

ALABAMA

TENNESSEE

KENTUCKY

INDIANA

ILLINOIS

NAS Glenview

NAF Detroit

MICHIGAN

OHIO

FLORIDA

NAS Whiting Field

NAS Cecil Field

NAF Mayport

NAS Jacksonville

GEORGIA

NAS Atlanta

SOUTH CAROLINA

NORTH CAROLINA

WEST VIRGINIA

VIRGINIA

NAS Washington D.C.

NADC Warminster

PENNSYLVANIA

NAS Willow Grove

NEW YORK

NAS Oceana

NAS Norfolk

NAS Patuxent River

MARYLAND

DELAWARE

NEW JERSEY

CONNECTICUT

RHODE ISLAND

NAS South Weymouth

MASSACHUSETTS

NEW HAMPSHIRE

VERMONT

NAS Brunswick

MAINE

Key

☆ Research and Development Centers
● Naval Air Stations
□ Naval Air Facilities
○ Training Bases

FLORIDA

NAS Key West

CUBA

JAMAICA

NAS Guantanamo Bay

HAITI

DOMINICAN REPUBLIC

PUERTO RICO

NAS Roosevelt Roads

ALASKA

NAS Adak

146

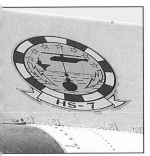

The 'Big Dippers' of HS-7 apply this graphic badge to their SH-3Hs.

HS-15 are known as the 'Red Lions', and use such a device in their unit badge.

Also based at Mayport are several SH-60B units, including HSL-48 'Vipers', one of whose aircraft is seen here.

HS-11 'Dragonslayers' operate the SH-3H Sea King with Air Wing One aboard the USS America. Most of the aircraft wear a toned-down colour scheme.

The 'Air Wolves' of HSL-40 act as the East Coast SH-60B Seahawk FRS. Very few SH-60Bs wear squadron markings.

The 'Tridents' of HSL-32 are based at Mayport as part of Helicopter Sea Control Wing One. Their aircraft wear a red Trident badge on the tailfin.

VR-24, known as the 'Lifting Eagles', or sometimes as the 'World's Biggest Little Airline', provide COD support to the Sixth Fleet.

Co-located HSL-34 are known as the 'Gray Checkers'. Their aircraft wear a black and white checkerboard fin-stripe, and an ace of spades on the fuselage.

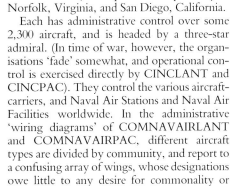

Many SH-2F Seasprites have now received toned-down markings on a tactical grey colour scheme. This one belongs to Det. 8 'The Rhinos' of HSL-36 'Lamplighters'.

Administrative Command

Administratively, command originates with the Chief of Naval Operations, and then runs through two area fleet commanders (Atlantic and Pacific) who control surface vessels, submarines, the Marines and Aviation. These are responsible for training and readiness. Aviation comes under the Commander Naval Air Force Atlantic (COMNAVAIRLANT) and the Commander Naval Air Force Pacific (COMNAVAIRPAC) headquartered respectively in Norfolk, Virginia, and San Diego, California.

Each has administrative control over some 2,300 aircraft, and is headed by a three-star admiral. (In time of war, however, the organisations 'fade' somewhat, and operational control is exercised directly by CINCLANT and CINCPAC). They control the various aircraft-carriers, and Naval Air Stations and Naval Air Facilities worldwide. In the administrative 'wiring diagrams' of COMNAVAIRLANT and COMNAVAIRPAC, different aircraft types are divided by community, and report to a confusing array of wings, whose designations owe little to any desire for commonality or logic. In the main, however, most of these

wings exercise control over shipborne squadrons only while these are shore-based between cruises.

Apart from the carrier-based units this includes the various ship-based helicopter units, operating aircraft as diverse as the SH-2F and SH-60B LAMPS platforms and transport aircraft like the CH-46 and CH-53. The various HSLs deploy helicopters to various types of ship on an as-required basis. SH-2Fs only go to the 'Knox'- and 'Kidd'-class frigates, and to the *Truxton* nuclear-powered cruiser. 'Spruance'-class ASW destroyers accept the SH-60B. The first two 'Ticonderoga'-class AEGIS cruisers take SH-2Fs but others in the class take SH-60Bs. Of the 'Oliver Hazard Perry'-class ASW frigates the first and third through 25th ships carry SH-2Fs, but the second and the 26th through 51st take SH-60Bs. The USS *Belknap* cruiser itself carries an SH-3D as a transport, but the other eight vessels in the class embark an SH-2F.

Despite the widespread introduction of the SH-60B, the Seasprite still has a long life ahead of it. A life-extension programme incorporating new GE T700 engines and revised avionics has resulted in the SH-2G. Six have been newly built, but most of the 97 required are to be produced by conversion of existing SH-2Fs.

The exceptions to this rule of administrative control are provided by the patrol wings, which often conduct operations and train from the same shore bases. On deployment the wings and their squadrons report to the area operational commanders. Atlantic Fleet Patrol squadrons currently maintain permanent deployments at NAS Bermuda (manned only by Reserve units); NAS Roosevelt Roads, Puerto Rico; NAS Rota, Spain; NAF Lajes in the Azores; and NAS Sigonella, Sicily. Pacific units staff deployments at NAS Adak, Alaska; NAF Misawa, Japan; NAF Kadena, Okinawa; NAS Cubi Point, Philippines; and NAF Diego Garcia. The patrol community has undergone a number of recent changes in the drive towards modernisation. In order to free late Orions for the re-equipment of some Reserve units, the patrol wings have been reduced from six to five squadrons, and squadron establishments have dropped from nine to eight aircraft.

The other community which uses the Orion is more secretive. Elint is the role of the EP-3E-II Aries II aircraft used by VQ-1 and VQ-2 at Agana and Rota, while highly modified P-3Bs are used by VPU-1 and VPU-2 at Brunswick and Barbers Point. The latter aircraft are painted to resemble standard P-3Cs (with painted-on sonobuoy launch tubes) and often carry spurious serials and squadron insignia.

Naval Aviation is administered overall by a three-star Assistant Chief of Naval Operations (ACNO Air Warfare or Op 05) in Washington, DC. His task is to implement the programmes of the CNO with respect to naval aviation, determining support requirements for aircraft and ships, and acting as CNO's principal advisor on aviation matters. The present incumbent is Vice Admiral Richard M. Dunleavy, a former A-3 and A-6 NFO. He does not exercise operational control, however, which lies in the hands of CINCLANT and CINCPAC, who are four-star admirals.

Commander Naval Forces Atlantic (COMNAVAIRLANT)

The mission of COMNAVAIRLANT is to provide combat-ready forces to fleet commanders operating from the North Pole to the Antarctic between the East Coast of the USA and the Indian Ocean. These forces fall under the operational control of the Second Fleet in the Atlantic, and the Sixth in the Mediterranean.

Reporting directly to COMNAVAIRLANT are Commander Tactical Wings Atlantic at Oceana, Commander Strike Fighter Wings Atlantic at Cecil Field, Commander Helicopter Wings Atlantic at Jacksonville, Commander Patrol Wings Atlantic at Brunswick and Commander Fleet Air Mediterranean at Rota, Spain.

COMNAVAIRLANT

Commander Tactical Wings Atlantic, NAS Oceana, VA
Fighter Wing One
Medium-Attack Wing One
Carrier Airborne Early Warning Wing 12
FACSFAC VACAPES

Commander Strike Fighter Wings Atlantic, NAS Cecil Field, FL
Light-Attack Wing One
Sea-Strike Wing One
FACSFAC Jacksonville
FEWSG
NAS Key West

Commander Helicopter Wings Atlantic, NAS Jacksonville, FL
NAS Jacksonville
NAS Mayport
Helicopter Tactical Wing One
Helicopter Anti-Submarine Warfare Wing One
Helicopter Sea Control Wing One
Helicopter Sea Control Wing Three

Commander Patrol Wings Atlantic, NAS Brunswick, ME
NAS Brunswick
NAS Bermuda
NAS Lajes
VXN-8
VQ-4
Patrol Wing Five
Patrol Wing Eleven

Commander Fleet Air Mediterranean
NAS Rota
NAS Sigonella
VQ-2
VR-22
VR-24

Commander Tactical Wings Atlantic
Fleet Area Control & Surveillance Facility Virginia Capes

Commander Fighter Wing One, NAS Oceana, VA

VF-43 'Challengers'	A-4F/J, F-5E/F, F-16N, T-2C	NAS Oceana/AD
VC-8 'Redtails'	TA-4J, SH-3G	NAS Roosevelt Roads, PR/GF
VC-10 'Challengers'	TA-4J	NAS Guantanamo Bay, Cuba/JH
VF-101 'Grim Reapers' (FRS)	F-14A/B	NAS Oceana/AD

Plus deployed Atlantic Fleet Tomcat units, nominally shore-based at Oceana:

VF-11 'Red Rippers'	F-14A	(CVW-6/AE)
VF-14 'Tophatters'	F-14A	(CVW-3/AC)
VF-31 'Tomcatters'	F-14A (TARPS)	(CVW-6/AE)
VF-32 'Swordsmen'	F-14A (TARPS)	(CVW-3/AC)
VF-33 'Starfighters'	F-14A	(CVW-1/AB)
VF-41 'Black Aces'	F-14A	(CVW-8/AJ)
VF-74 'Bedevillers'	F-14B	(CVW-17/AA)
VF-84 'Jolly Rogers'	F-14A (TARPS)	(CVW-8/AJ)
VF-102 'Diamondbacks'	F-14B (TARPS)	(CVW-1/AB)
VF-103 'Sluggers'	F-14B (TARPS)	(CVW-17/AA)
VF-142 'Ghostriders'	F-14B	(CVW-7/AG)
VF-143 'Pukin' Dogs'	F-14A (TARPS)	(CVW-7/AG)

Commander Medium-Attack Wing One, NAS Oceana, VA

VA-42 'Green Pawns' (FRS)	A-6E/KA-6D, TC-4C,T-34C	NAS Oceana/AD

Plus deployed Atlantic Fleet Intruder units, nominally shore-based at Oceana:

VA-34 'Blue Blasters'	A-6E/KA-6D	(CVW-7/AG)
VA-35 'Black Panthers'	A-6E/KA-6D	(CVW-17/AA)
VA-36 'Roadrunners'	A-6E/KA-6D	(CVW-8/AJ)
VA-65 'Fighting Tigers'	A-6E/KA-6D	(CVW-8/AJ)
VA-75 'Sunday Punchers'	A-6E/KA-6D	(CVW-3/AC)
VA-85 'Buckeyes'	A-6E/KA-6D	(CVW-1/AB)
VA-176 'Thunderbolts'	A-6E/KA-6D	(CVW-6/AE)
VA-55 'Sea Horses' 'War Horses'	A-6E/KA-6D	Decommissioned 1991

Commander Carrier Airborne Early Warning Wing 12, NAS Norfolk, VA

VAW-120 'Cyclones' (FRS)	E-2C/TE-2B	NAS Oceana/AD

Plus deployed Atlantic Fleet Hawkeye units, nominally shore-based at Norfolk:

VAW-121 'Bluetails'	E-2C	(CVW-7/AG)
VAW-122 'Steeljaws'	E-2C	(CVW-17/AA)
VAW-123 'Screwtops'	E-2C	(CVW-1/AB)
VAW-124 'Bear Aces'	E-2C	(CVW-8/AJ)
VAW-125 'Tigertails'	E-2C	(CVW-17/AA)
VAW-126 'Seahawks'	E-2C	(CVW-3/AC)
VAW-127 'Seabats'	E-2C	Decommissioned 1991/AK
VRC-40 'Codfish Airlines'	C-2A	NAS Oceana/JK

Commander Strike Fighter Wings Atlantic

VF-45 'Blackbirds'	F-16N, TF-16N, A-4F, TA-4J, F-5E, F-5F	NAS Key West/AD Det. at Cecil Field
VAQ-33 'Firebirds'	EA-6A, EP-3A	NAS Key West/GD
Fleet Electronic Warfare Support Group	EC-24A, NKC-135A	Waco, Texas
Fleet Area Control and Surveillance Facility, Jacksonville		

Commander Light-Attack Wing One, NAS Cecil Field, FL

VFA-106 'Gladiators'(FRS)	F/A-18A/B/C/D T-34C	NAS Cecil Field/AD
VQ-6 'Sea Shadows'	ES-3A	NAS Cecil Field

Plus deployed Atlantic Fleet Hornet units, nominally shore-based at Cecil Field:

VFA-15 'Valions'	F/A-18A	(CVW-8/AJ)
VFA-37 'Bulls'	F/A-18C	(CVW-3/AC)
VFA-81 'Sunliners'	F/A-18C	(CVW-17/AA)
VFA-82 'Marauders'	F/A-18C	(CVW-1/AB)
VFA-83 'Rampagers'	F/A-18C	(CVW-17/AA)
VFA-86 'Sidewinders'	F/A-18C	(CVW-1/AB)
VFA-87 'Golden Warriors'	F/A-18A	(CVW-8/AJ)
VFA-105 'Gunslingers'	F/A-18C	(CVW-3/AC)
VFA-131 'Wildcats'	F/A-18C	(CVW-7/AG)
VFA-132 'Privateers'	F/A-18C	(CVW-6/AE)
VFA-136 'Knighthawks'	F/A-18C	(CVW-7/AG)
VFA-137 'Kestrels'	F/A-18C	(CVW-6/AE)
VA-46 'Clansmen'	A-7	Decommissioned 1991
VA-72 'Blue Hawks'	A-7	Decommissioned 1991

Commander Sea-Strike Wing One, NAS Cecil Field, FL

VS-27 'Seawolves' (FRS)	S-3B	NAS Cecil Field/AD

Plus deployed Atlantic Fleet Viking units, nominally shore-based at Cecil Field:

VS-22 'Vidars'	S-3B	(CVW-3/AC)
VS-24 'Scouts'	S-3B	(CVW-8/AJ)
VS-28 'Gamblers'	S-3B	(CVW-6/AE)
VS-30 'Diamondcutters'	S-3B	(CVW-17/AA)
VS-31 'Top Cats'	S-3B	(CVW-7/AG)
VS-32 'Maulers' 'Norsemen'	S-3B	(CVW-1/AB)

Commander Helicopter Wings Atlantic

VX-1 'Pioneers'	P-3, S-3, SH-2, SH-3, SH-60B	NAS Patuxent River/JA
VRF-31 'Storkliners'	Ferry unit, no aircraft assigned	NAS Norfolk

Commander Helicopter Tactical Wing One, NAS Norfolk, VA

HM-12 'Sea Dragons' (FRS)	CH-53/MH-53	NAS Norfolk/DH
HM-14 'Sea Stallions'	MH-53E	NAS Norfolk/BJ
HC-2 'Circuit Riders'	CH-53E, SH-3G	NAS Norfolk/HU Det. Bahrain
HC-6 'Chargers'	CH-46D, HH-46D, UH-46D	NAS Norfolk/HW
HC-8 'Dragon Whales'	CH-46D, HH-46D, UH-46D	NAS Norfolk/BR
HC-4 'Black Stallions'	CH-53E	NAS Sigonella, Sicily/HC
HC-16 'Bullfrogs'	SH-3D, HH-1N	NAS Pensacola/BF
VC-6 'Skeet of the Fleet'	Pioneer RPVs	NAS Norfolk

This Fighter Weapons School (Top Gun) A-4 Skyhawk wears fake Iraqi air force markings. Top Gun operates a selection of A-4s, F-5s and F-16Ns, and even a single F-14 Tomcat, the latter simulating the Su-27 'Flanker's' long-range BVR capability.

Commander Helicopter Antisubmarine Warfare Wing One, NAS Jacksonville, FL

HS-1 'Sea Horses' (FRS)	SH-3G/H	NAS Jacksonville/AR

Plus deployed Atlantic Fleet Sea Kings and SH-60Fs, nominally based at Jacksonville:

HS-3 'Tridents'	SH-60F/ HH-60H	(CVW-17/AA)
HS-5 'Night Dippers'	SH-3H	(CVW-7/AG)
HS-7 'Big Dippers'	SH-3H	(CVW-3/AC)
HS-9 'Sea Griffins'	SH-3H	(CVW-8/AJ)
HS-11 'Dragon Slayers'	SH-3H	(CVW-1/AB)
HS-15 'Red Lions'	SH-3H	(CVW-6/AE)
HS-17 'Valkyries' 'Neptune's Raiders'	SH-3H	Decommissioned 1991/AK

Commander Helicopter Sea Control Wing One, NAS Norfolk, VA

HSL-30 'Scooters' (FRS)	SH-2F	NAS Norfolk/HT

Plus deployed Atlantic Fleet SH-2F squadrons, nominally shore-based at Norfolk:

HSL-32 'Tridents'	SH-2F	NAS Norfolk/HV
HSL-34 'Grey Checkers'	SH-2F	NAS Norfolk/HX
HSL-36 'Lamplighters'	SH-2F	NAS Norfolk/HY

Commander Helicopter Sea Control Wing Three, NAS Mayport, Va

HSL-40 'Air Wolves' (FRS)	SH-60B	NAS Mayport/HK

Plus deployed Atlantic Fleet SH-60 squadrons, nominally based at Mayport:

HSL-42 'Proud Warriors'	SH-60B	NAS Mayport/HH
HSL-44 'Swamp Foxes'	SH-60B	NAS Mayport/HP
HSL-46 'Grandmasters'	SH-60B	NAS Mayport/HQ
HSL-48 'Vipers'	SH-60B	NAS Mayport/HR

Commander Patrol Wings Atlantic, NAS Brunswick, ME

VXN-8 'World Travellers'	RP-3D, P-3B	NAS Patuxent River/JB
VQ-4 'Shadows'	EC-130Q, E-6A	NAS Patuxent River/HL
VPU-1 'Association of Old Buzzards'	P-3B	NAS Brunswick/SP
VP-30 'Pros' (FRS)	P-3C, TP/ UP-3A	NAS Jacksonville/LL

Commander Patrol Wing Five, NAS Brunswick, ME

VP-8 'Tigers'	P-3C	NAS Brunswick/LC
VP-10 'Red Lancers'	P-3C	NAS Brunswick/LD
VP-11 'Pegasus'	P-3C	NAS Brunswick/LE
VP-23 'Sea Hawks'	P-3C	NAS Brunswick/LJ
VP-26 'Tridents'	P-3C	NAS Brunswick/LK
VP-44 'Golden Pelicans'	P-3C	Decommissioned 1991/LM

Commander Patrol Wing Eleven, NAS Jacksonville, FL

VP-5 'Mad Foxes'	P-3C	NAS Jacksonville/LA
VP-16 'Eagles'	P-3C	NAS Jacksonville/LF
VP-24 'Batmen'	P-3C	NAS Jacksonville/LR
VP-45 'Pelicans'	P-3C	NAS Jacksonville/LN
VP-49 'Woodpeckers'	P-3C	NAS Jacksonville/LP
VP-56 'Dragons'	P-3C	Decommissioned 1991/LQ

Commander Fleet Air Mediterranean

VQ-2 'Batmen'	EP-3E	NAS Rota, Spain/JQ
VR-22 'Med Riders'	C-130F/ KC-130F	NAS Rota, Spain/JR
VR-24 'The World's Biggest Little Airline'	C-2A, CT-39G	NAS Sigonella, Sicily/JM

(VR-24 may be known as 'Lifting Eagles')

F-16Ns of VF-126 'Bandits' line up on the Miramar ramp. The squadron provides adversary training for West Coast units.

The Pegasus badge and appropriate 'We Deliver' motto of VRC-30.

A Grumman C-2 Greyhound of VRC-30 unfolds its wings. The Greyhound is the dedicated COD derivative of the E-2C Hawkeye airborne early warning platform.

VC-1 'Blue Alii' are based at NAS Barbers Point, Hawaii, from where their A-4s and P-3s perform adversary and fleet support duties.

This rattlesnake motif adorns the tailfins of VF-102 'Diamondbacks' F-14As.

The badge of VS-32 is an all-seeing eye set against a day and night sky, spotting a sub.

Right: 'The Privateers' of VFA-132 have had a number of different tailfin badges on their F/A-18s. The latest is a Pirate's ship.

This colourful VF-124 'Gunfighters' F-14 acted as an air show and display aircraft. Most of the West Coast FRS's Tomcats are in much more subdued colours.

VA-35 'Black Panthers' are an Atlantic Fleet A-6E Intruder unit.

A handful of KA-6Ds still wear grey and white colours, but most Intruders are as toned down as this VA-128 'Golden Intruders' A-6E. VA-128 are the COMNAVAIRPAC A-6 FRS.

VFA-125 is the Pacific Fleet Hornet training unit, turning out F/A-18 pilots for the US Navy and US Marine Corps.

VAW-120, known as the 'Cyclones', are COMNAVAIRPAC's Hawkeye FRS, training aircrew for all the Pacific Fleet E-2C operators.

The menacing shark badge shown here adorns the E-2C Hawkeyes of VAW-122 'Steeljaws'.

The Grumman TC-4C is equipped with A-6E radar and avionics and is used for the training of Intruder aircrew with the FRS, VA-128.

This is the insignia of Ocea Hawk operators HS-4 'Blac Knights'.

The badge of the **COMNAVAIRLANT SH-3 FRS, HS-10 'Taskmasters'**.

HS-12 are known as the 'Wyverns', and one of these creatures is their badge.

An underslung load of weapons is the badge of CH-46 operator, HC-11.

The Sea Kings of HS-10 'Taskmasters' wear a graphic 'crossed-out submarine' badge and act as the West Coast SH-3 FRS.

This HS-10 Sea King displays an overall dark grey toned-down colour scheme. The SH-3 is rapidly being replaced by the SH-60F.

The SH-3H has now been replaced by the SH-60F with HS-4, CVW-15's ASW/SAR helicopter squadron on board the 'Starship' Vinson.

The Kaman SH-2F Seasprites of HSL-33, known as the 'Sea Snakes', wear a blue and gold stripe on their tails. The unit is based at NAS North Island.

HSL-41, known as the 'Sea Hawks', fly the Sikorsky SH-60B Sea Hawk from NAS North Island, and from a wide variety of small ships.

The 'TT' tailcode identifies this SH-60B as belonging to HSL-43, this one wearing the markings of the USS Crommelin's ship's flight.

The North Island-based 'Angels' of HC-1 support the Pacific Fleet using a mixed fleet of CH-53s and SH-3s. All wear the tailcode 'UP'.

An HH-46A from HC-11's detachment 3, then operating aboard the USS Roanoke, lands aboard the nuclear-powered carrier USS Carl Vinson.

The 'Puckered Penguins' of VXE-6 operate Antarctic support UH-1Ns and ski-equipped LC-130 Hercules from Point Mugu.

VC-5 at NAS Cubi Point are known as the 'Checkertails' and operate a mix of Sea Kings and Skyhawks.

This 'Checkertails' A-4E Skyhawk wears toned-down unit markings. The Skyhawks provide adversary training services.

VRC-50, also based at Cubi Point, operate this C-2 Greyhound COD-bird in support of Pacific Fleet carriers in the area.

VRC-50's Greyhounds are augmented by a handful of US-3As, COD variants of the Viking ASW aircraft.

United States Navy

Commander Naval Forces Pacific (COMNAVAIRPAC)

COMNAVAIRPAC trains and administers all Naval Aviation units in the Pacific, administering all aircraft, carriers and aviation units assigned to the Pacific Fleet and providing combat-ready forces for the Third and Seventh Fleets, operating between the Indian Ocean and the West Coast of the USA. The Third Fleet exercises control over forces on the West Coast and in the Hawaiian area, while the Seventh looks after forces in the Far East and Indian Ocean.

Reporting directly to COMNAVAIRPAC are Commander Fighter/Airborne Early Warning Wing Pacific at Miramar, Commander Medium-Attack/Tactical Electronic Warfare Wing Pacific at Whidbey Island, Commander Light-Attack Wing Pacific at Lemoore, Commander Antisubmarine Warfare Wing Pacific at North Island, Commander Patrol Wings Pacific at Moffett Field (incorporating Patrol Wings One, Two and Ten), and Commander Fleet Air Western Pacific at NAF Atsugi.

COMNAVAIRPAC

Commander Fighter-Airborne Early Warning Wing Pacific, NAS Miramar, CA

Navy Fighter Weapons School (Top Gun)	A-4E, F-5E/F, F-16N/TF-16N	NAS Miramar
VF-126 'Bandits'	F-16N, A-4E/F, TA-4J	NAS Miramar/NJ
VC-1 'Blue Alii'	VP-3A, A-4E,TA-4J	NAS Barbers Point/UA
VX-4 'Evaluators'	F-14A/B/D, F/A-18A/C	NAS Point Mugu/XE
VF-124 'Gunfighters' (FRS)	F-14A/B/D, T-34C	NAS Miramar/NJ

Plus deployed Pacific Fleet Tomcat squadrons, nominally shore-based at NAS Miramar:

VF-1 'Wolfpack'	F-14A	(CVW-2/NE)
VF-2 'Bounty Hunters'	F-14A TARPS	(CVW-2/NE)
VF-21 'Freelancers'	F-14A	(CVW-5/NF)
VF-24 'Renegades'	F-14B	(CVW-9/NG)
VF-51 'Screaming Eagles'	F-14D	(CVW-15/NL)
VF-111 'Sundowners'	F-14D TARPS	(CVW-15/NL)
VF-114 'Aardvarks'	F-14A	(CVW-11/NH)
VF-154 'Black Knights'	F-14A TARPS	(CVW-5/NF)
VF-211 'Flying Checkmates'	F-14B TARPS	(CVW-9/NG)
VF-213 'Black Lions'	F-14A TARPS	(CVW-11/NH)
VAW-110 'Firebirds' (FRS)	E-2C, C-2A	NAS Miramar/NJ

Plus deployed Pacific Fleet Hawkeye squadrons, nominally shore-based at NAS Miramar:

VAW-112 'Golden Hawks'	E-2C+	(CVW-9/NG)
VAW-113 'Black Hawks'	E-2C	(CVW-14/NK)
VAW-114 'World Famous Hormel Hawgs'	E-2C	(CVW-15/NL)
VAW-115 'Liberty Bells'	E-2C	(CVW-5/NF)
VAW-116 'Sun Kings'	E-2C	(CVW-2/NE)
VAW-117 'Wallbangers'	E-2C	(CVW-11/NH)

Commander Medium-Attack and Tactical Electronic Warfare Wing, Pacific, NAS Whidbey Island, WA

VA-128 'Golden Intruders' (FRS)	A-6E	Whidbey Island/NJ

Plus deployed Pacific Fleet Intruder squadrons, nominally shore-based at Whidbey Island:

VA-52 'Knight Riders'	A-6E/KA-6D	(CVW-15/NL)
VA-95 'Green Lizards'	A-6E/KA-6D	(CVW-11/NH)
VA-115 'Eagles'	A-6E	(CVW-5/NF)
VA-145 'Swordsmen'	A-6E	(CVW-2/NE)
VA-155 'Silver Foxes'	A-6E/KA-6D	(CVW-2/NE)
VA-165 'Boomers'	A-6E/KA-6D	(CVW-9/NG)
VA-196 'Main Battery'	A-6E/KA-6D	(CVW-14/NK)
VA-185 'Knighthawks'	A-6E/KA-6D	Decommissioned 1991 (CVW-5/NF)

VAQ-129 'New Vikings' (FRS)	EA-6B	Whidbey Island/NJ

Plus all deployed Fleet Prowler squadrons, nominally shore-based at Whidbey Island:

VAQ-130 'Zappers'	EA-6B	(CVW-3/AC)
VAQ-131 'Lancers'	EA-6B	(CVW-2/NE)
VAQ-132 'Scorpions'	EA-6B	(CVW-17/AA)
VAQ-133 'Wizards'	EA-6B	(CVW-6/AE)
VAQ-134 'Garudas'	EA-6B	(CVW-15/NL)
VAQ-135 'Black Ravens'	EA-6B	(CVW-11/NH)
VAQ-136 'Gauntlets'	EA-6B	(CVW-5/NF)
VAQ-137 'Rooks'	EA-6B	(CVW-1/AB)
VAQ-138 'Yellowjackets'	EA-6B	(CVW-9/NG)
VAQ-139 'Cougars'	EA-6B	(CVW-14/NK)
VAQ-140 'Patriots'	EA-6B	(CVW-7/AG)
VAQ-141 'Shadowhawks'	EA-6B	(CVW-8/AJ)
VAQ-142 'Grim Watchdogs'	EA-6B	Decommissioned 1991

Commander Light-Attack Wing Pacific, NAS Lemoore, CA

VX-5 'Vampires'	TA-4J, A-6 AV-8B, F/A-18, OV-10A/D, AH-1J/T/W	NWTC China Lake/XE
VAQ-34 'Electric Horsemen' 'Flashbacks'	F/A-18A/B	NAS Lemoore
VAQ-35 'Grey Wolves'	EA-6B	NAS Whidbey Island/GD
VFA-127 'Cylons'	A-4E/F, TA-4J, F-5E/F	NAS Fallon
Naval Strike Warfare Center	F/A-18	NAS Fallon/STRIKE
VFA-125 'Rough Riders' (FRS)	F/A-18A/B/C/D T-34C	NAS Lemoore/NJ

Plus deployed Pacific Fleet F/A-18 squadrons, nominally shore-based at NAS Lemoore:

VFA-22 'Fighting Redcocks'	F/A-18C	(CVW-11/NH)
VFA-25 'Fist of the Fleet'	F/A-18C	(CVW-14/NK)
VFA-27 'Chargers'	F/A-18C	(CVW-15/NL)
VFA-94 'Shrikes'	F/A-18C	(CVW-11/NH)
VFA-97 'Warhawks'	F/A-18C	(CVW-15/NL)
VFA-113 'Stingers'	F/A-18C	(CVW-14/NK)
VFA-146 'Blue Diamonds'	F/A-18C	(CVW-9/NG)
VFA-147 'Argonauts'	F/A-18C	(CVW-9/NG)
VFA-151 'Vigilantes'	F/A-18A	(Not assigned)
VFA-192 'Golden Dragons'	F/A-18A	(CVW-5/NF)
VFA-195 'Dambusters'	F/A-18A	(CVW-5/NF)
VA-122 'Flying Eagles' (FRS)	A-7	Decommissioned 1991

Commander Antisubmarine Warfare Wing Pacific, NAS North Island, CA

VS-41 'Shamrocks' (FRS)	S-3B	NAS North Island/NJ

Plus deployed Pacific Fleet Viking squadrons, nominally shore-based at NAS North Island:

VS-21 'Fighting Redtails'	S-3A	(CVW-5/NF)
VS-29 'Screaming Dragon Fires'	S-3A	(CVW-11/NH)
VS-33 'Screwbirds'	S-3A	(CVW-9/NG)
VS-35 'Blue Wolves'	S-3B	(Not yet assigned/VS)
VS-37 'Sawbucks'	S-3A	(CVW-15/NL)
VS-38 'Red Griffins'	S-3A	(CVW-2/NE)
VRC-30 'Providers'	C-2A, UC-12B, CT-39E	NAS North Island/RW
HS-10 'Taskmasters' (FRS)	SH-3H/SH-60F	NAS North Island/RA

Plus deployed Pacific Fleet Sea King and SH-60F squadrons, nominally shore-based at NAS North Island:

HS-2 'Golden Falcons'	SH-60F	(CVW-9/NG)
HS-4 'Black Knights'	SH-60F	(CVW-15/NL)
HS-6 'Indians'	SH-60F	(CVW-11/NH)
HS-8 'Eight Ballers'	SH-3H	(CVW-14/NK)
HS-12 'Wyverns'	SH-3H	(CVW-5/NF)
HS-14 'Chargers'	SH-3H	(CVW-2/NE)
HS-16 'Night Hawks'	SH-3H	Decommissioned 1991
HSL-31 'Archangels' (FRS)	SH-2F	NAS North Island/TD

Plus deployed Pacific Fleet Sea Sprite squadrons, nominally shore-based at NAS North Island and Barbers Point:

HSL-33 'Sea Snakes'	SH-2F	NAS North Island/TF
HSL-35 'Magicians'	SH-2F	NAS North Island/TG
HSL-37 'Easy Riders'	SH-2F	NAS Barbers Point/TH
HSL-41 'Sea Hawks'	SH-60B	NAS North Island/TS

Plus deployed Pacific Fleet SH-60B squadrons, nominally shore-based at NAS North Island:

HSL-43 'Battle Cats'	SH-60B	NAS North Island/TT
HSL-45 'Wolfpack'	SH-60B	NAS North Island/TZ
HSL-47 'Saberhawks'	SH-60B	NAS North Island/TY
HSL-49 'Scorpions'	SH-60B	NAS North Island
HC-1 'Angels'	CH-53E, SH-3G, SH-3H	NAS North Island/UP
HC-3 'Pack Rats'	CH-46D, HH-46A/D	NAS North Island/SA
HC-11 'Gunbearers'	CH/UH-46D, HH-46A/D	NAS North Island/VR
HM-15 'Blackhawks'	MH-53E	NAS Alameda/TB
VXE-6 'Puckered Penguins'	LC-130F/R, UH-1N	NAS Point Mugu/XD

Commander Fleet Air Western Pacific, NAF Atsugi

Commander Fleet Air Western Pacific

NAS Agana, Guam
NAS Cubi Point, Phillipines
NAF Atsugi, Japan
NAF Kadena, Japan
NAF Misawa, Japan
NAF Diego Garcia

VC-5 'Checkertails'	A-4E, TA-4J, SH-3G	NAS Cubi Point
HC-5 'Providers'	H-46	NAS Agana/RB
VQ-1 'World Watchers'	EP-3E	NAS Agana/PR
VQ-5 'Black Ravens'	ES-3A	NAS Agana/SS
VRC-50 'Foo Dogs'	C-2A, US-3A	NAS Cubi Point
HSL-51	SH-60B	NAF Atsugi

Commander Patrol Wings Pacific

NAS Adak, Alaska
NAS Barbers Point, Hawaii
NAS Moffett Field
NAF Midway Island

Commander Patrol Wing One, Kamiseya, Japan

COMPATWING Det Diego Garcia
COMPATWING Det Misawa
COMPATWING Det Cubi Point
COMPATWING Det Agana

Commander Patrol Wing Two, NAS Barbers Point, Hawaii

VP-1 'Screaming Eagles'	P-3C	NAS Barbers Point/YB
VP-4 'Skinny Dragons'	P-3C	NAS Barbers Point/YD
VP-6 'Blue Sharks'	P-3C	NAS Barbers Point/PC
VP-17 'White Lightnings'	P-3C	NAS Barbers Point/ZE
VP-22 'Blue Geese'	P-3C	NAS Barbers Point/QA
VPU-2 'Wizards'	P-3C, P-3B	NAS Barbers Point/No code
VQ-3 'Tacamopac'	E-6A	NAS Barbers Point/TC

(VQ-3 will move to Tinker AFB.)

Commander Patrol Wing Ten, NAS Moffett Field, CA

VP-9 'Golden Eagles'	P-3C	NAS Moffett Field/PD
VP-31 'Black Lightnings' (FRS)	P-3C, UP/ TP-3A	NAS Moffett Field/RD
VP-40 'Fighting Marlins'	P-3C	NAS Moffett Field/QE
VP-46 'Grey Knights'	P-3C, TP-3A?	NAS Moffett Field/RC
VP-47 'Golden Swordsmen'	P-3C	NAS Moffett Field/RD
VP-50 'Blue Dragons' ('Ancient Mariners'?)	P-3C	NAS Moffett Field/SG

Above and below: VF-202 'Superheats' F-14A Tomcats wear high- and low-vis colour schemes, both with the Texan rudder flag.

Co-located with VF-202 at NAS Dallas are VF-201, nicknamed the 'Hunters'. Like VF-202 they are a Reserve unit, and a component of Carrier Air Reserve Wing 20.

The 'Blue Dolphins' of VFA-203 from Cecil Field are one of two F/A-18 strike units within CVWR-20, and carry the wing's 'AF' tailcode.

Stylised 'ND' tailcodes are used by the Reserve units of CVWR-30 on the West Coast. This F-14A belongs to VF-301, the 'Devils Disciples'.

The 'Fighting Omars' of VFC-12 at NAS Oceana operate their A-4Fs in the adversary role, supporting regular and Reserve Atlantic Fleet fighter units.

VFC-13 'Saints' are the West Coast Reserve adversary unit. Like VFC-12, they are administered by the Reserve Tactical Support Wing.

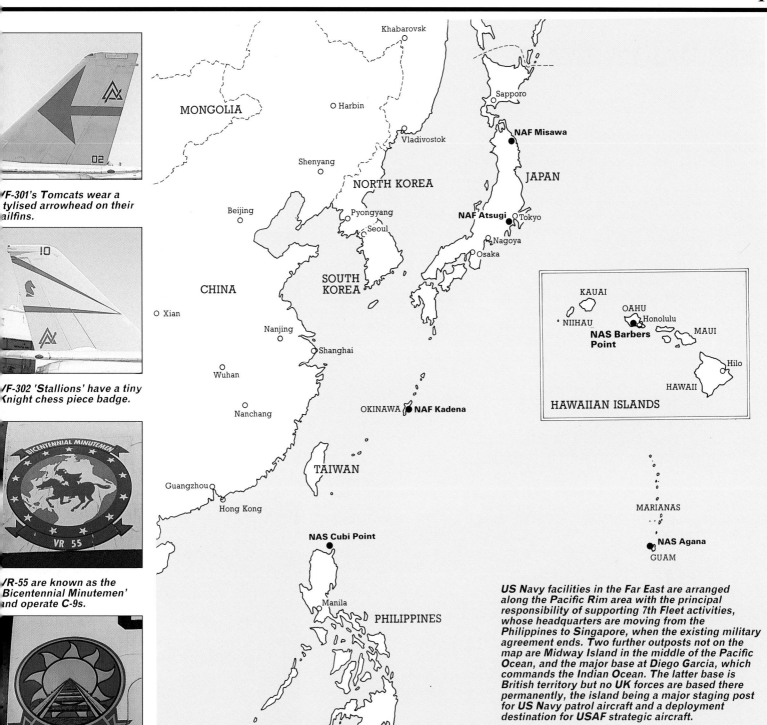

VF-301's Tomcats wear a stylised arrowhead on their tailfins.

VF-302 'Stallions' have a tiny knight chess piece badge.

VR-55 are known as the 'Bicentennial Minutemen' and operate C-9s.

The squadron badge of VR-58 'Sunseekers', a C-9 unit based at Jacksonville.

Khabarovsk

MONGOLIA

O Harbin

Sapporo

Shenyang O

Vladivostok

NAF Misawa

JAPAN

NORTH KOREA

Beijing O

Pyongyang O

NAF Atsugi

Tokyo

CHINA

Seoul

Nagoya

Osaka

O Xian

SOUTH KOREA

Nanjing O

Shanghai O

O Wuhan

O Nanchang

OKINAWA **NAF Kadena**

TAIWAN

Guangzhou O

Hong Kong

NAS Cubi Point

Manila

PHILIPPINES

KAUAI

OAHU

NIIHAU

Honolulu

NAS Barbers Point

MAUI

Hilo

HAWAII

HAWAIIAN ISLANDS

MARIANAS

NAS Agana

GUAM

US Navy facilities in the Far East are arranged along the Pacific Rim area with the principal responsibility of supporting 7th Fleet activities, whose headquarters are moving from the Philippines to Singapore, when the existing military agreement ends. Two further outposts not on the map are Midway Island in the middle of the Pacific Ocean, and the major base at Diego Garcia, which commands the Indian Ocean. The latter base is British territory but no UK forces are based there permanently, the island being a major staging post for US Navy patrol aircraft and a deployment destination for USAF strategic aircraft.

The most unusually named squadron in the Navy is VAW-78, the CVWR-20 E-2C unit. They are known to all as the 'Fighting Escargots'.

This C-9 wears the 'JS' tailcodes of VR-46 'Peach Airlines', who operate from Atlanta, Georgia.

Commander Fleet Logistics Support Wing detachment Washington operates this smart-looking C-20 Gulfstream III.

US Naval Air Reserve

The US Navy has a substantial reserve, the air elements of which report directly to Commander Naval Reserve, which in turn reports to ACNO Air Warfare in Washington, or to their respective operational commanders. Since 1970, the Naval Air Reserve (which includes vital medical and intelligence units, as well as aircraft/helicopter operators), has been re-organised to reflect a mirror image of the front-line fleet it is tasked with supporting and augmenting. It has two full Carrier Air Wings, backed by Patrol and Support Wings. The Carrier Air Wings CVWR-20 and CVWR-30 are not assigned to an individual ship, but would be recalled to serve with AIRLANT and AIRPAC respectively. They undergo their necessary periodic CQs (Carrier Qualifications or Car-quals) with carriers as they become available. At one time, it was proposed that one of the older carriers (e.g. *Coral Sea* or *Midway*) should be kept in service as a dedicated reserve carrier, but these plans proved too ambitious.

For a brief period beginning in the mid-1980s, in order to keep Reserve aircrew current on aircraft types which could not be made available full-time, Squadron Augmentation Units (SAUs) were formed as shadow identities for the relevant (F-14, A-6 and S-3) FRS training units. The MAU was the Patrol community's equivalent. Financial constraints led to the disbandment of these units in September 1991.

The Naval Air Reserve contributed seven squadrons to Operation Desert Storm, and 2,942 Reservists were mobilised, many of them medical and intelligence personnel. The seven squadrons included four transport units, an ASW unit, and two new combat support helicopter units.

Naval Air Reserve

Commander Naval Air Reserve Force, New Orleans, LA

Commander Carrier Air Reserve Wing Twenty, NAS Cecil Field, FL

VF-201 'Hunters'	F-14A	Codes from AF/100	NAS Dallas
VF-202 'Superheats'	F-14A (TARPS)	Codes from AF/200	NAS Dallas
VFA-203 'Blue Dolphins'	F/A-18A	Codes from AF/300	NAS Cecil Field NAF New Orleans
VFA-204 'River Rattlers'	F/A-18A	Codes from AF/400	NAS Cecil Field
VA-205 'Green Falcons'	A-6E, KA-6D	Codes from AF/500	NAS Atlanta
VAQ-209 'Skywarriors'	EA-6B	Codes from AF/604	NAS Washington
VAW-78 'Fighting Escargots'	E-2C	Codes from AF/600	NAS Norfolk

Commander Carrier Air Reserve Wing Thirty, NAS Miramar, CA

VF-301 'Devils Disciples'	F-14A	Codes from ND/100	NAS Miramar
VF-302 'Stallions'	F-14A (TARPS)	Codes from ND/200	NAS Miramar
VFA-303 'Goldenhawks'	F/A-18A	Codes from ND/300	NAS Lemoore
VFA-305 'Lobos'	F/A-18A	Codes from ND/400	NAS Point Mugu
VA-304 'Firebirds'	A-6E/KA-6D	Codes from ND/420	NAS Alameda
VAW-88 'Cottonpickers'	E-2C	Codes from ND/600	NAS Miramar
VAQ-309 'Axemen'	EA-6B	Codes from ND/604	NAS Whidbey Island

Commander Reserve Patrol Wing, Atlantic, NAS Norfolk, VA

VP-62 'Broadarrows'	P-3C	NAS Jacksonville/LT
VP-64 'Condors'	P-3B	NAS Willow Grove/LU
VP-66 'Liberty Bell'	P-3B	NAS Willow Grove/LV
VP-68 'Blackhawks'	P-3C	NAF Washington/LW
VP-92 'Minutemen'	P-3C	NAS South Weymouth/LY
VP-93 'Executioners'	P-3B	NAF Detroit/LH
VP-94 'Crawfishers'	P-3B	NAS New Orleans/LZ
VP-MAU 'Northern Sabres'	TP-3A, P-3C	Decommissioned 1991/LB

Commander Reserve Patrol Wing, Pacific, NAS Moffet Field, CA

VP-60 'Cobras'	P-3B	NAS Glenview/LS
VP-65 'Tridents'	P-3C	NAS Point Mugu/PG
VP-67 'Golden Hawks'	P-3B	NAS Memphis/PL
VP-69 'Totems'	P-3B	NAS Whidbey Island/PJ
VP-90 'Lions'	P-3B	NAS Glenview/LX
VP-91 'Stingers'	P-3C	NAS Moffet Field/PM
VP-MAU 'Rolling Thunder'	TP-3A, P-3C	Decommissioned 1991

Commander Fleet Logistic Support Wing, NAS Dallas, TX

Commander Reserve Tactical Support Wing, NAF New Orleans, LA

VFC-12 'Fighting Omars'	A-4F/M, TA-4J	NAS Oceana/JY
VFC-13 'Saints'	A-4F/M, TA-4J	NAS Miramar/UX
VAQ-34 'Electric Horsemen'	F/A-18A/B	NAS Lemoore/GD
VAQ-35 'Grey Wolves'	EA-6B	NAS Whidbey Island/GD
VR-46 'Peach Airlines'	C-9	NAS Atlanta/JS
VR-48 'Sky Pigs'	C-20	NAF Washington/JR
VR-51 'Flamin Hookers'	C-9	NAS Glenview/RV
VR-52 'Taskmasters'	C-9	NAS Willow Grove/JT
VR-54 'Revellers'	C-130T	NAS New Orleans/LA
VR-55 'Bicentennial Minutemen'	C-9	NAS Alameda/RU
VR-56 'Globemasters'	C-9	NAS Norfolk/JU
VR-57 'Conquistadors'	C-9	NAS North Island/RX
VR-58 'Sun Seekers'	C-9	NAS Jacksonville/JV
VR-59 'Lone Star Express'	C-9	NAS Dallas/RY
VR-60 'Volunteer Express'	C-9	NAS Memphis/RT
VR-61 'Islanders'	C-9	NAS Whidbey Island/RS
VR-62 'Motowners'	C-9	NAS Detroit/JW
CFLSW det. NOLA	CT-39G	NAS New Orleans/LA
CFLSW det. WASH	C-20, CT-39G	NAF Washington

Commander Helicopter Wing Reserve, NAS North Island, CA

HCS-4 'Red Wolves'	HH-60H	NAS Norfolk
HCS-5 'Fire Hawks'	HH-60H	NAS Point Mugu/NW
HM-18 'Norsemen'	RH-53D	NAS Norfolk/NW
HM-19 'Golden Bears'	RH-53D	NAS Alameda/NW
HS-75 'Emerald Knights'	SH-3H	NAS Jacksonville/NW
HS-85 'Golden Gaters'	SH-3H	NAS Alameda/NW
HSL-74 'Demon Elves'	SH-2F	NAS South Weymouth/NW
HSL-84 'Thunderbolts'	SH-2G	NAS North Island/NW
HSL-94 'Titans'	SH-2F	NAS Willow Grove/NW

This immaculate TA-4J serves with VT-7, the 'Eagles', who form part of Training Wing One at NAS Meridian.

Not all TA-4Js used in the training role wear training colours. This overall grey TA-4J of VT-7 is one such exception.

A yellow fuselage band marks this TA-4J as belonging to VT-22, the 'King Eagles', from NAS Kingsville. It is seen on the Lexington.

Chief of Naval Air Training

A huge technology-oriented force like the US Navy has a large requirement for training. The Chief of Naval Education and Training reports directly to the Chief of Naval Operations, and controls the various Training departments of the Atlantic and Pacific Fleets (COMTRA-LANT and COMTRAPAC), the Chief of Naval Technical Training (whose responsibilities include the training of air traffic controllers, aviation engineers and technical officers and enlisted personnel), and the Chief of Naval Air Training (CNATRA). CNATRA is responsible for the training of all pilots and NFOs, and for the indoctrination of flight surgeons and aerospace experimental psychologists. Engineer officers are trained at the Naval Post Graduate College at Monterey, while maintenance officers undergo training at Pensacola. Supply officers are trained at Athens, Georgia. Enlisted personnel attend Naval Air Technical Training Centers at Memphis, Lake Hurst and Meridian, while further specialist training is conducted at an ever-varying number of Naval Air Maintenance Training Group Detachments.

VT-19 'Fighting Frogs' provide intermediate jet training with their T-2C Buckeyes as part of Training Wing One at NAS Meridian.

T-2C Buckeyes from VT-4 'Rubber Ducks'. The unit is responsible for basic NFO training as part of Training Wing Six at Pensacola.

The T-44A is used by VT-28 and VT-31 as part of Training Wing Four at NAS Corpus Christi for multi-engine pilot training.

Training Wing Five at Whiting Field is responsible for primary turbine and rotary training, using the T-34C and TH-57.

The US Navy trains some 2,000 pilots and NFOs (Naval Flight Officers) per year. Recruiters operate a fleet of blue-painted piston-engined T-34B Mentors. Students join the programme either from the US Naval Academy at Annapolis (after a four-year, university-equivalent course), or from the Naval Reserve Officer Training Candidate Scholarship programme (conducted in 60 mainstream universities and colleges). On graduation from either of these programmes, the student is commissioned as an ensign in the regular Navy. The third source of students is the Aviation Officer Candidate Program, which takes enlisted men or civilians through the Officer Candidate School at Pensacola, these people emerging as Reserve Ensigns.

A six-week Aviation Preflight Indoctrination course follows before students are streamed to pilot or NFO training. Pilot training begins with a 20-week Primary Flight Training course on the T-34C Turbo Mentor at NAS Whiting Field, or at NAS Corpus Christi. Those destined for jet aircraft then go to Pensacola, Meridian, Chase Field or Kingsville for a 24-week Basic Jet training course on the T-2 Buckeye. All T-2s remaining in the inventory are T-2Cs,

An 'E' tailcode identifies these TH-57s as belonging to Training Wing Five. The type is used by HT-8 and HT-18 for basic and advanced rotary training, respectively.

The insignia of VT-4, 'Rubber Ducks', part of Training Wing Six at Pensacola.

although a handful of less powerful T-2Bs served with the undergraduate NFO training squadron, VT-10, until recently. A 21-week Advanced Jet training course follows at the same bases, with students transitioning to the TA-4J Skyhawk. The Skyhawk is used for the great milestone of the naval aviators student career, carrier qualifications (Carquals or CQs), although E-2 pilots complete a modified basic jet course and do CQs in the T-2C. The T-45 Goshawk is being introduced to replace both Buckeye and Skyhawk. On successful completion of the course, pilots are posted to FRSs for the F-14, F/A-18, A-6, EA-6B, S-3, C-9 or OV-10.

Pilot trainees destined for larger, heavier aircraft stay at Whiting Field or Corpus Christi for a five-week Intermediate Prop course before transitioning to the T-44 King Air at Corpus Christi for a 19-week Multi-engine course. Successful students go on to the E-2C or C-2, or to the P-3 or C-130. Future helicopter pilots undergo the same Intermediate Prop course at Whiting Field, before transitioning to the TH-57 for a six-week Helicopter Transition course and a 12-week Advanced Helicopter course at Whiting Field on the TH-1 and TH-57.

An increasing number of pilot trainees are female, who can be assigned to various shore-based aircraft types (theoretically including Adversary units) and to the C-2 VRC units, with which they can at least fly on to aircraft-carriers in the COD role.

All NFOs undergo the same 15-week Basic course in the T-2 at Pensacola, before some are sent for Interservice Undergraduate Navigator Training on USAF T-43s at Mather AFB. These will move to Randolph AFB, Texas, in 1993. These NFOs return to the Navy C-130 and P-3 fleets. All other NFOs undergo a seven-week Intermediate course on the T-2 and T-47 at Pensacola, before being streamed. The T-47s of Training Wing Six are in the process of being replaced by T-39Ns modified by Sabreliner Corporation. Contract irregularities mean that the T-39s will be used for only 18 months, after which Flight International will take over the contract using modified Learjets. Future F-14 Radar Intercept Officers stay at Pensacola on the T-2 and T-47 for a further 17 weeks. A-6 tactical navigators also stay at Pensacola, but their course lasts only 11 weeks. EA-6B crews undergo the same course, before a 12-week Electronic Warfare course. Overwater jet navigators for the S-3 also undergo an 11-week course at Pensacola. Future airborne tactical data systems officers for the E-2C go directly to one of the two FRSs at Miramar or Norfolk.

Other Naval Aviators receive their 'Wings of Gold' at the end of the appropriate training course, and before proceeding to a Fleet Replacement Squadron (FRS) for type conversion.

In order to screen candidates for naval aviator training, Recruiting Command operates some 51 piston-engined Beechcraft T-34B Mentors. Based singly (90 per cent of them at civilian airfields) close to major population centres, these aircraft are used to weed out applicants who may be prone to airsickness or who have any other aversion to flying. Four aircraft are based at Pensacola for training and as a reserve for when others are being serviced. The others are at the following locations: **Area 1** – Albany, NY; Boston, MA; Buffalo, NY; Harrisburg, PA; Newark, NJ; New York, NY; Philadelphia, PA; Pittsburgh, PA. **Area 3** – Macon, GA; Atlanta, GA; Columbia, SC; Jacksonville, FL; Louisville, KY; Miami, FL; Montgomery, AL; Nashville, TN; Raleigh, NC; Richmond, VA; Washington, DC. **Area 5** – Great Lakes; Chicago, IL; Cleveland, OH; Columbus, OH; Detroit, MI; Indianapolis, IN; Milwaukee, WL; Minneapolis, MN; Omaha, NE. **Area 7** – Albuquerque, NM; Dallas, TX; Denver, CO; Houston, TX; Kansas City, MO; Little Rock, AR; Lubbock, TX; Memphis, TN; New Orleans, LA; Oklahoma City, OK; San Antonio, TX; St. Louis, MO. **Area 8** – Los Angeles, CA; Phoenix, AZ; Portland, OR; Salt Lake City, UT; San Diego, CA; San Francisco, CA; Seattle, WA.

Chief of Naval Air Training

Commander Naval Air Training, NAS Corpus Christi, TX

Commander Training Wing One, NAS Meridian, MS (Tailcode A)

VT-7 'Eagles'	TA-4J	(Intermediate Strike)
VT-19 'Fighting Frogs'	T-2C	(Advanced Strike)

Commander Training Wing Two, NAS Kingsville, TX (Tailcode B)

VT-21 'Red Hawks'	TA-4J	(Advanced Strike)
VT-22 'King Eagles'	TA-4J	(Advanced Strike)
VT-23 'Professionals'	T-2C	(Intermediate Strike)
(VT-21 was to become the first T-45 unit during late 1991.)		

Commander Training Wing Three, NAS Chase Field, Beeville, TX (Tailcode C)

VT-24 'Bobcats'	TA-4J	(Advanced Strike)
VT-25 'Cougars'	TA-4J	(Advanced Strike)
VT-26 'Tigers'	T-2C	(Intermediate Strike)

Commander Training Wing Four, NAS Corpus Christi, TX (Tailcode D)

VT-27 'Boomers'	T-34C	(Primary Turbine)
VT-28 'Rangers'	T-44A	(Multi-engine Turbine)
VT-31 'Wise Owls'	T-44A	(Multi-engine Turbine)

Commander Training Wing Five, NAS Whiting Field, FL (Tailcode E)

VT-2 'Doer Birds'	T-34C	(Primary Turbine)
VT-3 'Red Knights'	T-34C	(Primary Turbine)
VT-6	T-34C	(Primary Turbine)
HT-8	TH-57B	(Basic Rotary)
HT-18	TH-57B/C	(Advanced Rotary)

Commander Training Air Wing Six, NAS Pensacola, FL (Tailcode F)

VT-4 'Rubber Ducks'	T-2C	(Basic Jet, E-2/C-2)
VT-10 'Cosmic Cats'	T-2C, T-34C	(NFO syllabus)
VT-86 'Sabre Hawks'	T-47A	(RIO, tactical & overwater navigation)
NFDS 'Blue Angels'	F/A-18/KC-130F	Naval Flight Demonstration Squadron/BA

Naval Air Systems Command

Inevitably referred to as Navair, the Naval Air Systems Command, headed by a three-star (aviator) admiral, oversees the development, production and procurement of all air-related equipment, including aircraft, aircrew and support equipment and armaments. Navair also oversees all modification programmes relating to existing aircraft and systems. Navair was created in 1966 from the Bureau of Naval Weapons, which in turn was formed in 1959 from the Bureau of Aeronautics and the Bureau of Ordnance.

Subject to Congressional approval, all US Navy aviation research and development is to be concentrated under a new organisation, the Naval Air Warfare Center, headquartered at Crystal City near Washington, DC. It will oversee the work of an Aircraft Division (at Patuxent River) and a Weapons Division (split between China Lake and Point Mugu). The existing separate technical commands will lose their present status and will report to the new organisation. These commands were, for the record, the Naval Weapons Evaluation Facility at Kirtland AFB, New Mexico (which is likely to close); the Naval Air Development Center at Warminster, PA; the Naval Air Propulsion Center at Trenton, New Jersey; the Naval Weapons Center at China Lake; the Naval Air Engineering Center at Lakehurst; and the Pacific Missile Test Center at Point Mugu. The Naval Air Test Center, Naval Research Laboratory and Navy Test Pilots School (all at Patuxent River) will form the Aircraft Division.

Naval Air Development Center

The broad task of the Naval Air Development Center at Warminster, Pennsylvania, is to enhance technology, improving existing aircraft and systems by refining equipment already in use. The NADC has been heavily involved with ASW development (their work led to the P-3C updates and to the LAMPS project), and with the Aries Elint/EW modifications to the Orion, and with instrument and avionics development.

NADC	UP-3A (with S-3 avionics), P-3C, F-14A, NCH-53A, T-2C, NA-7C?	Warminster, PA

Naval Air Engineering Center

The Naval Air Engineering Center at Lakehurst, New Jersey, conducts programmes of research, engineering development, testing, evaluation and systems integration, as well as procurement and fleet engineering support for aircraft launching and recovery systems, landing aids and support equipment for aircraft and weapons systems.

Naval Coastal Systems Center

The Naval Coastal Systems Center incorporates the Naval Diving and Salvage training centre, and the Navy Experimental Dive Unit. Aircraft operate in a purely support role.

Naval Coastal Systems Center	H-53	Panama City, FL

Naval Weapons Center

The Naval Weapons Center at China Lake is a major research development and test centre for naval weapons, primarily concerned with naval air warfare. The NWC includes full range facilities (including nuclear range facilities) and deals with all types of ordnance, guided and unguided, powered and free-fall. To support these tasks, the NWC operates a large fleet of aircraft including substantial numbers of unmanned target drones. The NWC parents a number of smaller units, including VX-5 'Vampires'.

NWC	F/A-18A/C/D, AV-8B, A-6E, A-7E/TA-7C, NTA-4J, QF-4N, QF/86F, T-39D, AH-1W, UH-1N	China Lake, CA

VT-10 'Cosmic Cats' use their T-2C Buckeyes for teaching the NFO syllabus. They come under Training Wing Six at NAS Pensacola.

VT-10's badge is a 'Cosmic Cat', complete with aviator shades and bone dome!

The badge of VT-86 is a winged sword with spectacular lightning bolts.

A TA-4J and T-47 from VT-86 hold formation. The T-47A Citations are operated under contract, and are being replaced by T-39 Sabreliners.

The US Navy's T-47As wear standard red and white training colours, with star and bar national insignia and 'Navy' titles but with civil registrations.

The Naval Flight Demonstration Squadron, as the 'Blue Angels' should be more formally known, fly F/A-18s as part of Training Wing Six at Pensacola.

This EP-3A (SMILS) is operated by the Pacific Missile Test Center at Point Mugu as a range control aircraft. Other Orions serve with the NATC and the NDC.

The PMTC operate a number of F-14A Tomcats and F/A-18 Hornets as launch aircraft for the various missile tests. All wear the PMTC badge.

The McDonnell Douglas QF-4N Phantom is gradually replacing the QF-86 as the primary unmanned target drone in use with the PMTC.

This anonymous-looking CT-39G Sabreliner is used for communications and VIP transport duties. Sabreliner operators include VRC-24, VRC-30, VRC-40 and VRC-50.

This unusually painted T-34C Turbo Mentor is used by the NAS Cecil Field base flight. A large number of T-34Bs are used by Navy recruiters to provide candidates with basic air experience.

One of only two RC-12Ms, this aircraft serves with the Roosevelt Roads Base Flight. The other is a range control aircraft at Point Mugu with the PMTC.

Naval Weapons Evaluation Facility

The Naval Weapons Evaluation Facility is based at Kirtland AFB, near Albuquerque, New Mexico. Its task is to test and evaluate, and support nuclear and conventional weapons, mainly in the development of delivery methods. It assists in the trials of some naval aircraft.

NWEF	A-6E, F/A-18	Kirtland, NM

Pacific Missile Test Center

The Pacific Missile Test Center at Point Mugu tests and evaluates naval missiles, including air-to-air and air-to-ground weapons, providing development, engineering, logistic, training and range support. It parents the Pacific Missile Range Facility at Barkings Sands, Hawaii, which operates an RC-12M and UH-3As. F/A-18s and F-14s are used as launch aircraft and for chase duties.

PMTC	F-14A, NF-14D, F/A-18A/B,	Point Mugu, CA
	F/QF-4N, A-6E, RP-3A, EP-3A,	
	RC-12M, A-7E, TA-7C	

Naval Air Test Center

The Naval Air Test Center at Patuxent River, Maryland, tests and evaluates aircraft, systems and weapons systems to determine their suitability for service use. Its prime responsibility is for strike and ASW aircraft and helicopters, but also tests and develops systems, servicing procedures and even computers. It has a wide variety of aircraft types on charge for trials, and

to support such trials. In the latter category is the service's sole Convair 880, used as an inflight-refuelling tanker and for ASW trials. VX-4 'Evaluators' based at Point Mugu operates as part of the NATC.

NATC	F-14A, NF-14D, F/A-18A/C,	Patuxent River, MD
	AV-8B, A-6E, E-2C, S-3,	
	AH-1W, SH-2F, SH-3H, VH-3A,	
	CH-53E, SH-60B, HH-60H,	
	HH-60J, TH-1L, T-45, Cv.880	

Naval Research Laboratory

NRL in Washington is a scientific research facility, consisting of several laboratories, whose assigned aircraft are operated from Patuxent River, Maryland.

NRL	EP-3A, RP-3A, EP-3B, P-3C	Patuxent River, MD

Naval Test Pilots School

With so many test establishments, the US Navy has a requirement for large numbers of test pilots and flight test engineers. It therefore trains its own at the Naval Test Pilots School at Patuxent River. The school enjoys an excellent reputation, and receives students (on an exchange basis) from the US Air Force, Britain, France, and a number of other countries. The unit operates a large and varied fleet of aircraft and helicopters to give students the broadest possible experience.

NTPS	F/A-18B, T-2C, T-38, T-39D,	Patuxent River, MD
	OH-6A, UH-60A, HH-65A,	
	U-21A, NU-1B Otter, U-6	
	Beaver, X-26A	

Miscellaneous units

AUTEC Detachment	H-1, UH-3A	Andros Island, Bahamas
BF NAF Atlanta	UC-12B	Atlanta,GA/7B
BF NAS Norfolk	UC-12B/M	Norfolk/7C
BF NAF Dallas	A-4, UC-12B	Dallas/7D
BF NAS Jacksonville	UC-12B, SH-3	Jacksonville/7E
BF NAF Brunswick	UC-12B, UH-1N	Brunswick/7F
BF NAS Whidbey Island	UC-12B, SH-3	Whidbey Island/7G
BF NAF Fallon	UC-12B, UH-1H	Fallon/7H
BF NAF Alameda	UC-12B	Alameda/7J
BF NAF Memphis	UC-12B	Memphis/7K
BF NAF Point Mugu	UC-12B, HH-46A	Point Mugu/7L
BF NAS North Island	UC-12B	North Island/7M
BF NAF Washington	UC-12B	Washington/7N
BF NAS Key West	UC-12B, SH-3	Key West/7Q
BF NAS Oceana	UC-12B, SH-3	Oceana/7R
BF NAS Lemoore	UC-12B, UH-1N	Lemoore/7S
BF NAS Moffett	UC-12B	Moffett/7T
BF NAS Cecil Field	UC-12B	Cecil/7U
BF NAS Glenview	UC-12B	Glenview/7V
BF NAF Willow Grove	UC-12B	Willow Grove/7W
BF NAF New Orleans	UC-12B	New Orleans/7X
BF NAF Detroit	UC-12B	Detroit/7Y
BF NAF South Weymouth	UC-12B	South Weymouth, Maine/7Z
BF NAS Cubi Point	UC-12B, UC-12F	Cubi Pt. Philippines/8B
BF NAF Sigonella	UC-12M	Sigonella, Sicily/8C
BF NAF Rota	UC-12M	Rota, Spain/8D
BF NAF Roosevelt Roads	UC-12B, RC-12M	Roosevelt Roads, PR/8E
BF NAF Guantanamo Bay	UC-12B	Guantanamo Bay, Cuba/8F
BF NAF Mildenhall	UC-12M	Mildenhall, England/8G
BF NAF Kadena	UC-12B	Kadena, Okinawa/8H
BF NAS Agana	UC-12B	Agana, Guam/8J
BF NAF Misawa	UC-12B	Misawa, Japan/8M
BF NAS Patuxent River	SH-3D/G	Patuxent River
NAS Bermuda	UP-3A	Bermuda
NAS Keflavik	UP-3A	Keflavik
CINCAFSE	VP-3A	Sigonella
CINCLANTFLT	VP-3A	Norfolk
CINCPACFLT	VP-3A, UP-3A	Barbers Point
CNO	VP-3A	NAF Washington
BF=Base Flight		

INDEX

Picture credits

Front cover: James Benson. **4:** D. Lamarque. **5:** M.J. Gerards, Aldo Ciarini (two). **6:** John van Benten, Graham Robson. **7:** Kees van der Mark, Willy Scheungrab (three), Paul Jackson. **8:** P.J. Cooper, Jon Lake, P.J. Cooper, Paul Jackson. **9:** Georg Mader. **10:** Herman Pieterse, Carlo Marcora, McDonnell Douglas via Robert F. Dorr (RFD), P.J. Cooper. **11:** via Austin J. Brown. **12:** Ron K. Cembrowski, Graham Robson, P.J. Cooper. **13:** McDonnell Douglas, via RFD. **14-15:** Sergei Skrynnikov /Avia Data. **16:** John Gourley, Tim Laming. **17:** Sikorsky (both). **18:** via RFD, John Gourley, US Navy via Peter B. Mersky (PBM). **20:** William J. Mondy (three), John Gourley. **21:** William J. Mondy (three), John Gourley. **22:** Hermann Buttigieg. **23:** Hermann Buttigieg (two), John Gourley, US Coast Guard, John Gourley. **24:** Joe Cupido. **25:** Joe Cupido (four), via RFD. **26:** Grumman, John Gourley. **28-29:** Grumman. **30:** John Gourley. **31:** John Gourley, Grumman. **32:** John Gourley. **33:** John Gourley, Grumman. **34-35:** Sergei Skrynnikov/Avia Data. **36-37:** Michael Pugh. **38:** Michael Pugh. **39:** Joe Cupido, Captain Mark Hasara via RFD, Michael Pugh. **40:** McDonnell Douglas, McDonnell Douglas. **41:** James Benson, McDonnell Douglas. **42:** McDonnell Douglas. **43:** McDonnell Douglas via Bruce Robertson, McDonnell Douglas. **44:** McDonnell Douglas. **45:** NASA, Hughes, McDonnell Douglas, US Air Force. **47:** 32nd TFS, Paul Bennett. **48:** McDonnell Douglas, US Air Force. **49:** McDonnell Douglas, Paul Bennett. **50:** McDonnell Douglas, McDonnell Douglas, McDonnell Douglas. **52:** McDonnell Douglas, US Air Force, McDonnell Douglas, US Air Force. **53:** McDonnell Douglas, McDonnell Douglas via Michael Stroud. **54:** Robbie Shaw, McDonnell Douglas (three). **55:** McDonnell Douglas. **56:** US Air Force, Richard Gennis, Joe Cupido. **57:** US Air Force. **58:** US Air Force via RFD, US Air Force. **60:** McDonnell Douglas, US Air Force (three). **61-62:** US Air Force. **67:** Michael Pugh. **69:** McDonnell Douglas, R.L. Ward. **71:** McDonnell Douglas. **72:** Captain Mark Hasara via RFD, Paul Jackson. **73:** Peter Steinemann, Robbie Shaw. **74:** Edwards AFB via Paul Bennett, Joe Cupido, McDonnell Douglas. **76:** James Benson. **76:** Robbie Shaw, Stephen J. Brennan/Eagle Aviation Photos, C. Rosher/TRI. **77:** 3rd Wing, John Gourley, Jeff Puzzullo, Associated Press, Robert J. Leavitt. **78:** via RFD, Peter Wilson, McDonnell Douglas, Jeff Rankin-Lowe, David Donald. **79:** David Donald, Jeff Puzzullo, R.L. Ward, Robert J. Leavitt, McDonnell Douglas. **80:** Richard Gennis, via RFD, Paul Bennett (two), Joe Cupido, Tieme Festner. **81:** Joe Cupido, René van Woezik, McDonnell Douglas (two), Paul Bennett. **82:** McDonnell Douglas, Michael Stroud (two), Peter R. Foster, William Turner/TRI, Jeff Puzzullo. **83:** William Turner/TRI, via RFD, RFD, Doug Remington. **84:** Richard Gennis, William Turner/TRI (two), Jeff Puzzullo (two), Paul Bennett. **85:** Doug Remington, James Benson, Peter R. Foster, RFD. **86:** David Donald, RFD, via RFD. **87:** C. Rosher/TRI, James Benson, Robert J. Leavitt (two), McDonnell Douglas. **88:** Steven D. Eisner (two), Paul Langshaw/Eagle Aviation Photos, US Air Force, Joe Cupido, via RFD. **89:** Jeff

Puzzullo, Joe Cupido, Jeff Rankin-Lowe, via RFD, Graham Robson, Don Abrahamson via Bob Archer, J. Sjoersdma. **90:** via RFD, David Donald (three). **91:** Paul Bennett, 36th TFW/PA, Chris Ryan, David Donald, 48th Fighter Wing. **92:** Tom Kaminski, Ricky Rizzo, Jeff Puzzullo, J. Sjoerdsma, Michael Pugh, James Benson. **93:** via RFD, Bob Williams via RFD, Jeff Rankin-Lowe (two), Jack Callaway via RFD. **94:** James Benson (two), C. Rosher/TRI, Joe Cupido (two), Stephen J. Brennan/Eagle Aviation Photos. **95:** McDonnell Douglas (three). **96:** McDonnell Douglas, Peter Steinemann (two), Robbie Shaw (two). **97:** Peter R. Foster, Robbie Shaw (three). **98:** McDonnell Douglas, Yves Debay, Captain Mark Hasara via RFD. **100:** Peter Steinemann. **101:** Indian Air Force, Peter Steinemann. **102:** Indian Air Force, Peter Steinemann (three). **103:** Peter Steinemann. **104:** Peter Steinemann. **105:** Indian Air Force, Peter Steinemann. **106:** Peter Steinemann, Indian Air Force. **107:** Peter Steinemann (two), Indian Air Force. **108:** via Mike Verier. **109:** via Mike Verier (two). **110:** via Mike Verier. **111:** LLAM via G. Kromhout, via Mike Verier. **112:** Mike Verier. **113:** via Mike Verier (two). **114:** via Mike Verier (four), Martyn D. Swann. **115:** via Mike Verier. **116:** via Mike Verier, David Donald. **117:** Robbie Shaw. **118:** via Mike Verier. **119:** via Mike Verier, Bryan Wilburn via Mike Verier, Israeli Aviation & Space Magazine. **121:** P.J. Cooper, Peter Steinemann. **122-125:** via Mike Verier. **126:** via Mike Verier (three). **127:** via Mike Verier. **128:** via Mike Verier. **129:** via Mike Verier (three). **130:** M.J. Gerards, Martin Baumann. **131:** Martin Baumann, M.J. Gerards. **132:** M.J. Gerards (two), E. de Kruyff (two). **133:** M.J. Gerards, Georg Mader. **134:** H.J. van Broekhuizen (three), Harry Berger/ MAPN. **135:** H.J. van Broekhuizen, Harry Berger/MAPN (two). **136:** Martin Baumann. **137:** Gerard Keysper, René van Woezik, Georg Mader. **138-139:** Gerard Keysper. **140:** US Navy via Peter B. Mersky (PBM), Grumman, Richard Gennis. **141:** Robbie Shaw (three), via RFD, US Navy via PBM (two). **142:** Robbie Shaw, US Navy via PBM (four), Michael M. Anselmo, RFD. **143:** Jeff Wilson, Jeff Rankin-Lowe (two), Robbie Shaw (two), US Navy via PBM. **144:** Graham Robson, Robbie Shaw (two). **145:** US Navy, US Navy via PBM (four), Robbie Shaw, US Navy via PBM (four), Paul Langshaw/Eagle Aviation Photos, US Navy, Richard Gennis (two), Jeff Wilson. **147:** Jeff Wilson, Jeff Rankin-Lowe (two), Robbie Shaw (two), US Navy via PBM. **148:** Stephen J. Brennan/Eagle Aviation Photos. **149:** General Dynamics via PBM, Robbie Shaw (eight), Peter R. Housden, Graham Robson, US Navy via PBM, Stephen J. Brennan/Eagle Aviation Photos. **150:** Robbie Shaw (six), US Navy via PBM. **151:** Robbie Shaw (six), PBM, US Navy (two), US Navy via PBM. **152:** RFD, US Navy via PBM, R. Housden, Graham Robson, Peter Wilson, Robert L. Lawson via PBM. **153:** Steven D. Eisner (two), Robbie Shaw (two), PBM, US Navy via PBM. **154:** Richard Gennis (two), US Navy via PBM. **155:** Richard Gennis (two), H.J. van Broekhuizen (three), via PBM. **156:** Robbie Shaw (three), US Navy via PBM, J. Callaway via RFD. **157:** Robbie Shaw (three), David Donald (three), John Gourley.